To Jay,
a lady who is interested
in everything,
all the best
Pat Basso.

TRAVELS WITH M

Patricia Basso

MINERVA PRESS

ATLANTA LONDON SYDNEY

TRAVELS WITH M
Copyright © Patricia Basso 1999

All Rights Reserved

ISBN 0 75410 782 5

First Published 1999 by
MINERVA PRESS
315–317 Regent Street
London W1R 7YB

Printed in Great Britain for Minerva Press

TRAVELS WITH M

This work has been written by Patricia Basso under the guidance of her long-suffering travel mate, Michael Clark, known as 'M'. It is a very frank record which we feel will stimulate, entertain and even enlighten, but hopefully will not offend in any way.

Survival Gear for the Trip

Girls/ Ladies	Boys/ Gentlemen
6 knickers	6 knickers
4 tee-shirts	4 tee-shirts
2 skirts	2 shorts
1 trousers	2 trousers
1 dress	2 shirts
1 sandals	1 sandals
1 trainers	1 trainers
1 jumper	1 jumper
1 anorak	1 anorak
2 pairs socks	2 pairs socks

Two small soaps, toothpaste, talcum, deodorant, shampoo. One lot in hand luggage to use on hot journeys with spare pair of knickers and small towel. One lot in backpack.

Torch, candles and matches in case battery expires. One toilet roll for each week; as used, the space can be filled with presents and souvenirs. Loo rolls are multi-purpose.

Anti-malarial tablets (can make you feel nauseous), mozzie repellent, Anthisan for when they do get you. Don't scratch.

Large towel, sun cream, aftersun, plasters, sunglasses, hat. Anti-vomit, anti-runs, anti-water bugs (what a lot of antis).

Hostel sheet (get inside and it acts as a good mozzie

net). Foil survival bag. Good one litre water carrier. In very hot climes you may need to drink one litre every hour. A little electric pot boiler and enamel mug to sterilise water. Tea bags, milk sachets and powdered fruit juices. Box of Dioralyte will replace all the body needs if you have the runs; tastes foul but can save your life.

Plastic plate, knife (sharp), fork and spoon. Poly bags (if only to annoy other hostellers on early morning departures). Seriously, they are useful for dirty, soggy or smelly items.

Notebook, pens, pencils for that diary and all those addresses. Lonely Planet Country Survival Guide and large map of country. Small magnifying glass to read map names and timetables. Money/ passport/ travellers' cheques belt to wear around your tum. Small camera plus films – we met travellers who had traded in their larger cameras for smaller ones. Foil to wrap exposed films to keep them out of the heat – it works.

Backpack with detachable daypack. Travel pillow and earplugs!

Our Trip Round the World or Pink Hat and White Knickers!

Flight, Sunday, 15th January, 1989

Well, we did make it after dire warnings about sharks, jellyfish, sand-flies, spiders in loos and octopuses which end all your cares and worries in thirty seconds! Simon and Debbie saw us off, with the former actually acknowledging that we were on the way when he saw the boarding passes. First stop New York for a few hours before on to Los Angeles for the Grand Canyon.

Actually sitting on the plane it seems impossible that less than two weeks ago we were having our last Open House weekend before moving. Saturday, 30th December was our third Bless the World gathering with twenty-one of us just thinking and talking about man and the world and hoping to reinforce the positive energies. Sunday, 1st January was the last in a long line of afternoon tea madnesses with various neighbours. What a lot of fun and happiness we have had as wall as cementing solid friendships for the future. Some helped Michael move large furniture to the garage ready for the horsebox the next day.

Monday, 2nd January with Mum and Dad and Mum's shepherd's pie which was enough to feed a streetful of furniture removers. I did begin to wonder about the usefulness of M as he picked up Henry Moore bits of drainage pipe and asked why we were not taking them.

With the next lot not moving in until July I very kindly left a few chairs and mattresses to make the place looked lived in.

Tuesday, 3rd January, and Doreen opened her soup kitchen at noon. Then it was 'Drain the Water' time. It turned out to be 'Let's Make the Kitchen Really Clean' time. We forgot how slow the drainage is and after packing the final load returned to find the kitchen awash. Water streamed off the units like Niagara Falls. The floor had never been cleaner. A quarter of an hour later, all was dry but I could still hear a Chinese torture drip. The large drawer by the sink was a watery tomb and stuck fast. A mighty wrench brought the drawer plus contents to the newly dried floor.

'One of my better ones,' said Michael.

I pinched myself several times and then collapsed into laughter, as I realised it was not one of those deadly dreams you have about a forthcoming big event and all that could go so wrong. M had an emergency dental appointment so I drove the horsebox to Walton, sixty miles.

'You'll be okay,' said Mum, 'people always respect horses in transit.'

I was not convinced because the way it was packed I was more likely to be stopped by the RSPCA for having cardboard boxes over their heads as that was all you could see.

The next week at Walton was spent sorting out nearly twenty hurriedly packed dustbin bags before they went in the loft and ten large loads of washing at the launderette so that nothing gathered little squatters in the next few months. M made all the travel arrangements and then it was 'How many ways to pack a backpack time'. Apparently they are not called rucksacks any more. Our four-way backpacks are great; they can be worn as backpacks; carried as shoulder bags, or transported as a suitcase (one way for giants and one way for midgets like me). What with M and Pat carrying them it's like the start of an Irish invasion. M had to commute to London for a week to sort out visas. The Indian Visa Centre was a sign of things to come; just like an Indian railway station from the film *Gandhi*. The visa itself is one big illegible smudge with the permit to visit Darjeeling in handwriting above. We decided to buy body belts for money and other valuables, as you could have an arm torn off. Once or twice I did wake up in the night wondering why I was embarking on this next misadventure.

John and Donna in Adelaide had asked for three metres of fibrefill material to make a sleeping bag for their latest arrival. Seems incredible to me that in the whole of 'we love outdoor life' Australia this stuff is unobtainable. So what's the problem? The problem is the amount of space occupied by three metres of fibrefill.

'No problem,' says M, as he stuffs it into a Sainsbury's carrier bag and sucks out the air with Mum's fifty-year-old Goblin hoover in reverse and Mum sitting on the whole lot as he does it.

Great but as he switches the Goblin off, Mum starts to rise like a Yorkshire pud. So we leave it with a bit of air until I point out that it could burst its way out of the backpack. M 'boots' it one and it goes off like a bomb. Point made. Just what you need on an aeroplane!

Next tactic? Hoover air out again but truss it with cord as you go. Poor old fibrefill, no escape now and packed in the bottom of the backpack like a tightly rolled leg of lamb.

Very boring as no weird characters to describe at Gatport Airwick, as Gillie calls it. Going into a jumbo jet is like going into a school assembly with life-saving manuals instead of hymn books. One strange fellow slept with a mask on during the lunch and just woke up for the film. I didn't bother with headphones but M was very quiet watching women leaping in and out of waterbeds. The earphones just seem to be a load of screeching as modern technology doesn't allow for good reception if you sit over the engines! M has given up in the hope of getting his £2 back or he'll take the headphones for the next flight. It'll be the airport not the Heathfield police after him. We did cause some consternation at the X-ray screen as I waved two of thirty films like castanets to avoid the rays, not having read that the new machines do not damage films. The number of films to take has been like an A level maths course:

M: 20 x 24 exp = 480 = 5 photos per day
Pat: 10 x 36 exp = 360 = 4 photos per day

So can you work out how many days on the trip?

US Here We Come

New York, rather Newark Airport. Immigration okay, no Mafia connections on the computer. Customs working to rule so we joined two queues. M won. I was behind a fellow who had half the Tower of London stashed in his duvet: brass sword, poker, snuffer, kettle, and so on. A bit concerned when our luggage to Los Angeles was a case of handing it over to a van rental. Then M set off the alarm with his metal spec case. Saw the NY skyline, possibly the United Nations and Empire State. Arrived in LA after fourteen hours' flying. Chaos but luggage had not been absconded by the van rental. M very efficient at using US phones. LA must consume as much electricity as the whole of UK but it was impressive from the plane and driving through the harbour area. A super shuttle – a type of minibus-taxi, took us miles to the hostel. Have now seen the sprawl and smog from a good viewpoint, as the hostel was up in the hills next to the bell presented by Korea and the biggest in the US. Amusing ads such as the one to the family guidance centre – divorce in seven days! Adjusted ourselves to hostel life. Our chore was to make sure everyone was up at 8.30; not easy.

Monday

Took local bus to centre of LA to find Greyhound bus station, usually in the downtown area. Spent a few hours wandering around. Just like TV and as the taxi driver said last night, 'Not a place I'd choose to live in'. Oil wells with 'nodding donkeys' rise up anywhere especially in car parks. Living in an American city, it strikes me, can only offer materialism as there is nothing else, except to abandon reality and 'drop out' in the parks and alleys. It is hard to believe that I am seeing *Hill Street Blues* for real. It is all so vast and impersonal; I cannot see how people find any overall purpose to their lives. I think this trip will make me realise how lucky I am to be part of a community and family. One lady on the bus said how the Grand Canyon made you realise how fragile and transitory we humans are.

You almost need to be bilingual in LA as so much Spanish is spoken. It's trilingual in the Greyhound station, as they have another language called the tannoy system. As M says, how anyone ever finds the right bus at the right gate, heaven knows. Anyway, we managed it, having watched the world go by: ladies putting their hair in rollers before the night coach journey, a mum with several children and all their belongings in a dustbin bag, and the man limping along with an odd boot and shoe. Reached Flagstaff at 7.30 and took another bus to the Grand Canyon.

Our first glimpse of the Grand Canyon will never be forgotten. The whole spread, the colours, the feelings of time and space it brings is awesome. I shall forever remember the feeling of being lifted from the present. The rocks are as old as two billion years, although the Canyon has only been created in the past three to six million years, – relatively recently! The Colorado River is one mile down and at one point the Canyon is seventeen miles across. The South Rim is the better edge to look from.

At Mather Point you can see fifty miles of the Canyon. Have to remember that the first step off the rim is 3,000 feet. Can do mule rides to get closer to the Vishnu Schist rock at the bottom; it takes one day down and one day up.

The schist is the stuff two billion years old. As one guy said, the Empire State Building could get lost there. The platform floor is desert and before 1963, when the gates of the Glen Canyon Dam were closed, the river carried half a million tons of silt and sand through every day, now a mere 80,000 tons a day. Yet it has not stopped men walking all through, such as Fletcher in 1963. He took two months, while before him Butchart spent eighteen summers covering over 15,000 miles. Fletcher admitted it was frightening looking up from the river at the towering walls of black schist and to feel the darkness closing in at night.

At the Tusayan Ruins it is reckoned some thirty Indians lived there for fifty years or more then left. In fact, the Indiana lived in and around the canyon for centuries before other people ever saw it. In 1869 Major Powell told the world of his first geological expedition and now there are about three million visitors a year. The main concern is to preserve the timelessness of the Canyon against the hazards of the modern tourist – for instance, no chair lift or cable car; just the poor old mules. By the way when resting the mules you must make sure their heads are out to the canyon in case something on the trail alarms them and they leap out. What a shame there was ice on the trail and we could not use the mules.

Wednesday

Walked twelve miles but every one hundred yards gave us a totally different view of the Canyon. Amazed how the movement of the sun changed the appearance of the same view on the way back. Saw the luminous pinks of the sunset but it was too cold to linger. Luckily the hostel is very warm with heating in the dorms and a huge log fire in the sitting room. Quite a culture shock going into hostel life after thirty years. The young people are amazed at our trip and think it's great. One lot said they wished they had such 'with-it' parents. Mind you, we have a bit of a laugh getting in and out of the upper bunks. Still, I did manage a bit of contact with M in his top bunk this morning. Only one rest room at this hostel with a label to turn: 'He/Man' or 'She/Woman'. M wondered about us going in together but I reckoned that would cause confusion.

I was surprised how you get used to living in and out of a backpack and drying your knickers overnight on the end of the bed. The dorms are mixed and nobody seems to care. I stood in the hall chatting to one chap for half an hour while folks squeezed past – so what? I was in my nightie waiting to flip the loo label the 'She/Woman' side.

Went in my first US food store. New words like 'jelly' and 'jello'. Mannie from London gave us a lift in her blue Beetle cars which she had bought in Austin, Texas. Quite a 23-year-old travelling all round US by car on her own. Her grandfather was a travel addict and left her his money but she had to use it for seeing the world, not boring things like mortgages. Great fun and also very mind broadening, this travel game. So far discussed teaching's modern hazards, incest, women's rights – all in English, French and German – plus the novelty of the middle-aged who travel à la backpack; cheeky young things. M has a great time chatting as well as we do not always stick together so that we can compare notes later. What a lot of memories we shall have, verbal and visual.

Now on a chat about nuclear problems 'cos we were at the Canyon when the US Air Force went over twice with sonic booms. Round the Canyon it sounds as if the world has ended. Wondered what effect it would have if a nuclear wotsit encountered the Grand Canyon. We all decided it would, be better for the nuclear wotsit to encounter a US city instead and leave the Canyon alone for a few more years. Its time and space has that effect upon you.

Now in Sedona talking about the power of crystals and rocks. Vortexes emanate from the rocks which give psychic forces. Centre of the New Age. Moved to incarnation and lessons to be learnt. Even in stuckout Flagstaff many people 'channel'. Flagstaff seems like the last outpost before leaving the material world to enter the power of the Grand Canyon.

Found some good comments in the hostel book:-

1. It's a bloomin' great ditch. It's a flippin' big hole.
2. We have something like this in Hong Kong, blocks of concrete rising up.
3. The walls of the Canyon possess a timeless quality, they don't need man.
4. Puts man and his puny creations to shame.
5. Must have taken ages to dig out. Where did all the rock go?
6. Don't worry if you can't make it to the bottom, it's only a short fall.
7. Worth the pain and the mule shit.
8. The Grand Canyon is Lady Earth lifting up her dress.
9. Does anyone know what time it is? Does anyone really care?
10. The Grand Canyon mirrors the deep complex nature of the human psyche.

So somewhat sadly we left the Canyon.

Thursday

Bus to Flagstaff. Had a couple of hours to wander around. It was like a cowboy outpost, shacky and very dusty although there was snow. You could feel the grit in your teeth.

Crossing the roads is terrifying. If the red hand is lit up

you don't go. If it's the virginal white man you go, but the trouble is he doesn't show up very well and the time allowed to cross is for Olympic runners only. Then down to Phoenix through 'mesa' country – desert, scrub and the odd range of mountains to go over. Unusual views of small canyons and large cacti everywhere. Even more unusual names such as Bumble Bee, Horse Thief Basin and Bloody Basin for the small mobile home outposts. Phoenix had some outstanding architecture with emphasis on curves and arches. Waited for bus to LA and kept trying to visualise and feel the Grand Canyon to reinforce the memory.

Counted out $5.96 in about fifty different coins to use them up for two burgers. Bit of a bother as I acquired the giggles and dropped them all. M was his usual patient self and continued to use his expertise on the Greyhound timetable. Heaven knows where we would be if I did it, as I'd get the wrong line every time. We're sitting next to a couple obviously in the heights of marital disharmony and M is also reading an Arizona freebie called Singles. Perhaps we should have passed it to the couple next door. They've had a great battle about what to eat. He thought she should have chicken, so she has stomped off to get chicken even if it makes her sick. They are now attacking each other from separate tables. M has found a new partner in the paper: 'very beautiful, very spiritual'; but as you have to pay $5 for everyone you reply to, I'm safe.

Greyhound was overbooked so it was non-paying kids on laps. Driver was great. Said he was surprised to have a full house as usually he has to talk to himself at this time of year. Had a bit of a discipline problem 'cos in Arizona you can smoke, not pot or cigars, in the back three rows but not at all in California. Some sneaky tried it on a couple of times so the last warning was basically 'Fag out or you out'. Bit like a school outing. At times there was a smell like burnt socks, sweaty ones at that. M said it was a fellow on pot behind a barricade of cardboard boxes as a smoke-screen.

Friday, Time: 2 a.m.

LA Greyhound station. Very scary with all the hangers-about. Phoned for shuttle and as we went out we were bombarded by taxi touts going down like the Stock Exchange. A little guy with cleaning cloth and a spray said, 'I'll take you.' We let him hand us over and the shuttle driver gave him a tip. Quite a trade this, collecting shuttle clients. The driver said he wouldn't hang around the station for long as you could end up quite headless. He meant it. Must admit I was a trifle scared in the loo as I mumbled to myself about the current shortage of toilet paper and the person next door immediately shoved some under. As I picked it up I noticed very large feet in very heavy shoes emerging from under very tough blue jeans. Wrong loo? Pulled myself together and strode out, followed by an extremely pleasant, chatty lady. Fancy her feet being even bigger than mine.

Like the Greyhound, the flight to Honolulu was over-booked by six. M said they'd start bartering air vouchers and cash for people to fly later. 'Don't be daft,' I said. He was right. Started at $200 domestic tickets and ended at $500. Pays to wait but it worked.

US has been quite a revelation. Met some lovely people but I do feel it is too large for the majority to care about anything but themselves – a quest for survival which involves a great deal of materialism and waste. Some can only survive by moving on. Like Mike, the hostel warden, who tried to teach for a year but has settled for less financially. He feels the Grand Canyon puts it all into perspective and he is trying to develop the Canyon programme for schools. The hostel was very basic but the human atmosphere was deep. He and M had a long talk about crystals, energy forces, and so on. There were even New Age shops in Flagstaff so it would seem that many Americans are looking for something more than just a life of disposables.

Saturday

Honolulu. The warm air hits you as you step off the plane. Had to buy mango juice drinks to get change for lockers for luggage. For the first time I had to produce proof of identity; passport not enough. The driving licence was okay but slight confusion when asked which state. Still, in the end England seemed to do. Perhaps New England would have simplified matters. Took the bus to Waikiki Beach. Swam and sunbathed. Hard to realise we were on a Pacific island. Hostel full so treated ourselves to a $56 stay in the Continental Surf, eleven floors up. Great view down the shopping streets, well-designed tower buildings, interspersed with many trees, flowers and unusual water features. Three-hour evening stroll round the arcades. Innumerable shops at five different levels, outdoor lifts and escalators. Music, flame torches and fairy lights made it all very romantic and I loved every, minute of it. Quite a time to be in the US as yesterday Bush was inaugurated as President. Also today is the start of the Chinese New Year: clanging cymbals, drums, firecrackers and lion dances chasing-bad spirits out of homes and shops in Chinatown to clear the way for a *Kung Hee Fat Choy* – A Prosperous New Year to You.

You'd need to be prosperous to buy some of the goodies – even Irish crystal or eelskin leather goods. The latter is not endangered and conger eels are popular grub. One thing hard to find is proper Hawaiian grub, probably to avoid an LA-type smog. Its distinctive feature is the use of an *imu*; an earthen pit lined with kiawe wood and lava rock that steams and smokes as no other oven can, except a very ancient Rayburn. The imu is dug a day ahead by gathering and heating kiawe wood and lava rocks. Banana stumps are cut and prepared for lining the imu. The pig is stuffed with sizzling rocks wrapped in leaves and wire and placed in the imu with fish, yams or breadfruit. When the pig is removed hours later it is called kalua pig and is ono – delicious. Usually followed by coconut pudding called *haupia*. A sit-down dinner with entertainment is called a *luau* not to be confused with *aloha* which means welcome.

Not that we felt very welcome on their public transport. We went all round the island on 'the bus' for a total cost of $2.4 which was cheap but, we paid for it in tellings-off. First bus we had to be shown how to screw up the dollar note before putting it into the cash capsule. No wonder their notes get so tatty. Next bus it was get your bags on your knees. Third bus, we were told off for eating nuts. By the fourth bus we had got the hang of it. The service was efficient but the drivers were miserable. The trip included Dolphin Bay where the other half stay at the Hilton. Fun looking at blowholes in the volcanic rocks and the surfers from the coral sand beach. Much more exciting seeing them live than on film, some really daring.

Back to the airport past Pearl Harbour. You can see the sunken remains of the *Arizona* and a wall of marble with the engraved names of the 1,177 crew members killed on 7th December, 1941. A 1,760 lb armour-piercing bomb sunk her in less than nine minutes. Our last unhelpful driver dropped us a good walk from the airport, but we consoled ourselves with the thought that we needed the exercise before our longest flight of eight hours to Auckland. The flight was delayed by two hours so we treated ourselves to nosh costing $5 and then had a romantic stroll in the Airport Gardens. Their gardens were a mixture of different types – Hawaiian, Chinese and Japanese – lit by flame torches with water pools filled with massive carp. Then back to earth as we tried to sleep like a couple of dossers on the benches. Free earphones because of delay so I managed to watch half of *Crocodile Dundee II*. Not very good with earphones, must have abnormal ears. M was very happy as we had two films all 'for free', although he still had the other earphones.

Seems hard to believe how far we have come in a week. Even more amazing is the voyaging of the Polynesians for thousands of miles to Hawaii; no compass, just guiding their canoes by the sun, stars, waves, currents and birds. Now it takes computers and they don't always get it right. Even with M's fancy world time watch we are not too sure if it is Sat/22 or Sat/23, Sun/22 or Sun/23 or could it even be Mon/23/24?

Usual plane homework of forms, this time an agriculture quarantine form for NZ. Wanted to know if we had animals (alive or dead), meat, skins, feathers, wool, eggs, cultures, shells, hair, honey or bone. We declared we had been on a farm so should be fun. Even got sprayed on the plane so they must be a very hygiene-conscious lot; no farting for three weeks. Dare M admit to once having had fowl pest. Also no weapons allowed, handguns, flick knives or swordsticks. Doesn't mention cannons. We could have a 'ball' with them. Do they have a sense of humour in NZ, I ask, or is this all 'deadly' serious?

New Zealand

First taste of NZ is one of great efficiency and above all helpfulness. Shuttle to hostel. Susanna on reception a total ray of sunshine. Booked for us at Rotorua and Wellington. Gary at Wellington sounded super, insisted we stay for the night so transferred hostel booking. Organised money, bus and even M's playing-up camera. One Fast Foto shop told us about a camera repairer.

He must have a business connection with him because when we arrived the repairer said, 'Ah, the man from England with the shrunken Pentax.'

'Very, painful,' I commented, but he fixed it.

Every third shop is a Fast Foto. Hostel in the Parnell area, which is Auckland's answer to Happy Hampstead. In the 1900s it was a desirable address but then deteriorated until a businessman realised this was a shame. He bought and renovated dilapidated villas and turned it into a chic shopping centre. Century-old bricks pave the way into quaint courtyards and all sorts of shops nestle in the labyrinth of alleyways and wooden bridges and balconies. Very fascinating. The hostel itself was like a posh hotel, only a year old with every possible amenity.

Tuesday

Somewhat thrown as we lost Sunday except for a couple of hours early in the morning. Visited the Memorial Museum up on the hill. This housed a Maori Exhibition with a large, beautifully carved meeting hall and an enormous boat carved out of one trunk of wood, 83 feet long. They certainly know how to use wood with loving care; all part of acquiring mana or spiritual power. Problem was that others tried to pinch *mana* so hence the need for large-sized war canoes. Walked miles round various bays. Certainly a very pleasant place to live. Not many places where you could take a photo of a large, tepid (heated geothermally) swimming pool near a dual carriageway with park, trees and skyscrapers in the background. Sounds ghastly but it is all so clean; it seems perfectly natural.

Visited Kelly Turton's Underwater World. Kelly was always fascinated by the undersea world. Made money by reclaiming wreck treasures, gold, and so on. Then used his wealth to convert old sewage drains into underwater world. You walk under a plastic dome 7 cm thick while moray eels, crayfish, sharks and massive stingrays swim around and over you. The underside of a stingray as big as yourself is really something with its breathing flaps, just like Concorde. The technology of nature is really revealed here. I had no idea that sharks had such lovely smooth skins and of course they have their blood detection radar system – one part per million.

The World was opened in 1985 but poor Kelly died seven weeks later from a heart attack. However, he knew that in those few weeks one hundred thousand people had already seen the results of his tribute to a world very few can see. M had a long chat with a pink pig-fish which couldn't keep its eyes off him. Several people remarked on 'that man who is talking to that fish'; I wasn't too sure whether I belonged to them or not, although it was rather lovely, a large bearded gentleman and a round pink fish with beautiful eyes. The moray-eels looked evil but apparently they are not after food but like to be chatted to

24

and stroked. There were some other big jobs called wobbe-gongs, like frilly sharks, but we were woebegone because all we saw was a tail well camouflaged in a rock hole. In smaller tanks they had coral-consuming starfish which just spread their stomachs over the coral leaving a nasty scar; very large lobsters and delicate little seahorses. In all a beautiful experience. Well done, Kelly.

Just found out a bit more about the Maori warship. Made of totara wood it took one hundred warriors to paddle the giant vessel. Young men started their careers in the most vulnerable seat in the prow, moving back one seat after each battle, assuming of course that they survived the confrontations.

Wednesday

Coach to Rotorua. Steamy, patches and a smell of sulphur. Another friendly and well-equipped hostel. Afternoon at Whakarewarewa Thermal Reserve – Whaka to the locals 'cos they can't spell it. Saw our first shooting geyser and boiling murky mud pools. Even the bushes have steam coming out of them through little holes in the ground. Very weird as are the Maori figure wood carvings in which no part of the human anatomy is neglected. M was nearly run over as he stood in the road trying to get the right angle for a good photo. The thermal water we found too hot to touch in some places. The people of the Maori village there use the water for heating, cooking and washing. Even geysers have personalities. Most spectacular was Pohutu (Maori for explosion) and we were lucky to see it in action. Next to it is the Prince of Wales Feather Geyser, smaller, but it always starts off shortly before Pohutu. Then the latter makes its big splash, generally 20 metres, but can be 30. Very erratic, can be nine times a day or only twice. Usually lasts for 20 minutes although one long eruption lasted fourteen hours.

We had one twenty minute session.

Rotorua is a very touristy place, hundreds of motels, despite the everlasting pong of rotten eggs and the fact that many people feel that the Sulphur City is sitting on a time bomb.

Thursday

So you don't believe it, but we hired bikes and cycled over 30 km. Half of it was walked because it was up a mountain.

This is it, I hoped, I won't have to walk Muslim-style ten paces behind M. Normally I have to take one and a half steps to his every one. No, I lost again because the wheels of my bike were two-thirds the size of his, so I was quite a few revolutions behind, especially up the hills. Strange the number of coincidences. Yesterday in the bus station loo I happened to comment to one lady that the harbour at Auckland was very like Portsmouth. Another lady exclaimed that she had come from there in the 1960s. Today as we struggled up the hill I remarked that one side of the road looked like Scotland and the other the Yorkshire Dales. Five minutes later we met a fellow who had come from Yorkshire in the 1950s. Great consolation he was as he told us we were not nearly at the top.

'Oh, well,' I said, 'at least the wind will be behind us for coming back.' To which he replied:

'It'll have changed by then.'

Just as well he was wrong. The morning's 15 km took nearly three hours, the afternoon's only one.

All this was to see the buried village of Te Wairoa. How I didn't have to have M buried I'll never know. He's a bat out of hell on a bike, meandering into the middle of the road or overtaking me and smacking my bottom; encouragement, he calls it. Went down past the Blue and Green lakes, except that they both looked grey because it was cloudy and drizzly. The buried village was occupied by Maoris and Europeans until the night of 10th June, 1886, when Mount Tarawera erupted and covered the village and 5,000 square miles with ash, lava and mud up to two metres. One hundred and fifty-three people died and the pink and white natural terraces were no longer there as a major tourist attraction. The tohunga (high priest) had foreseen a disaster but the Maoris thought he had brought it on. They refused to dig him out of his hut but four days later Europeans rescued him. He died soon after, reputably at the age of one hundred and ten. There was a line of aspen poplars which have grown up from fence posts. The tops of the old posts can be seen sticking out from the base of the trees.

Also some very impressive waterfalls, 83 metres, with a cave to go through at the foot. The whole site is still being excavated but so far they have the various whares (huts), smithy, bakery and wooden remains of the sightseers' hotel with a bed 'imbedded' in the ash.

Decided to revitalise our aching limbs with a 40°C thermal bath. Really soporific. We seemed to have managed a great deal at Rotorua, including the City Museum. Heaven knows how many kilometres we did by the end of the day, killermetres more like. Sorry, that was M's joke. I think it's the ice creams going to his brain cells. It's very difficult to move him past an ice cream shop. Exotic tastes such as boysenberry are an absolute must.

Friday

Last wander around Rotorua. Saw Rachel's Spring, a mere 100°C. Named after Rachel who committed suicide in a boiling mud pool nearby.

Decided to go mad as we had a half-price discount ticket and have a private thermal pool, round at that. Censored.

Bus to Poirirua, fifteen minutes from Wellington. Met by Gary, married to Pauline, second cousin to M. Beard like M, same non-materialistic attitude except when it comes to hoarding in sheds – creator in wood and metal like M. Pauline away to look after her mum and dad as both flat on their backs. Gary is the Baptist minister and the close-knit community made us very welcome.

Saturday

Painted signs for the church music festivals, cleared Gary's garden and generally tried to make ourselves useful. In the evening we were invited to Gaynor and Vernon's for a beautiful supper. A real laugh with them; Suwe; Ruth; their children William six, Alexandra three; Ben and Sotoria, and of course little Hannah, a ten-month old poppet belonging to Vernon and Gaynor. Great mix of nationalities and yet they all make a great joke of each other's colours.

Innocently I asked if they wanted a chocolate chip cookie and they all fell around the floor laughing. Gary explained later that this was a bit like an Irish joke. Ben was a real character, a 22-year-old Fijian recently become a Christian. He was a Pied Piper with children and during Sunday church led ten of them to feed the ducks in the lake nearby.

Also a great one for puns, graded according to how many people recognise them. If it's only Gary it's an A+ joke but if it is really corny it becomes an X grade. After a round of really bad Rugby jokes M rated it XV. Only Gary, got that to start with so that made M's XV an A+ joke. Ben had been a rough street guy, but to see his massive stature gently cuddling tiny Hannah you would never know it. We felt that we had known them all for years, not just twenty-four hours. It will be a real wrench to leave on Monday.

Sunday

Morning Service – all singing and congregational participation: something that some of our churches could copy. Then lunch with Gary when we talked about all things material and spiritual. Just discussing the feasibility of Moses dividing the waters when Sue rushed in from the church to say the waters had divided from the Baptismal tank. Gary had forgotten that he had left it filling for the evening. So there we were with dustpans and buckets scooping up water which had moved from the front of the church to the entrance at the back.

Gary laughed it all off by saying, 'Well it's not as bad as last time.'

It was the second time he'd done it in three years.

Ben leapt around shouting, 'He's done it again!'

Picked up Gary's daughters, Adele and Johanna, from the airport. Aged eight and six they are a total enchantment, so fresh and loving. Experienced our first Baptist baptism – very moving. Then the girls invited a bundle of kids for juice and biscuits; just like being a proper mum again. From the warmth of the whole church it is hard to imagine that this is a very deprived area, with broken homes, unemployment and hard guys on the street. Gary has been attacked a few times. One time he went in to defend a kid who was having his head bashed on concrete. When the police arrived, Gary didn't press charges, so the attackers apologised but not the victim, who felt cheated. He was being chastised for teasing a mentally handicapped member of the gang and was aware he had gone too far and his punishment was therefore justified.

Another time a large fellow went for Gary and in the end Gary said to himself, Lord, help me to look him in the eye. Suddenly the man withdrew and from then on word spread amongst other toughies to avoid the eyes of the 'preacher man'. So despite the cleanliness and general air of a reasonable standard of living, NZ has its share of problems, even curfew areas. Gary certainly does a grand job in his area.

Monday

Farewell to Gary in his 'rattles everywhere' twenty year-old Bedford van and on to the boat for a gloriously sunny boat trip of three hours to the South Island. Caught up on reading homework about the Maoris. Definitely a warrior lot with the losers ending up as slaves or pot roast. At that time not many animals around so enemies were a good wide source of protein. Tasman did not stay long after several of his crew were cooked. According to legend, ten great canoes arrived in NZ in the fourteenth century. The names and landing points of all the canoes are remembered and most Maoris can trace their ancestors from these, although there were some earlier Maori migrations – the moa hunters. The moa, a huge flightless bird, twelve feet high with human-shaped legs and outsize feet, is now extinct.

The first temporary European seal and whale hunters were a bit of a rough lot. They introduced disease, prostitution and created such a demand for preserved heads that Maori chiefs chopped off slaves' heads. One chief Heke, got a bit fed up with the English and kept chopping down their flagpoles. The clever English covered their flagpoles in iron, so for good measure Heke burnt Kororareka instead. Most of the English were pleased about this because it was a rather scruffy hole.

NZ is a very socially minded country. Apart from wide intermarriage, women had the vote twenty-five years before the UK. Also pioneered pensions, minimum wage laws and child health services. Maoris had no written language but communicated in art and song. Early missionaries compiled a fifteen letter language with each syllable ending in a vowel to give the lyrical overtone. WH is a soft F so Whaka is fat you make of it!

Forgot to mention that Gary took us to a couple of viewpoints to look over Wellington. Most impressive, although concrete towers are replacing older buildings. Original wooden houses in the various creeks but the new suburbs are creeping out quite a way. We both preferred Auckland as it seemed more planned and community based as well as traditional, although less spectacular. Mind you, we are both a bit anti-cities and I'd still rather have London or Lincoln any day. A decent cathedral seems to give a city some enduring solid point of reference.

Tuesday

After yesterday's beautiful boat trip and then seven hours in a very hot, broken-down air-conditioned coach, we arrived at Cousins Clark in Christchurch. Great deal of family gossip although they were both suffering from bad backs. We did the equivalent of hostel chores. M did a load of gardening including the kiwi trees. Cousin Chummie told me all about the different pruning treatment needed for male and female kiwi trees.

'Oh dear,' I said, 'it sounds very complicated. You'd better tell Michael himself.' Turns out he was having me on.

Pauline (Gary's wife) took us on a guided tour of Christchurch, or misguided, because by the time Chum and Eve had given various directions and M had the map as well we did get a little confused. Pauline is tiny, six stone, but she has no end of patience, a real sweetie. Saw the Botanic Gardens and the Antarctic Exhibition. Christchurch is the HQ for Operation Deep Freeze and supplies

31

are ferried from the airport to US bases in the Antarctic. Saw Amundsen, Scott's relics, plus an original stuffed husky. Then stuffed ourselves with a cream tea in the octagonal tearoom which keeps being set on fire.

Wednesday

Pauline led us up a trek as a joke training for the four day Milford Track. All because I said I didn't fancy the latter. Why? Because it's sand-flies, possibly rain and floods, plus perilous bridges. Anyway, we went up the Sugar Loaf, behind where they live and from where you see Lyttelton Harbour. The harbour itself is the drowned crater of a long extinct volcano and the walk is called the Crater Rim Track. Not much sun but plenty of geophysical wind and M got burnt.

Thursday

Coach to Queenstown. M a bit poorly from yesterday's exposure but recovered by 6 for his ice cream. I knew he was a bit off because he didn't fancy one earlier. Queenstown is a lovely place by the lake with sharp, rugged blue mountains all around. Hostel crowded and kitchen a bit of a muddle but it really is amazing to see what people cook, especially the Japanese, mounds of it. Chum, Eve and Pauline gave us a blessing send-off and I must admit Christchurch was a more traditional city. It even had a cathedral in a cathedral square. Problem was that every city bus went through it so we had trouble finding the correct bus.

No city bus in Queenstown as you can walk, bike, raft, jet-boat, fly, gondola lift or smelly, smoky steamer around as everything is so compact. The steamer eats up one ton of coal every hour. Lake Wakatipu is not a smokeless zone so far as the SS Earnslaw is concerned. After all, she was built at the beginning of the century and actually carted over in sections from Dunedin, 283 km away. Queenstown's name comes from Ireland because many of the early gold-diggers were Irish.

On the way to Queenstown our very kind coach driver stopped at all sorts of interesting places and events. There was the little Church of the Good Shepherd by Lake Tekapo, built in 1935 of stone and shingle gathered near the lake. It is a memorial to the original shepherds but it is unique because the long window behind the altar has the view of the lake and the mountains behind. The lake itself is a brilliant turquoise, even on a cloudy day, because the glacial rock powder contains minerals which cause the blue reflection. No need for a stained-glass window in this little church. Later on we stopped again to watch Bungee jumping from the Kawarau Suspension Bridge. You pay about £25 for the privilege of a leap backwards from the bridge held by an overgrown piece of elastic. The elastic is attached to a piece of rope tied round your ankles.

You then hang upside down until you are collected by the yellow dinghy. All this for a certificate and the money goes towards the Restoration Fund for the Bridge.

'So what?' you say, and I reply 'The drop was around 180 feet in a gorge with a very fast river below.'

They get a free T-shirt as well. Standing on the bridge itself was enough. Mind you, perhaps it would be better to do one bungee jump and get it out of the way than four days of flies-and flood on the Milford Track. Would be a lot cheaper as well.

Friday

Queenstown is a bit of mix with posh hotels around the lake and the hostel rabble nearby. We explored a bit and planned. M is really good at the planning, even the weather fits. Tried the lake fitness course – twelve points with equipment like parallel bars, rope, ladders, and so on. All very carefully worked out by the experts until M thinks up other fun games for each section. You are supposed to rate yourself as 'Very Fit', 'Fit' or 'Unfit'. The way we tried it we were the 'Un-unfit'. Picnic lunch on a rock stuck out on the lake. A helicopter kept going over us. I think they wondered if we were stranded. Took the gondola lift 2,500 feet up. I'd never done it before but M had when skiing. A feat of engineering and feet worth of view from the top. Cup of tea and cream cake with a really romantic view; what a holiday of a lifetime. Sometimes very hard to believe that it is happening to me. Then we had a very unusual walk up a gorge; known as One Mile Creek. Rained like mad so it seemed like the rain forest with unusual fantail birds swooping from overhanging rocks.

Last night we were in single-sex dorms, tonight together again in two-pair unisex room with own loo and shower. Must admit I'm not so keen on being separated from Big M now but I'll have to be ready for it when we reach India.

Saturday

We decided to explore Arrowtown, a few kilometres from Queenstown. It was an old gold town in the 1870s and you can hire a pan (looks like a wok) for $1.50 as there are little bits of gold left to find. Decided to hire our pan from the original 1862 general store but he sent us to his rival pan leaser because he was shutting the store to go for a game of golf. Anyway, off we trundled up the gorge towards the site of another old gold settlement, Macetown. We had to ford the River Arrow several times but if we had done the whole 13 kilometres we would have had to cross it twenty-two feet-killing times. Trucks, minibuses and even motorbikes go across the river; in fact, more traffic than most of the

NZ roads. M had a great time panning for hours. He even forgot about the sand-flies; our first encounter. One coach driver said, 'Don't kill 'em, just fan 'em or else twenty-seven plus of their relatives will appear for the funeral!'

Excitedly we returned our pan and asked the expert to assess our 'finds'. 'Sorry,' he reported, 'iron pyrites.' Still, at least we can say we have tried for gold.

In the Arrowtown Museum I found a lovely book about Macetown as well as instructions for 'Grandma's Washday' and 'The Husband's Commandments'. The settler women certainly had to be tough. Who needs a washing machine when all you had to do is build a fire in the backyard to heat a kettle of rainwater; shove one whole cake of shaved soap in boiling water, rub dirty spots on board, take things out of kettle with broom stick handle, wrench, pour, wrench water in flower bed, scrub porch with hot soapy water, hang out clothes, turn tubs upside down. After all that, Instruction 14 says: put on clean dress, smooth hair in side combs, brew tea, set and rest and rock a spell, and count blessings! You certainly had to count your blessings according to the Husband's Commandments:

> Thou shalt have no other husband but me, whom thou didst vow to love, honour and obey, for I saved thee from old maidism and rescued thee from the terrors of single blessedness. When thou goest out with thy husband thou shalt not wear a crinoline or any other dangerous machine likely to come in contact with his shins.

Not that gold-diggers' wives were likely to wear crinolines. One daring, lady, Adie, would wear a long riding skirt, and in the winter, after fording the river several times, the skirt would be splashed and frozen stiff by the time she arrived home. When taken off the skirt would stand up straight on its own and have to be thawed out. Generally the women accepted a way of life according to the last commandment:

Blessed are they who expect nothing, for they shall not be disappointed.

So no more grumbling, girls.

Macetown grew, flourished and died all in fifty years. The population peak was three thousand with four hotels, four stores, school, post office, blacksmith bakery, bootmaker and even a public hall. Road access was perilous and at points was built on dry stone walls, 500 feet high. The River Arrow was frozen most of the winter. Horses had special frost nails to grip the ice. Life was hard but imaginative with mine names such as Morning Star, Black Angel and Homeward Bound.

Families were large and concerts, dances and parties provided fun. One Macetown character was Doc, a real social fellow despite being a gambler. Probably just as well that he found the largest nugget ever, 16 oz worth about £300 today. He was very fond of children and on Christmas mornings put on a party for the children. Each child had a Christmas card, a drink of raspberry vinegar and cakes to eat. Sometimes he had afternoon tea parties for the ladies and baked the cakes himself. Sadly he never got married.

Many were very fond of animals, such as Billy. He read an ad in the local paper and sent for a 75-cent saddle, a tremendous bargain for his horse. Great was his disgust when he received a bicycle saddle. Quite often children nearly drowned playing near the river, like Vi who was only saved because someone saw her red patchwork dress floating downstream. Juvenile delinquents like Ned and his mates would corner a bull, tie a hat on its head and let it rampage down the main street. The constable from Arrowtown came up to find the culprits but they all absconded for the afternoon.

The lure of gold kept them all going. The prospect of a good find is like a drug. I must admit M was well hooked to his pan. I didn't like to tell him that it usually took a shift of a ton of rock or quartz to yield an ounce of gold, sometimes more. Coach to Te Anau Hostel, run by a very kind but firm elderly lady – perhaps a retired teacher! Great fun listening to her telling a six-foot-plus, non-comprehending German male how to wash the kitchen floor properly: plenty of hot water and not too much soap.

Sunday

Today was the Milford experience. Through snow-clad and glaciated mountains to the Milford Sound which should be called the Milford Fjord. Why? Geography Lesson I: sounds are valleys made by water. Fjords are made by ice. Anyway, whatever, the scenery was magnificent and compensated us for not being able to go on the trek as it was booked up until March. The Fjord is 22 km long with sheer peaks all around. We were lucky as we left Te Anau in cloud but it was all sun and fluffy white clouds for the launch trip. On the way to the Fjord our driver stopped several times so that we could take pictures of rainforests waterfalls, massive rock holes, avalanche scars, earthquake landslides (6.5 one last year) and the Homer Tunnel. The latter was started in the 1930s by five road diggers with picks, shovels and wheelbarrows and finished in 1953. I was okay as I had thirty shots left but M had only about half that. On the way home our driver asked those who had run out of film to put their hands up, so I made M confess. I think the driver had shares in Kodak or Fuji.

Back to the hostel. You can always detect a hostel be-tween 5 p.m. and 7 p.m. because the cooking smells go out for miles. One Japanese nearly set fire to the place frying his uneaten lunch roll from the day before for breakfast; lettuce and all. I hope they leave the kitchen tidy tonight as we have a night chore of cleaning it up, as we need to get the coach to Mount Cook around 6 a.m. tomorrow. Yes, it really is a holiday.

Monday

Up at 5 a.m. but slight panic as coach did not appear until 6.45. Bank Holiday as Waitangi Day, anniversary of some agreement between the English and Maoris, neither of which really stuck to it. Anyway, we think the driver has had a bit of a lie-in. Mount Cook has a superb hostel. Good walk to the foot of the Mueller Glacier. Could hear the ice creaking and shifting. The section on the mountain had beautiful shining blue and white but the bit gouged out at the bottom looked like a council rubbish tip. Mount Cook itself was impressive known to the Maoris as Aorangi – cloud piercer. On the Kea Point Walk to the glacier were the 'home-blown' flowers and fruits; all within a couple of miles of mountain ice, as well as lupins of all shades, thistles as well as raspberries and red and white currants. On the way back we had a fruit feast for a premature pudding. Shall not forget the awe-inspiring view from our hostel room; rugged mountains less than a mile.

Tuesday

Went on the Governor's Bush Walk for a last view of Mount Cook then coach to Twizel, change Tarras, change and finally Wanaka. Beautiful lake of yet a different blue. Having done a bit of homework I had a strong urge to go up Mount Iron so although we had run late and it was after 5 p.m. I dragged M off. The view was unique – a total round panorama of rivers, valleys, lakes and mountains. No other viewpoint could ever beat it and yet it was only 527 metres high. From it we could see the Maze and Puzzle Centre. They reckon more than a quarter of a million people have got lost in the three-dimensional maze since it was set up a decade ago. The names get better and better. There's Mount Aspiring and the Gin and Raspberry Stables nearby. I'm just about mastering all the Big T centres of the area – Taupo, Te Anau, Tekapo, Timaru, Tutukaka and there is even a Te Puke in North Island. Still very lucky with the weather considering the west can be much wetter. Even luckier to have had a good day at Milford Sound as the average rainfall there is 6,325 mm per annum! Spoil-sport M has converted it to 20 feet. I thought it sounded more impressive in millimetres. It's still a lot of rain.

Wednesday

Walk round Lake Wanaka, very peaceful. Try to get in four hours' good walking even if on a coach trip. So moving pattern is walk before and after coach or a long one before or a long one after. Today on to Franz Josef. Beautiful drive first to Fox Glacier. From Fox to Franz is 25 km. Very interesting but the fact is that between them the road goes up and down along a narrow ridge and there are 365 bends in those 25 km. Unusual walk called the Terraces which was through the native rainforest. Large trees, often dead, become a place for other creepy-crawly trees and heavy mosses. Cool and quiet with the evening sun glistening through the upper branches. We branched off to the Callery Gorge Bridge. Steep rocks and rushing green water below with a suspended swinging bridge about 60 feet up. M says 40 to 50 feet, but he still wasn't keen to stand on it for long, especially when I started to make it sway. Have to get my own back for the tricks he plays on me like 'bind-weed going anti-clockwise in NZ and clockwise in UK'.

After supper we had a really remarkable walk in the

dark. Think what you like, but in fact it was to see thousands of glow worms nestled under over-hanging tree roots and in bushes. Their whole life cycle is really extraordinary and you feel a sensitive respect for these tiny florescent technological creatures. After hatching the minute larva immediately emits a bright, almost blue light. It then makes a horizontal nest in the shape of a tunnel made of mucus and silk. This is suspended by silk threads and forms the runway for the larva. Then we have the most astonishing biological engineering. From its lair the larva lets down vertical fishing lines, up to seventy, from 1 cm to 50 cm depending on the location. Each line has droplets of mucus at regular intervals to catch small insects lured by the light. The larva breaks through its tunnel to bend down and haul in the line with its victim. Thousands of larvae with their lines lit up like millions of diamonds provide a very spectacular curtain of light drops. When the larva is mature it removes the lines and parts of the nest and suspends itself vertically for pupation. The female is often fertilised soon after hatching and while still clinging to the empty skin.

Males survive for twenty-eight days but the poor young female dies within three days of laying eggs. Sound, light, humidity and temperature can cause the glow-worm to switch its luminosity on and off at will. Nevertheless, life goes on as uninterrupted as possible, fishing lines are cleaned, repaired and lengthened. When you consider their size, their ingenuity is truly a miracle of nature, that we humans could never create on such a fine scale. It certainly makes you think, and as you hear and see the effects of man slashing the rainforest it makes you feel very sad. So many aspects of nature are vanishing for ever. It is thought that the greenhouse effect is causing rapid changes in glacial movements. Even here the Franz Josef Glacier has increased its pace of retreat. A plane that crashed in 1943, 3.5 km from the terminal face of the glacier, made it to the bottom 6.5 years later – a speed of 1.5 metres a day. It has been known to move 5 metres a day but now in 1989 the average is 3 metres, which is still twice the speed of 40-odd years ago, so you could collect your plane in half the time. Now we have heard that daffodils are already blooming in London. Does make you wonder what is going to happen and travelling around like this makes you realise how much the world has to lose in natural beauty. Yet seeing the effects of volcanoes, earthquakes and avalanches, which is more vulnerable in the long run – man or nature?

Thursday

Although Greymouth was named after some Sir Grey fellow, the name is totally apt on a geographical basis; a grey river enters a grey sea bordered by a grey stony beach. Even the weather was grey to start with and the town seemed really dreary after all our beautiful scenery of the past week. I kept trying to visualise where we had been to keep the memories alive and I'm glad I have tried to soak in everything I have seen. Leaving the mountains, valleys, forests, lakes and all the varied colours to arrive at Greymouth, I must admit, was a shock. It has made me even more determined to appreciate my luck in being able to see so many wonderful places as we travel on. Even the sand-flies have not been so bad and perhaps the Maori philosophy has it right – When God created the West Coast he filled it with beautiful mountains, lakes and forests and an abundant supply of greenstone. Then lest man should grow complacent in the midst of all this beauty he introduced the sandfly to remind men of their essential mortality.

Perhaps we had this philosophy in mind when we combed the Greymouth beach and found smooth stones of many colours; many of them very small and hidden by the larger grey ones. So even Greymouth gave us a tangible souvenir of colour. Actually, we were looking for that Maori greenstone, and here we go again to find an assessor, as M thinks he may have found some. As it turned out, my dark green rough lump was it.

Friday

Coach to Nelson. Incredible service these coaches do provide. They deliver post, newspapers and even plastic bags of shopping to rural homes. This driver was the most adept we have seen at delivering newspapers to the gate. He threw them out of his window left and right. Right was easy enough, I suppose, but to do the left he put his arm out and round and threw them in front of the bus. Every paper landed in the middle of its prospective drive. He also had half a dozen primary school kids to pick up and he knew each one by name and character. One seven-year-old lad was being trained on right hand paper throws with a short lesson on the slipstream effect. I think he was trying to interest young Jason in something, as apparently when asked what he does at school the answer is invariably 'swimming' or 'nuffin'.

Followed the Buller River valley and saw the lines where after five months of rain last year it rose by over 60 feet. Perhaps it should be called the Fuller River. Before that we had a quick stop at Punakaiki for the Pancake Rocks. The limestone rocks look like giant layers of pancakes and the waves lash around caverns below the rocks and up through massive blowholes. Around the area you can still see the scars of the 1968 7.3 scale earthquake – one whole mountain just slipped away. Apparently one fisherman on the shore saw his boat and the water it was on disappear down a hole and then reappear. He decided to make a quick getaway. Even now if you explore local caves and it rains you have to get out fast before you drown.

Hostel was full in Nelson so we had a tramp round to find a place. Then treated ourselves to a $6.50 meal – £3 each in the Toby Jug pub. That included a drink and on our one-course plate we had fish (M had groper steak), curried rice, sultanas, beans, normal and mini sweetcorn, apple, orange, lemon, peppers, spam, lettuce, tomato, cucumber, cottage cheese, courgettes, and of course chips – eighteen items in all (two kinds of beans). M's groper was a bit like haddock. He had hoped for a bigger grope studying boobies on the Ta Huna beach where women can bathe topless but the tide was right in leaving no beach. Actually, people who object to the toplessness – not the groping – can make an official complaint to the police which may be upheld. Can't see the point of it all. Sorry, a very poor joke.

Saturday

Off to Picton. Third time we bumped into Liz from Surrey. Second time at Queenstown I had said I wished we had taken her address. So we had a good old comparison chat on the boat about our South Island trips. Arrived Wellington and had a walk to see the beehive, alias the government HQ and the rest of the Botanic Gardens we did not see with Gary. Beautiful flower beds with a dense concentration of bright colours. Phoned Gary and he was really glad to hear from us as he had been poorly and Pauline was still looking after her mom and dad.

'Real neat to talk to you,' he said and we made promises to see each other again.

It will be sad to leave the beauty and friendship of NZ in a day's time. Not really met any undesirable people except the old bat this morning who arrived at 8.40 for the 8.30 bus. Driver pointed out that she had held him up.

'It says 8.40 on my ticket,' was the reply.

'But 8.30 on the timetable,' was his reply.

Eventually the ticket was checked, yes, 8.30.

'So what,' said Madam Bat, 'I'm here.'

A few kilometres on she realised she had left something so our long-suffering driver stopped at the next store and phoned for it to come on the next bus. Another fellow on the way to Mount Cook had a bundle of picks, crampons, ice axes, and so on which nearly massacred the driver as he put them on. The owner told him to be careful as they were valuable. It was as much as I could do not to tell him he should keep his lethal 'klingons' or whatever in a tough bag. Again the driver was a monument of patience, for which I verbally commended him. Anyway, my thoughts must have got through as a little later the klingon owner did admit he should perhaps carry them all in a bag. Mind you these drivers do have some queer freight at times – dry cleaning, queen bees, chickens. Once I thought we had a pig up front but it was a passenger baby making funny noises.

Sunday

Twelve hour coach ride from Wellington to Auckland. Would have been eleven hours but at the last loo stop we managed to leave a lady behind. She was probably still looking at the cafe's Rogues' Gallery of photos of all the coach drivers in NZ, hundreds of 'em mounted all around the walls. City bus to our first friendly hostel. Quite a laugh as two old dears, male and female, hadn't finished their ice creams when the bus arrived. They asked if they could bring them on the bus and the driver said it was okay as he did not think they would behave like teenagers with them. Somehow the old boy dropped his all over the passageway and we all got the stifled giggles while he rummaged and scrounged around for tissues. Then the old girl got the giggles but not so stifled. They were worse than any teenagers but the driver was the usual height of NZ

44

diplomacy and pretended not to notice any of it.

I have decided that New Zealanders do have a great sense of humour, obviously inherited, if you read some of the things their ancestors got up to. The poor Chinese in some of the old gold towns had some good pranks played on them and yet the Europeans had a deep respect for the Chinese. When building their huts the Chinese knocked out the bottoms of bottles and inserted the bottles into the walls. During the night they urinated into these and the urine ran from a tin guttering into a drum to be used as a fertiliser. Local lads would block up the necks of the bottles with mud with disastrous results for the Chinamen whose bunks were built alongside the walls. The Chinese also used to gather dried grass which they tied into bundles and carried home on their backs to use as bedding. Sometimes the lads would sneak up behind them, set the grass alight and then run off. Yet on the death of a Chinese person every white person attending the funeral was given a small gift of something which had belonged to the deceased.

More than a century on there are still no real social barriers in NZ. Everyone makes fun of everyone else. It is said that NZ is forty years behind modern societies; maybe in its 'no need to rush attitude', especially amongst coach drivers; and in its multitude of old cars such as brightly coloured split windscreen Morris Minors; but when it comes to good-naturedness, helpfulness, consideration and kindness they are light years ahead.

Ayers and no Graces in Australia

Monday

With sadness we left NZ wondering if we would receive the same gracious treatment anywhere else. Usual immigration homework forms to fill in on the plane. This time Australia wanted to know if we were carrying fungi, bamboo – alive or dead, or parts of – or hatching eggs of reptiles or insects, and so on, plus feathers, hairs or semen. You can imagine M's answer to the last and he's only prepared to give it up to a very attractive young nubile. I can see trouble ahead! Actually we had a few teabags and did wonder if they should be declared as 'parts of plants dead' and were the actual bags 'articles manufactured from wildlife' such as turtles, crocs, elephants and rhinoceros?

Thank goodness we have not visited an abattoir in the last few months or life would be really complicated. As it is I think we shall be well 'knackered' by the time we get through immigration. I was right, we did have trouble all day in Melbourne. The guide books say its architecture is a disaster, that's not all. Mind you, it was the down under equivalent of Friday 13th – Monday 13th. On the agricultural clearance form dearest M put down that we had been on a turkey plucking farm before Christmas. That did it; red pen, red lights and finally three Australian Agricultural Control Officers in fits of laughter attempting to search us for feathers.

Every hostel was full so we ended up in what was once an old railway hotel converted into a backpackers' residence. We got the address wrong and M ended in a topless bra – sorry, Freudian slip – topless bar. So the BP place was really something, next to Chinatown, paper peeling off the wall, doors caving in and large holes in the bathroom floor. Dumped our stuff and went to the hostels HQ to do future bookings. Building gutted. Tried to phone but walked several blocks to find a phone with an earpiece. Booked up Sydney after another trek dodging the trams, which run down the middle of the pedestrians only Mall – another Melbourne booboo. Then to the Greyhound who shilly-shallied about the validity of our pass, but that was put right. Success, we found a super steak meal for £3 each. Ambled back and even M was too tired to view the goods on offer on film at the Shaft Sinema nearly opposite our salubrious lodgings. Having come from the gentleness of NZ to the bustle of Oz, we experienced quite a culture shock. A dress rehearsal for Bangkok?

Tuesday

Not much sleep as traffic, sirens and shouting went on all night. Bit like trying to sleep with Hill Street Blues on full volume. Later found out that Russell Street, where we were, together with two others, has the worst crime record in Melbourne. Glad we went to bed early. Up early, two-hour walk round Melbourne and still not very fond of it. Glad again to leave on the coach for the eighteen hour ride to Sydney. Fairly monotonous scenery and rather bumpy ride. So far not over impressed with Oz but we do have a laugh about it all.

Wednesday

Arrived Sydney 5.30 a.m. Looks better than Melbourne,

more space and better planned. Really luxurious hostel with own reasonable restaurant and swimming pool with sunning area on the roof.

Bought a $7 run-around ticket and went on buses, trains and boats like mad. Boat all round harbour and saw the familiar Sydney Bridge and Opera House. Apparently the latter is falling down in parts. Nevertheless, both were impressive although we were rather perturbed by the non-shutting of doors on the City Line. They just tell you to hold on tightly. Went to Manly Bay, lovely beach and surfers. Attractive places for Sydneyers to escape to at weekends. Then wandered around the dock area to find the Wayside Chapel run by a friend of our friend, Ruby, the Reverend Ted Noffs.

Ted had been especially concerned with drug abuse and felt that the problem was being tackled too late. He established the Shepherd of the Streets programme in 1978 with Government aid, in which a team of people search for runaways. They are given a temporary haven and help and if feasible they are reunited with their families. It reaches out to over six hundred families every year. There is also the coffee house open day and night to anyone, but it brings together young people, down-and-outs and even the likes of us, who had a cup of tea and a chat there. The Little Shoppe is run by local women every day to sell donated goods but its other purpose is as a line of communication.

Ted is ill at present but we may be able to see him tomorrow or his son, Wesley. The running of the Life Education Centre is by Wesley, although his father founded it in 1979. The Government and other authorities have now increased the service and about half a million children a year are seen by the service worldwide. There are mobile units with visual aids, games, and so on which aim at the five to twelve age group.

It is progressive programme on the physiology of the

body through a transparent anatomical manikin called TAM; fun but with a serious message. The approach is purposely non-shock but makes the children aware of the incredible structure and systems within them. They are encouraged not to abuse their most prized possession and to make decisions based upon their own well-being, not upon peer pressure or advertising influences. Anyway, we had a look at the chapel and heard how at Christmas four thousand people came for dinner, rich and poor together. The better off provided chickens, hams puddings and so on, and of course, being summer they were able to make it a street party with dancing and Christmas music. It started with less than one hundred in 1964 and now nobody in the area is lonely at Christmas. We do have caring groups in Britain but this little chapel centre takes some beating and there is no form of religious moralising. Ted Noffs believes that we are part of the family of man, which in turn is part of the one great source of life that created the universe. We are all evolving souls and there have been many spiritual leaders in Christianity, Buddhism, Sikhism, Judaism, Islam, and so on. Every religion is like a coat but what is more important is the body underneath. Put the many coloured coats together and you have the rainbow of man. We are unique individuals with our own group interpretations of creation.

Came back for a freezing swim in the roof pool which really cooled us down. Then made more use of our travel tickets to go to a £2.50 'eat as much as you can help yourself to Chinese'. Included soup, bread and butter, tea and coffee. We were well and truly stuffed so had a walk round Darling Harbour before staggering back. Coincidences continue as I shared a room with two girls from Brighton. They were fascinated by what we are doing. There was also a Swedish girl who had just spent two years working in a drug rehabilitation centre run like a very posh holiday camp-cum-boarding school. I told her about the Wayside Chapel and then until 11 p.m. we had a very interesting discussion. One of the Brighton girls was a nurse and with her experience she said she felt very sorry for some of the drug dependents but not all. The other was a secretary and I admired her honesty. She felt that most of them should be able to use more self-control in the first place. So like a sociology lesson we moved from families, to love, to God and ended up back at the need for family caring. So much for an early night. Had to decide whether to leave the door open for a bit of air plus a possible bit of 'rape and pillage' or to stifle. Settled for the latter as it was less effort.

Dear M was a bit miffed the next day when he saw the three girls were blonde twenty-year-olds. He said he'd have swapped with me to protect them and I'd have had three young men to protect me. I'm sure!

Thursday

Forgot to mention our walk through the Botanics where a possum in a tree trunk let us go really close and was highly delighted when M rewarded him with banana, safely stuck on the end of a stick. Not sure if it was a gliding possum as it did not jump. Gliders have a flying membrane between the elbow and the ankle and their long, well-furred tail also helps, acting as a rudder to steer their flight. The best flyer is the 'Yellow-bellied, which with a body length of 280 mm can do over 100 metres in one leap; a sort of flying carpet.

Early start to get our cheap tickets' worth. Bus and train over the bridge to North Sydney. Idea was to get quick boat back to circular Quay, or Qway as M calls it just to confuse people. Some union thing or other meant you had to take a round trip to a place called Meadowbank. An hour later we reached the aforementioned Meadowbank and got off to try for a speedier form of transport back to the Qway. Here we met our great fun, bearded, very helpful, singing bus driver. He had three passengers; M, myself and a 'my sight is not so good as it was' elderly lady. While keeping up the patter he actually took a detour to take us to a better bus stop as we had just missed the train. He called us a couple of drovers as we were on Day Rover tickets and asked where we came from.

'England, oh, yes, where the Queen lives unless she's in Scotland shooting shags. Oops, sorry, I mean stags.'

'Don't think he was very keen on taxi drivers as the faint-sighted lady said she was going on by taxi and he retorted that he thought all taxi drivers should be taxidermitised. All this between long Caruso renderings of 'When I grow too old to dream' and similar songs expressed with great fervour and a few of his own ideas. Censorship again. Very much one of life's characters. What with him and the Odd-Job in Woolies we were coming to the same idea – Thursday, 16th February, 1989 was going to be a 'lets keep bumping into loveable nutters day.'

Odd-Job in Woolies? M noticed that Woolies did a good brekker for £2 and there was a bearded fellow in a funny hat partaking of his bacon and eggs, already giving a loud verbal treatise on the state of the world. The manageress asked him politely to lower his voice, whereupon he told her to mind her own business. Of course we got the giggles and received larger portions because we commented we had not expected free entertainment with our breakfast. His final effort, before he stamped out was to tell the manageress to go back to where she belonged, in the kitchen, so that he did not have to look at her ugly face. I was a little worried when a little later M bought a similar Lawrence of Arabia hat, supposedly for Alice Springs. What with that and the beard, is he trying to qualify as a nutter?

Further panic in the afternoon as M got back two films, totally blank. Took shrivelled Pentax to another repairer who swore there was nothing wrong with it. Meanwhile we had taken another film to a different developers, so the repairman – was he psychic – said, 'Stay cool, have an ice cream, relax until you collect the film.'

It was okay so back we went to complain to lot number one who sent us to the developing centre. Long technical explanation then it occurred to us that in one of Pattie Poo's 'Let's have a luggage sort-out' the films had got muddled; yes, you've got it – two unexposed films. We found the proper two and had them done later in the 'Soho' King's Cross area. Thank goodness, they were beautiful prints. As usual M saw the funny side and decided we had joined the nutters of Sydney, but I decided no more luggage sort-outs; we stay in an easy-to-find muddle. I think I have had more than enough of Fast Foto shops.

Went round the area called the Rocks. Has some of the oldest buildings in Australia. Was a pretty seedy area haunted by larrikins (Australian hooligans) until razed by an outbreak of the bubonic plague. Now being restored including the old courthouse famous for the 1935 shark case. An escaped convict was identified by his tattooed arm found in a shark's belly. Wandered by the Harbour Bridge which some say is like an overgrown coat-hanger. Completed in 1932 at a cost of £10 million, it is continuously being repainted. More expensive is the Opera House whose Harbour setting enhances its grandeur. As a feature I like it because you can add your own interpretation, shells, sails, and so forth.

In fact, for a city we both enjoyed Sydney for its extensive waterfront, beaches, old places, modern architecture, transport, atmosphere, culture and the people. We were even given an ice-cold Diet Pepsi as part of an advertising campaign. They had one week in Sydney, that is, one van, three guys, one girl to dispose of eighteen thousand cans. Apparently not as easy as it sounds, except when a school outing comes by. Great fun and they all yelled 'Bravo for Diet Pepsi, down with Coco Cola'.

Last evening wander round in interesting King's Cross area'. Farewell Sydney and thanks for a couple of fun days.

Friday

Writing not so good as I am trying to catch up on coach between Sydney and Adelaide, another twenty-hour ride. M is watching the afternoon video, three hours of the 'Battle of the Bulge' I shall have to watch the same battle if I keep nibbling on these long rides. I'm fed up looking for kangaroos. Had a chat to the driver about the wire mesh over his windscreen and the big iron bars in front of his engine. The mesh is protection against big birds and the other is a roobar grid.

'Rhubarb,' said I, 'the kangaroos are a con trick.'

'Wait, till dusk,' he said, so I am keeping myself awake writing this. You can tell it's hot as the pen keeps blobbing. At this rate we'll be one big blob at Alice. Nevil Shute must have used a pencil for his novel *A Town Like Alice*. Still can't believe we are actually going there.

So we thought we had left the Sydney nutters behind. One has escaped into the back of the coach and every few minutes sends forth clouds of hairspray. I've told the driver and M has done a further reccie under the guise of going to the loo. Seems to be a heavily tattooed, lacquer sniffer and multi-beer can alcofrolic. Coming up for a fuel stop when we shall see what happens. Think our frolicky friend realised he had been sussed because at Wagga Wagga he disappeared and the police came on the coach to remove the evidence. Then we had a male role call to eliminate who he was.

Roo-search time again. Keep being deceived by tree stumps. Apparently could see emus so it's an emuroo search now and dusk is sure a-coming. Competition to see who spots what first, but M is cheating as he has gone up front pretending to talk to the driver. At 7.40 we saw a collection of emus. Quite a thrill to see them in their own wide open space, not in a poky zoo. Seem to be a playful lot. Tame emus have been known to pull the tails of sleeping dogs and then to run as fast as possible. They even play tag.

Female is a bit of a layabout as she lays her eggs and then slopes off. Dad incubates the eggs for ten weeks and hardly leaves them, hence losing a lot of weight in the process. The young emus stay with Dad for a couple of years. Mum usually joins a group of nomadic non-breeding birds. As emus cannot fly they have to run at rates up to 50 kph. At full pace an emu stride can measure 3 metres. Defence is a swift kick or two, or knocking down their prey, such as dingos and then killing them by repeatedly jumping on them. Have a special feather pattern to cope with temperatures from 45°C to 100°C. The eyes are protected from dry, sandy winds by a translucent inner eyelid which moves from the corner of the eye nearest to the beak, outward. I don't think we shall see a roo now so here endeth today's nature lesson. No roos but a beautiful dusk and sunset over miles of scrubland dotted with odd trees, a real feeling of space, almost infinity glowing all around you.

Saturday

Settled in at John and Donna's, Adelaide, with Renata a very bright four-year-old and Martin, a very steady-eight-month old. They took us to a local reserve so that we could see our roos, koalas and emus and even touch them. The roos looked very awkward, except when they moved quickly. The koalas were much prettier than their pictures and ever so docile. Again nature has done a good job on environmental adaptation. Their most favoured trees are gum trees but they contain poisonous oils. So they have an appendix which helps digestion by growing to a world record length of two metres. Also saw some dingos. They look like ordinary dogs although there are signs of wildness in their eyes. They even have a form of social hierarchy based on the survival of the fittest. It seems that NZ gave us every kind of scenery whilst Oz gives us every unusual aspect of animal life. Asia will probably give us the social.

Sunday

All walked round to the paper shop. Renata organised us into a crocodile. We did look a strange lot, four large adults being told what to do. M and John tried to escape round a corner but she soon sorted them out. A real character is our Renata, determined we live every moment, whether we like it or not.

John took us on a guided trek through the mangrove forest. Mangroves are trees which survive between the sea and the land. Twice a day the high tide brings around three metres of sea water so it is an area of swampy mud, quicksands and salt everywhere.

So how do these overgrown types, almost like rhododendrons, survive these salt baths? Firstly they have aerial roots or spongy, fingerlike projections called pneumatophores (try saying it). They store air for when the soil is waterlogged. Many mangroves produce seedlings from the fruit while it is still attached to the tree. The tree can tell from the pressure on the roots when the tide is low, so that it can drop the seedling. In the next twelve hours it has established itself enough to withstand the next saline invasion. The leaves have special glands which remove salt, and you can see the excreted salt crystals ready to be washed off in the next rain. There are also the older suicide leaves which store up salt and then drop off. You can only go through on the special boardwalk, 7,305.5 boards in all.

Saw flights of black swans, as well as sandpipers, semaphore crabs and mud whelks. First encounters with 'mozzies', blood and all. Can't think why, but it was John and M they got, not us girls. Home via a fun park. Renata organised us again. M too fast on large slide, hit the bottom – the slide's and his own!

Monday

Writing this on the way to Yulara – Ayers Rock. M went to town to fix the next stage to the Alice, as they say. I spent the day with Donna and the children. John took us to the beach for a sunset. It was our first view of a very large Australian beach. Some of them are over 100 km long.

Tuesday

John, M and I got up at 2 a.m. to see the total eclipse of the moon. I thought it would be black but it was like a pinky-orange ping-pong ball just suspended above us. Yet another Australian experience. Wandered around Adelaide, very fine, wide, tree-lined streets. John, Donna, Renata and Martin joined us for fish and chips before we got on the coach at 7.30 p.m. Sad to leave them.

Wednesday

On the Stuart Highway, the last part of road to be sealed on the main route between Adelaide and Darwin, just 3,014 km. The Stuart was the worst part to do as it had been scoured lower than the surrounding country by successive tyre tracks of the preceding eighty years. It gently slopes and curves to relieve driver boredom, as well as to avoid Aboriginal sacred sites. Realignment from the old track has saved 150 km. Every little helps because it really is the back of beyond, although there are solar-powered, vandal-resistant, free phones about every 80 km. Do Oz vandals really go that far? Passed through Coober Pedy, established in 1915 when young Willy Hutchinson found some 'floaters' – pieces of opal. The name is Aboriginal, meaning 'white fellow's hole in the ground'. Harsh desert and extreme temperatures have prompted residents to live in underground dugouts. An extremely inhospitable area, even water has to be brought in.

Back to 'floaters', this time in Adelaide. Three take away vans, the only ones allowed, serve burgers, and other such delicacies, and also floaters. These consist of thick green pea soup in a bowl with a hearty meat pie floating in it. Sounds revolting but even the dinner-jacketed audiences from the Festival Centre indulge in these for a post-performance snack. Back to Coober Pedy where the churches and some of the motels are underground. Nearby runs the Dog Fence or dingo-proof fence, only 9,600 km long. By the fence you can find fossilised shells 100 million years old, a reminder that Oz is an island continent. Some island!

Now the only water the central area of the island has is ten inches of rain a year. Apparently when it does rain plants grow and flowers bloom at record speed to complete their life cycle before the dry returns. There is even a frog that goes into a sort of freeze underground for years on end and only pops up when there is some reasonable rain. Bit like the odd bare rocky outcrops which appear now and then in the short, straw-coloured grass and rusty desert soil. It really is rust coloured and goes an amazing orangey-red at sunups and sundowns. Not a cloud to be seen, only the road and infinite line in front except for the boredom reducing bends. Seen a couple of road trains, massive treetop height and 50 metres long. Wouldn't want to meet one of them on a dust track in a mini-moke. M is thinking about hiring a moke in the Alice, only £8 a day. Anyone for a dust bath?

Arrived at Yulara; very hot; had swim in cold pool. Then out to see Ayers Rock and the Olgas. The latter consists of thirty-six large domes which were most likely all one large dome many times larger than the Ayers. Mind you, since its appearance nine-tenths of Ayers Rock has eroded away although it is still a 9 km walk around the base; 2 km of this includes going round the edge of four sacred sites, two for men, two for women. The whole area has been set out and is managed by full co-operation between the Oz Government and the Aborigines. There is still a resident Aborigine community of around one hundred and fifty with their own area. Many of them work in conjunction with the Park leaders or rangers. The traditional Aboriginal way of burning in small patches to clear the old spinifex grass is still carried out. Then softer grasses and plants regrow and smaller mammals return. The Rock itself is over 500 million years old and you can see how the layers have been tilted up by some massive earthquake. We watched the effect of the sunset and the magic change of colour. The gorges, cracks, broken lumps and holes create weird shapes and shadows so you can see why the Aboriginal Dreamtime legends evolved around these intrusions. Tjukurpa is existence itself, past, present and future. It is the law which governs behaviour. Various parts of the rocks represent results of bad behaviour, such as the Torn Ear, a result of aggression. Each child is assigned a legend at birth and all through childhood they learn their own legend. Then later on they learn others but each one having his own legend to pass on ensures their continuity. The spirit of life is important for existence and if they feel they have wronged, they release their spirit and allow themselves to die within a few days. Their culture is closely guarded and only passed on during walkabouts, so not overmuch is known by the world outside. The problem now is that the young ones often attend school so will their culture be lost? Will one hundred years see the end of a ten thousand year existence? Even the Rock is eroding at the rate of an inch a year.

Unbelievably, a bit of rain revives all kinds of wildlife, much of which preserves itself underground between one-yearly showers. We were lucky as there was a bit of rain a month before so the area was really green. Usual adaptation of plants such as the desert oaks with vertical spindly leaves to avoid evaporation. Also a bloodwood eucalyptus which sheds real blood when stabbed or sawn. Got a lovely gory picture of a hole in a red lumpy mass. Six hundred types of eucalyptus or gum tree. The driver, Hans, is a great sport. For ten minutes he rambled on about the one and only very unique rubber tree. All eyes right and what did we behold – one dead tree all covered in tyres. Defunct tyres line the road as the heat of the road tears them apart. Periodically young offenders on community work are sent out in trucks to collect them up. Perhaps that's why the SOS phones have to be vandal proof.

Watched the sunset at Ayers Rock. Sunsets are better in winter so Hans only gave it five out of ten. Seemed all right to us. He then told us about tomorrow's early morning climb of the Rock with many dire warnings. It is not to be taken with health problems or fear of heights. Average of two persons per annum perish apart from other accidents. Chain to hold on but the path is steep and slippy as well as being prone to gusts of wind. Over the past ten years out of twenty fatalities, fourteen were due to heart attacks, four blown off, and two falls. Last year a German visitor strayed from his party on one walk and was found four days later like a shrivelled prune with all his body cells reduced by sixty per cent. We decided not to do the climb!

I was afraid of being kippered to the same colour as the Rock and M very gallantly said he would not want to leave me behind. As it was one fellow, when we would have gone, fell and had to be taken to hospital. The wind had bowled him over.

Thursday

Trip round the base of the Rock to see Aboriginal cave paintings, gorges and waterholes. Also heard a great deal more about the wildlife of the desert. Wildlife on the Rock includes shield shrimps whose fertilised eggs lie on the rock face until it rains. The female shrimps hatch first, ready to lay more eggs for the male to fertilise before the dry returns. The eggs may lie in limbo for as long as ten years. The problem is that the ten inches rain ration may come all at once and the area is then very susceptible to flash floods. It seems very strange to drive through arid country with innumerable flood warning signs. The aborigines used to be able to 'feel' when the rains were coming and would disappear to safe places. Now with more integration with whites they have become rather desensitised and stay put. Exposure to alcohol and cigarettes has not helped.

Five-hour bus to Alice Springs and a good chat to Hans. As we thought, the dust tracks around Ayers are used as the last resting for dying Greyhound buses. The rough surface and potholey ruts make them rattle like mad. You have to hold your hand baggage as it leaps off the rack. Although the outside temperature was 38°C I had goose pimples by the time we reached Alice because of gaps around the door.

Super motel, TV, pool, tea-maker, and so on all for £8 a night each. Here for three nights and M has found out that he can watch *Rumpole*, *All Creatures Great and Small*, *Dr Who* and *Hill Street Blues*. Despite watching the box in the altogether it is hard to believe that we are thousands of miles away from UK in the middle of the Oz outback.

Friday

General mooch around Alice. Bought bright pink sun hat to match my nose and M bought a navy one, both with Alice Springs on them. Arranged bush trip for tomorrow and then looked at the River Todd – totally dried up. They say if you see the Todd twice nearly full of water you are classed as a permanent resident.

Alice is bigger than I expected with a cool leafy shopping mall and even cooler, leafier arcades. Visited the Flying Doctor Station. The idea was first encouraged by Reverend Flynn who used to travel around the outback by camel in 1912. It was not until 1927 that it could take off properly when Traeger invented the combination transmitting and receiving set powered by a small generator driven by bicycle pedals. Now there are fourteen bases to serve over two million square miles of sparse settlement. Over one hundred thousand patients are given medical attention each year and nine thousand are transported to hospital. Vaccination clinics are also run as with a round trip of six hundred miles nobody would bother.

Back for a cool swim and lunch. Then a very warm stroll to the Olive Pink Reserve. Poor M thought it would be full of olive and pink-coloured plants toning in with the desert. It was named after Olive Pink who started it. She was one of your old types. A firm campaigner for Aboriginal rights, she thought nothing of interrupting court proceedings if she considered that tribal custom was not being taken into account. Other times she would smuggle sweet biscuits into Alice Hospital to the Aboriginals. Once she was refused access to the Aboriginal section of the gaol so she barged past the stunned guards. She refused to pay the fine, demanding to be gaoled. The head gaoler paid the fine himself so that he did not have the task of restraining her in his gaol. Although city bred and afraid of lightning and thunder, spiders and snakes, she spent weeks at a time, often on her own wandering amongst the Aborigines in the outback; usually, she admitted to her friends, 'scared half to death'. To make her point at various times she would send politicians bunches of attractive blooms but very poisonous. Even in death she has become a rebel. For some unknown reason her headstone faces west, while all the others face east.

Climbed a hill near the reserve for a good view all round Alice. Saw the tame wallaroo, not a wally kangaroo, which the warden has hand-reared. It pootles off at night and spends the day at his house. Watched the sunset from the Anzac Memorial and really felt it was the centre of the great Australian island.

Saturday

Early start in Toddy's rough and ready bus to go along the Western Macdonnells. Ron, our even more bearded than M driver, started by asking us if we had our croc-repellent. Saw Simpson's Gap, a rock cleft cut by a river that hardly ever runs. Must have taken ages. Tried to watch rock wallabies jumping from boulder to boulder but they are very quick and tone in with their surroundings. Saw Standley Chasm whose near-vertical walls almost close over you. Noon sun lights the bottom for a very few seconds, the only sun it has all day. Ormiston Gorge and a cool swim with the fish in the waterhole. Then Toddy provided lunch of ham salad finishing with a cup of real billycan tea. No need for Earl Grey here – it had its own smoky flavour and was blacker than any railway tea.

Then a hair-raising ride over dirt tracks and dry river beds to Redbank Gorge. This involved a good one-hour hot sun march so I rested and pondered under a tree. M said it was most unusual as the sides were highly polished by the sand which was carried in the water. He had to wade waist-high and hold his hat and camera above his head. Nevertheless, out of all the young ones he was the first back. Not a very comfy ride for M as his lower region is still rather tender and banned from slides for ever more. Hope he's fit for Asian transport. A chat with a North-ampton lass in the motel laundry, revealed that it leaves a lot to be desired, as do the hotels. Even class I hotels have rats thrown in for free. Another fellow today said he found India a bit soul-destroying so we may try to have more time in Thailand; do Ruby's charity visits in India and do a quick bunk to Nepal. That's if Indian transport has bunks or do we have to stand all night?

On the way back our new driver stopped by a tree, took out his wheel wrench and we thought the worst. He threw it into a tree several times and down came a collection of lumpy 'bloodwood' apples, an Aboriginal delicacy which only a few of us were brave enough to try. Why only a few brave among so many? A little grub lives there, female, pale green jelly type. She lays eggs in the apple and the male feeds her through a small hole. If you are really lucky you can see the minute larvae as well. There were a few quick conversions to vegetarianism. Back to the motel for M's *Rumpole* and *Upstairs, Downstairs* put on especially for me.

Sunday

Final wander around Alice before a last midday swim and on to the coach to Townsville. Longest ride of all – twenty-seven hours. Visited the arts centre and found out a few more Aboriginal legends. The equivalent of Satan was a guy called Punukuparli, who stabbed his brother, Tapara, in the eye with a forked club. Three days later Tapara appeared as the moon and the shadowy spots are the scars. Also Tiwi carvings on ironwood. Tiwi means 'human beings' although their philosophy is one of protection for themselves and their brothers. Many of the carvings are throwing clubs and ceremonial barbed spears. Good country to send convicts! Papunya art is more gentle in its abstract representations of everyday life and the old Dreamtime stories. Many of the paintings are laid out on sand using ochres, clay, ash and plants.

From art to science and the Aviation Museum in the original Alice Springs Airport Hangar. Interesting display of planes lost in the outback and found years later. A Wackett plane which went more than 40° off course in 1961 was found in 1965 with the pilot's last few days recorded on the wing. The plane has been restored so I asked what had happened to the diary on the wing. Apparently it had last intimate thoughts to his wife so it was repainted as well to protect her privacy. A small kookaburra plane also went missing in 1929 and was finally resurrected in 1978. The irony is that Anderson and Hitchcock in that tiny plane had gone to look for Kingsford-Smith. They perished but Smith reappeared a few days later, unharmed.

Had a chat to a lovely Belgian couple who had retired early from their own business. No kids but two mothers they have to go home for now and again. Told them about all our eight times twenty-plus year-olds but they reckoned it was easier to abandon kids than mothers. Good advice about Thailand; even had a guidebook on how to obtain your women. Trouble was it was in French so I translated it for M, a précis, of course. It seems there are three main sources – bars, massage parlours and boxes reserved for women. Also warns you never to go in a car with a woman as you may never be seen again. A very friendly, fun couple of hours, although she was my age with multiple sclerosis.

Over 2,000 km of flat territory to be covered between Alice and Townsville. Plenty of termite hills break the landscape but that is about all. First stop Ti-Trees which was a cafe and an animal sanctuary where you could share your sandwich with a wedge-tail eagle and watch two bossy emus chasing a baby roo, until it found a haven under a cart. Then Tennant Creek, which was first settled when a wagonload of beer broke down and the drivers decided to make themselves at home while they consumed their misfallen cargo. Then bus changeover at guess where? Three Ways – garage, shop, cafe and that's all and as all travellers say, 'Bloody miles from nowhere.' Yet like our old English Three Ways, many travellers meet here. From then on we pulled away from central Australia, which somehow had a different kind of soul magic, a reassurance of eternity.

Monday

I think M is wishing he had a bigger 'bumpy' after all those bumpy miles and my ankles have swollen beyond any definition. M busy assessing feasibility of cheap local night flights in Thailand, more time for the ladies, Arrived at Mount Isa, one very smoky chimney stack from melting copper because the town consists of one very rich copper, silver, lead and zinc mine. Deposits discovered in 1923 but it still looks a somewhat unfinished town. Early morning video which coach 'creep' M managed to get going merely by turning on the set. The driver had already had to unlock two elderly ladies from their bedroom so I think he was wondering what he would have to do next.

M gets a bit bored at times. He has already thought of 101 uses for an inflatable travel pillow including an instant sex change. Now he's trying to see how many flies he can trap in his beard. Can't blame him really as the only feature for miles has been the 'goals' for passing drivers to hurl their drink cans into in an attempt to keep the roadside tidy. It's still a bit messy at times with cattle carcasses at various stages of decomposition. Drivers have to be very careful because the silly creatures often change their mind in the middle of the road, or stand for ages thinking about it.

Tuesday

Wandered around Townsville – pretty place a bit like South of France Riviera towns, even a casino. Town dominated by Castle Hill which only needs a few metres more to be classed as a mountain. Mad Townsvillers are taking up loads of rubble to add the extra but it doesn't seem to work as several years have only added a few centimetres. M is having to make decisions where to stay for the Barrier Reef, to dive or to snorkel. I'll just stick to glass bottoms, boats of course. Sent home a parcel of photos, books and over fifty postcards for Mum to post as it's over 50p a card. Parcel cost £17; postcards would have cost £25. That's how we afford trips around the world, but we are trying to keep to our budget of £3,000 for everything for three months. M has worked out that our down under bus pass has meant that all our NZ travel was free. Last glimpse of Townsville and the Sugar Shaker – Sheraton Hotel shaped just like one. The shopping mall was fun as it had a large-size chess-board, snakes and ladders, and backgammon.

Arrived Cairns at 7. Surrounded by Backpackers mini-buses touting for customers. Makes a change from the usual struggle with the luggage. Looked at local tours to the Reef. Great fun reading the local freebies as each has a Thinkspot, some even have two!

THINKSPOTS

- Few of us use the direct route to find the love and appreciation for which we so deeply long. It's okay to ask.

- Love each moment of today. It's all you have. Yesterday is gone and tomorrow is only a maybe.

- Twenty jobs half done are not worth one well done.

- You may be content with what you have, but never with what you are.

- A person who never makes mistakes usually makes hardly anything else.

- If the young were wise and the old enthusiastic the earth would be a paradise.

Wednesday

For £20 each we sailed in a catamaran to the Low Isles from Port Douglas. M fulfilled his dream of being among the corals and fish of the Great Barrier Reef. It was quite beyond his expectations. I chickened out on account of there being a great deal of sea, sun and salt as all activities were straight from the boat with fathoms below us. Watched M boom-netting: going along behind the boat hanging on to a net at six knots. Hard part was jumping on to the net in the first place although there was a secondary rope. Tough titties if you missed that. Plenty of them as well as the girls went in topless although our lady leader lost her bottoms as well. Of course, M went in without hesitation, he's so brave. Apparently it's a lovely feeling bouncing along the refreshing water in harmony with a dozen or more sets of bouncing boobies. Joking apart, M said it was the most wonderful experience of his life to be amongst the coral and fish of all colours. He was the strongest swimmer there and this time he was the catamaran creep, rescuing snorkels from twenty feet below.

After a super prawn, chicken, salad help yourself several times lunch, all included, M went off with the lady leader for more advanced exploration and to feed the fish by hand.

Had his thumb bitten by a spotted purple emperor, who was supposed to have taken the chicken. Most of the fish eat anything; bones are crunched, pineapple skins are hoovered up. Then his erotic swim with his topless lady leader. This involved diving down, brushing the 'soft, cuddly, furry coral with its pink, feathery tentacles with your body'. He should have gone bottomless. He also saw clams which if you put your hand in close rapidly. Don't panic, it doesn't get amputated but takes twenty minutes to be released, which is not very useful with a two-minute survival snorkel.

So now M is really looking forward to his deeper scuba-dive on Friday while I go out in a semi-sub. He will need tomorrow to recover from his sunburn. Put on his full block cream but it seems you can still burn after twenty minutes and six feet down in the sea. Found another use for the blow-up pillow, under your still all virgin white buttocks. Perhaps it's just as well he didn't go bottomless after all.

Thursday

Have to keep changing pens as they sort of come and go in the heat. Think this one has expired already. M not too good but insisted on mooching into the town for money and to fix up the coach to Brisbane. Swithered about taking a short cut through a new shopping arcade and are we glad we did. Brand new Thai airline office beckoned to us. Really helpful young lad checked our flight tickets. Just as well as we thought we were flying out on Monday 7th, not at all, it's Tuesday 7th. Then he noticed that the flight ticket was from Brisbane. Had we thought of going straight from Cairns as the plane stops there anyway? M's sunburn was tickled pinker as it meant he could do more diving. Then miracle number two we were able to change the exit

Thailand flight to a week later, so we could have two full weeks. Amazing how a split-second decision can change everything. Now we don't have the 26-hour ride to Brisbane.

Visited Cairns Museum and acquired some more Aboriginal culture. Certainly a survival system with the gentle Dreamtime beliefs on one side and aggressive protective instinct on the other side. Bulrush roots made a cord to strangle humans but with a sharp point about 15 cm long, kangaroo leg bone origin, attached to one end. The bone was slid under the victim's neck, put through a loop at the other end of the cord and quickly drawn tight. Skulls were also used as water carriers, preferably those of close relatives rather than those of strangers. Old people were well cared for and respected for their tribal wisdom. Mourning always included frantic displays of distress. In some areas women scratched their faces and bodies and beat each other, while the men cut deep wounds in their thighs with stone knives. Somehow or other they felt they were to blame for the death as it was not seen to be a natural event: rather a paradox as they lived in complete harmony in their natural environment. Today you can see the loss of pride in many of them as they wander aimlessly around places like Alice Springs, often half or totally drunk. What is civilised?

Did a bit of reading homework for my semi-sub Reef trip so I get my money's worth. Hope to see some of the following in safety! Horrid stonefish – has thirteen natural unlucky venom injection systems along its back. Saved if you're number fourteen.

Macneills assessor: brilliant blue, male incubates eggs in its mouth. Takes about fifteen days during which he has no food, just like our friend the emu. Women's lib seems to be well ahead in parts of the animal world. Often swims upside down.

Goatfish: change patterns according to mood or time as

a signal. Subdues its stripes so it can feed in peace.

Gulf damsel: visits shrimp cleaner stations in large sea anemone. Sits quietly while the shrimps clean it without touching the anemone's tentacles.

Ocellated goby: go around in pairs, excavate holes beneath dead coral. Take turns at house cleaning bringing out pieces of dead coral and mouthfuls of sand to dump outside.

Flasher goby: very well named, has a long spine on the dorsal fin which can be erected very quickly. A dirty mac colour, it only flashes at night.

Other gobies are fussy about the kind of bottoms they live on. Fire gobies prefer hard bottoms, crossed gobies like broken rubble bottoms. I think the human M fish would prefer to have no bottom at all as his sunburn is giving him a fiery bottom. By 7 p.m. he felt well enough for one of his 'help yourself to all you can pile on the plate in one go' Chinese meal.

Friday

Both set off for our trips to Fitzroy Island. Met each other for half an hour after M had done a trial dive and passed. Saw him off, after somehow he had acquired chewing gum on his foot and then deposited all over the boat. So the coral only grows a couple of inches but do the fish really have to resort to gum? My semi-sub was great. The fish and the corals are really electric colours. I can see why M is so enthralled by his diving although he did return a bit the worse for wear after a rather rough ride back. Still he did ever so well on his dive as he had a lot more air left than the other first-timers and the same as the expert divers. The instructor was most impressed and it meant that M saw a greater variety of fish and coral.

Saturday

Shopping and collected 1900 baht, about 40 to the pound. Later read the Thai guide to discover we are only supposed to take in five hundred each as they are keener to have foreign currency. So I shall be stuffing baht up my knickers, which is probably good practice for setting myself up in the Street of a Thousand Cut-Rate Prostitutes! Then went on a tropical rainforest tour and it rained so we really got the atmosphere. Must have been awful being troops in the war in areas like that. Weird trees climbing up each other and webs with spiders of hand-size spread in the middle. Tasted a few highly coloured exotic fruits and saw equally highly coloured butterflies. Fascinating were the fruit bats or flying foxes. Great clumps of them hang from the tops of trees fanning themselves with their wings to stay cool. Make a hell of a noise chattering all the time. Goodness knows how they still have the energy to fly at night. Wingspan is about two feet and they do all their activities upside-down – hang, fan, chatter and even copulate, but then they are down under batties!

Crystal Cascades was a gorge in the rainforest with waterfalls and pools. Rocks are used as water slides, high-dive platforms and trees are used for jump-off ropes. Had a swim but had to plan my exit as the water rushed at the edge. It was a case of going upstream, being carried down and leaping out in time. Lazy evening, even ate in our room using the camp set. For £5 between us we have a twin room with fan, fridge and a plug for our little pot boiler. Who needs Trust Houses at over £30 a night?

Sunday

Caught the Cairns to Kuranda train which had the original carriages of nearly one hundred years ago in beautiful wood with leather seats. The railway winds in and out of the tunnels along the edges of hairy gorges and over the Stoney Creek Bridge strung up hundreds of feet. To celebrate the completion of the bridge, John Robb, the chief engineer, organised a full banquet on the bridge itself. No speeches, however, as the waterfall was too noisy. Not like today's waterfall higher up, the Barron Falls, where much of the water is devoured by the hydroelectric scheme. Every day when the train arrives they open the hatch so that the visitors can see something of what nature intended. The building of the railway was a great feat which took nearly ten years for 70 km. Landslides, floods, mud, and so on made various contractors give up until Robb took over. Hands, buckets, shovels, dynamite and fortitude tackled the mountains and jungle. On the whole the workers were cooperative except that at one point they formed a sort of union, the United Sons of Toil, to demand 9s a day. Their pay was raised from 8s to 8s 6d a day.

Met at Kuranda by our guide for the day. It was Lee again from yesterday so we were well looked after. Not sure about his nationality but he looks almost part Indian with soft brown eyes and his hair tied back. A very knowledge-able young man who obviously 'lives' the tropical rainforest. We sat at the front of the minibus and he and M had some really good 'natural' discussions. He showed us the curtain fig tree which took about five hundred years to grow. It started by seeding on another tree, then by sending down thousands of aerial roots it stabilised itself and finally killed off its 'home' tree. This rotted and fell so a curtain of roots was left.

Cool swim and tried to see turtles at Lake Barrine, a volcanic crater lake. Lee showed us more of the Aboriginal survival fruits. Also led us up the tropical forest path telling us how one explorer kept on the right side of cannibalistic Aborigines. He would watch Chinese immigrants working and rush up to seize one. The Aborigines preferred Chinese as the latter's diet of rice and veg meant they had more tender flesh than the meat-eating British. Your first Chinese take-away! He did warn us, however, about the stinging tree. Romantic heart-shaped leaves, size of your palm, Latin name something or other *Morida* and murder it is. The merest brush produces a stinging through microscopic hairs, which is sheer agony for four days, causes glands to swell and even fits can occur. Having just survived the four days you have to be very careful for nearly a year as fresh contact with cold water can start the stinging off again. Lee had been caught slightly and nearly went mad with it. There are some warning notices but not enough as he showed us some growing at the side of the road. You hear about spiders, crocs, snakes, and so forth, but this is far less obvious and far more lethal.

Then he took us off the usual day trip route to see a really good Tableland view. It was over a three-valley meeting-point but it was also at the local hang-gliding take-off platform. Lee strung up the training harness from a tall over-hanging tree, gave us a demo and asked for volunteers. Great stuff, I thought, and without thinking I volunteered first. Lee told me what to do, like keeping your bum down, pushing your feet on the back rope and stretching out into the harness as you swing off. With great delight M helped him to pull me back and then push me off. It was a wonderful feeling, swinging out horizontally, arms aspread, over the Mountainside towards the valley below, 5000 feet down, I had several swings, then when the young 'uns saw the oldie had survived and even enjoyed it, they wanted a go. Not all of them. M very kindly stood back as I think he realised that this was one daring thing I could do, having been such a wet duck at the snorkelling. It's just a question of what you like a lot of around you, water or air!

The next stop was M's turn, boomerang throwing. Fortunately Lee was left-handed so he had both types. M was pretty good as they all came back within a few yards, except his last throw, which landed on a 'not very pleased' lady's car. We did point out that she had parked after us and must have been aware of the hazards. After all, Australia is full of notices saying, 'Beware of Falling Rocks, Coconuts, and so on' so she must have realised that a minibus full of foreign would-be boomerang experts needed no warning sign. Anyway, Lee was not very sympathetic and we were all more worried about any possible damage to the left-handed boomerang. On the final leg home Lee gave us his last little talk about the rainforest inhabitants as someone asked about snakes. No poisonous snakes, only constrictors which usually only consume things they can swallow. However, there are ten-pounder jungle rats, scorpions and centipedes a foot long. Good material for tropical nightmares. I think Lee was quite sad to say goodbye to M as he had asked some good questions and they were on the same environmental wavelength. Of course M had been the minibus creep again, opening doors and gates. Another unusual outing of ten hours for £15 each.

Monday

Sheets of rain as you never saw before, so that washed out M's last chance to snorkel. Apparently you can get seasick snorkelling. In between the sheet rain sessions we wandered around the town. Bit like strolling through a sauna. Not worth wearing a raincoat as you got wetter inside from perspiration than from the rain. M drew the line at me shopping in a swimsuit but it would have been lovely. During the sheet rain we sorted out our packing. M did Thai travel plans and I had a go at the language. Easy to remember how to be polite – end your sentence with 'khrap' if you are a man and 'kha' if you are a woman. M mastered that one very easily.

In the afternoon we walked about 6 km to and from Botanic Gardens. It's remarkable how many jungle trees can grow on each other at one time. Just as they reach the light they are strangled by others below; some grow a foot in a day. Watched two lads trying to grow in mud. They were wading in river bank mud beyond their knees and elbows. Even the most ardent rugby players could never look like they did. They were crab catching. We watched the mud crabs coming in and out of their holes and pushing off any intruders. Another creature resident in this area is the cane toad, alive in the sugar cane or stuffed in souvenir shops. In 1935 the Queensland Government being a 'canny' lot, imported a sackload of cane toads from Hawaii to combat the greyback beetle, which was destroying the sugar cane crop. The mission was a failure as the beetles could fly and the cane toad could not. Now the toads are more of a pest and ingenious methods are used to try to eliminate them without a great deal of success. The best seems to be one farmer filling an old washing machine sunk in the ground. They fall in and he puts them to sleep: law of increasing returns as he can sell them for stuffing, have a new washing machine each year and more old ones to catch more toads. Probably becomes richer that way than from sugar harvests. Small-scale sugar is no longer worthwhile and many farmers are selling land for building. The Japanese are buying like mad as they seem to have a 'yen' for it! As one Australian said, 'We don't mind 'em coming on holiday, we don't mind them selling their stuff here, but we don't want 'em bloody living here!' Very forthright are Australians.

Tuesday

Packed up. Bit sad to leave our room of a week. Wasn't

posh but we had fun in it. Spent last few dollars, leisurely lunch at hostel pool, goodbyes and taxi to airport. Runway built over former mangrove swamp. Thai Airlines computer broken so it took over an hour to check in. On plane, M and I in middle of rows one behind the other. He is surrounded by young female blondes, while I have the geriatrics. Difficult to get his attention as he is switched on already, although he has already communicated with me to swap headsets. His left ear is bust and he can only hear half the instruments. I would have thought he would have been better to concentrate on the blondes. No, too intellectual, they're doing a crossword.

In between he is making eyes at the Thai hostesses to collect as many free bags of nuts as possible, as if we didn't have enough luggage.

Tied up in Thailand

Started to read about Bangkok so that the culture shock from boomerangs to Buddhism is not so great. The Thai people seem to be gentle with one special guiding proverb: 'Do good and receive good; and do evil and receive evil'.

We all received a beautiful mauve orchid on the plane, just like velvet. I am plucking up courage to say 'Thank you' in Thai, but you have to remember whether each word is a rising or falling tone, level high, moderate or low tone. Thank you phonetically is 'cup Coon' with a falling tone. Use the wrong tone and the meaning is totally different. I seem to recall really useful words very easily, such as *Prick Key Noo* which are peppers that look like mouse droppings and are hotter than any curry.

Made my first Thai phone call to ask if there was a room. The answer was in English – no. More success with the next; £2 for a double. Taxi all through Bangkok, narrow alleys choked with people and families, washing, cooking, old chairs, bikes, and so on. Our room was a waffle box with a grubby, threadbare futon and two inside bolts. It was our first encounter with a hotel of ill repute. Great activity all night long.

Wednesday

Wandered about to find a slightly better place. We were prepared to pay more but found the James Guest House for the same price but much better. Very friendly with own little restaurant on the forecourt. Bangkok is like going into a big bang; the noise is like a mass of discos. Motorbikes minus silencers, in fact, everything minus silencers and horns that seem to go at the slightest provocation. The traffic is perpetual with no regard for other drivers and pedestrians. The speed and dodging of bikes, cars, buses and the thousands of three-wheel motorbike engine tuk-tuks is mind-blowing. The latter is like a souped-up dodgem car.

Started our cultural 'bit' by visiting the Wat Sakret Temple with the Golden Mount. This is an artificial mud and brick hill with a *chedi* on top. A chedi is a monument built to house a Buddha relic. There are Buddhas everywhere with lots of peeling gold leaf and appeals to you to donate towards the purchase of a new stamp-sized piece of gold leaf to be stuck on reclining, sitting, standing, fasting, fattened and even what look like 'ducky' Buddhas. During World War II concrete walls were added to stop the hill eroding. Not that the Buddha there was that large compared with the reclining Buddha in Wat Po. This is 46 metres long, 15 metres high and five hundred years old, made of plaster round a brick core and finished in five million stamp-sized pieces of gold leaf. Mother-of-pearl was used to decorate the eyes and massive feet which portray 108 different signs of a Buddha – *laksanas*. Galleries which go between the four inner chapels contain over four hundred life-size gilded Buddha images. Within this oldest and longest wat in Bangkok there are over ninety chedis, a sermon hall, a Buddhist Philosophy School and even a massage school.

I remarked that the masseuses were using their elbows in some places and M replied, 'Reckon they're using everything possible.'

Supper in the guest house courtyard cooked by our little

Thai girl, who keeps coming up to give us a hug. She helps me with my Thai and seems pleased that I try. I think she fancies M's beard and she says I remind her of her mum. For £1 each we had sweet and sour chicken with veg and rice, a giant fresh pineapple pancake and an ice crush fruit drink. The bahts certainly go a long way and we were able to watch it being cooked. The washing-up is done in large aluminium bowls on the ground alongside the cooking area. So what if Bangkok is a bit niffy at times, it doesn't seem that bad and the Thais are very clean. The worst smell was the fish market.

M is working away reading and planning. He is Plan Chief and I am Pack Chief, him on the maths and me on the language. Amazing how within a few hours a new culture becomes part of you. After a couple of 'goes' you remember to take your own paper. The loos are low like bidets, unflushable, so there is a trough of water under a tap with a metal or plastic bowl in it. The showers are in the same cubicle. Thailand develops your squat muscles. The Thais must have really good muscles as they sit on six inch stools to wash dishes and clothes, sew and many other jobs. The young ones don't even bother with stools.

Wandering down back alleys we did get some stares, M with his beard and me with my reddish hair, especially from babies and toddlers who always give you a large smile. We were able to see how many Thais live and work in the same room which opens directly on to the street. Often Grandad is working with the television on, Grandma is minding the baby, Mum is cooking for her side street cafe, Dad is fixing bikes, radios or whatever the trade is, and older kids are helping in between clips on the earhole from one adult or other. Certainly the extended family life here, doing everything to make money, welding old scooter petrol tanks, hand-printing, bookbinding and even rewiring electric motors by hand. One family had obviously run out of children for Granny, as she was having to screw large bolts on to rods. One street was nothing but woodyards and wood products and as it was the lunch break, there were loads of prostrate bodies sleeping on planks. Thais sleep anywhere.

Thursday

M has decided to become a Buddha. His sunburn is now peeling off in strips. Pity it's not gold leaf. What a sight as he parades around the room pretending to be a Buddha, stomach stuck out. Off to the Royal Palace. M had to put on long trousers, so it was just as well we carried them with us, although there was a booth with a sign 'Long Pants to Rent'. Apart from the famous Emerald Buddha there are temples, corridors, and shrines all covered in glittering mosaic tiles. Even the smallest windows are like jewelled caskets. The Emerald Buddha, around 75 cm high, is made of jade. High above other gold ornaments and statues it sits in its glass case which gives it an aura of mystery. First recorded in the fifteenth century it was said to have been covered in plaster and gold leaf. It was transported here and there and during a storm it lost the plaster covering. The jade is far more effective as gold Buddhas are rather common. There was a heavy feeling of reverence in this shrine from the built-up devotion. To me it was rather overpowering, not a real feeling of joy like we had in Gary's Baptist Church. The Buddha has a jewelled wardrobe. The King changes the Buddha's clothes for the hot, cool and rainy seasons. There is a ladder up the back for him to go up – too bad if he has vertigo.

Then bargained for a ride to the smarter shopping area. The tuk-tuk driver got fed up with the traffic and dropped us off a block before, but what luck, as it was opposite a book shop, where I could buy phrase books for Thai and

Nepalese. Saved us looking so we made our way to Jim Thompson's house. Jim, an American, loved Thailand and was responsible for the revival of the Thai silk trade after the Second World War. He also had old houses moved from other parts of Thailand so they could be preserved with other Asian works of art. Proceeds go to Bangkok's School for the Blind. In 1967 Jim disappeared rather mysteriously in Malaysia and has never been seen since. The house is alongside a klong (canal) at the end of a sleazy soi (larie) and yet once you are in the grounds you could be miles from Bangkok.

More transport bargaining to another wat nearer home. This was the Temple of the Golden Buddha, a 3-metre, 5.5-ton solid gold Buddha image. This we felt was more heartlifting than the others. It was graceful and gleaming. It was not until thirty years ago that it was discovered that it was gold. While it was being moved to a new building the plaster exterior fell off when the whole image was accidentally dropped by the crane. The theory is that the plaster was put on to protect it against the Burmese hordes. Also a courtyard with fifty-three bronze Buddhas, copies of styles from all over Thailand and other Buddhist countries. A first course in Buddhist Iconography, or what, I would term becoming 'Buddha-Bound'!

Decided to walk home to work up a good appetite. Stood on the corner to get our bearings. Could not understand why the street names did not tally with the map. There was the wat, the bridge and the klong but where was the street we wanted? Then we looked at the wat entry ticket and guess wat? We had been brought to the wrong wat in the first place. We had wanted to see the Golden Buddha anyway but it was not in the wat, what we thought it was in the first place! Easily done as there are over four hundred wats in Bangkok alone. By then it was rush hour and we were nearly killed several times trying to cross the roads. 'See Naples and Die,' they say. I can find a substitute for that. Equilibrium restored by a very tasty supper at James. M tried a plummy thing which when you broke the stone was bright purple inside. It was called something like 'Mafia'. Usual pancakes. They seem to be larger each time. M thinks our little lass is trying to fatten us up. At 40p he reckons there is very little profit. We watched our girl cooking. M had a fit when he saw her chopping pineapple in the palm of her hand. Fair enough but she chats away while she does it by touch.

Friday

In Thai I got us to the station and in Thai I got us two tickets to Ayutthaya. Chatted to an English-speaking Thai who helped me with some pronunciation. He then made me read a whole sentence on my own and it was all correct. Really satisfying. At Ayutthaya we were 'met' by a young lad and his tuk-tuk. Tried to put him off but eventually succumbed to his 'I take you nice place for 10 baht.' Usual simple place with hardboard walls but these had plaited bamboo on the outside. While I sorted us out, M did a deal with Bot to take us out for three hours for 300 baht, less than £8. I think he must have been 'sent' because he saved us from 16 km of hot, dusty, noisy cycling and 'Are we at the right wat?' Bot knew exactly where to take us.

Ayutthaya is virtually an inland island, at the confluence of three rivers with a wide canal to complete the circle of water. From 1350 to 1767 it was the capital of Thailand. Visitors from all countries abroad said it was the most illustrious city in the world. Bits of the old walls appear everywhere, even in people's gardens with washing strewn over them. Mind you, washing gets dried everywhere, even on the railway sleepers. Washing also gets done everywhere, including bodies. At Bangkok Station we saw two baby boys having their botties washed at a tap on the railway line. The same tap then provided water for the train loo. In this country nothing is wasted.

Back to the wats and Buddhas. Becoming a little confused but we did see one very large Buddha which was originally covered in gold, 250 kg of it, but that was melted down by the Burmese conquerors. Then saw a 60-foot sitting Buddha, massive he was; one finger about the size of M. Last one for the day was the Sleeping Buddha outside, 45 yards long. The postcards show a somewhat tatty fellow made in stone with patches of gold. Now he is radiant white, with lots of devoted ladies using pickaxes around him working on the newly found excavations.

I am writing this on a terrace by the river. Watching geckos up to ten inches long, walking along the rafters catching mozzies in the light. If you are really lucky you can have a ghekko in your soup. One fellow has now described a handsized spider seen in the loo. The tales grow worse. One girl on a boat in a Bangkok klong passed a dead body, all bloated. Common occurrence; Thais point and laugh. At least it was gone by the return journey. We haven't braved a boat yet. Apparently you have to cover your mouth as the speed and dodging, like the street traffic, mean you can swallow mouthfuls of 'klong'. The boats are long and narrow, driven by large car engines on the end of a long pole at the back, no silencers of course, average speed 40 mph. No wonder you don't have a chance if you fall in. *Kow pak kai* for our supper, not cow-pat but chicken, veg and rice. Usual chat with other travellers and exchange of tips. 'Seen it, been there, done it, got the T-shirt!'

Saturday

A day in the life of a Thai train. Ayutthaya to Chiang Mai, over twelve hours. Stood for two hours to start. 'Sit up and beg' shiny, plastic sweaty seats. Thai travel life includes dogs, cardboard boxes and bowls of food. Constant stream of family sellers with drinks, dubious meat on sticks, dough balls, nuts and fruit. If you buy the meat it is inserted into a home-made newspaper bag plus a small poly bag of rice, cold. We were either very brave or desperate as we bought a dough ball stuffed with what looked like earth but tasted like very bitter, grouty chocolate. Last hour was more fun as the loo flooded. No problem as the guards constantly mop the floor after sweeping up the rubbish. 'What a tidy nation,' you exclaim. That's what we thought, until we saw all the rubbish evicted out the window, glass and all.

Then some young fun Thai lads sat opposite us with an English dictionary. We exchanged 'How are you?'; 'What is your name?' and the numbers one to ten. There were frequent roars of laughter and fallings off the seat when I tried my Thai.

Then the guard came to help me; M reckoned he fancied me as he kept saying I was velly goot. Chiang Mai was like Cairns with minibuses touting for hotels. Our choice was quite good except for pillows like camel's humps.

Sunday

Recovered from yesterday's trainathon. More very old wats and Buddhas. Not so crowded and more peaceful despite a good few *farangs* (foreigners) on the streets. There would be more farangs but some are in jail for drug smuggling. Thai Monopoly game – pay fine or go to jail. The more we see the more we realise that Thailand has extremes. The Buddhist ideology is supposed to be one of gentleness and yet outside nearly every wat there are women and children asking you to set a bird free. Tiny birds are caught in small wicker baskets and you pay so many baht to release one.

Who knows how long the old Buddhist standards will

survive? M was cross when he missed a photo that would have said it all. It was a large golden Buddha standing outside, surrounded by ordinary and poorer homes and just visible through a haze of television aerials. M has observed that the aim seems to be to acquire goods that can earn you more money such as some form of motor transport and then the next essential is the television. Thai children are being well exposed to the Thai version of Eastenders.

Even the monks have their televisions and cigarettes. It used to be that socially every Thai male should be a monk for a short period of time. Average used to be three months, now it is often as short as a week. Probably about 20,000 monasteries and 150,000 monks. Wat a lot! Looking around I think the number will drop as the next generation considers the loss of earnings. There are two sects, one stricter than the other. Thammayut monks may only eat once a day before noon, and only what they have received in their alms bowls. Mahanikais eat twice before noon and may accept side dishes. Understandably there are thirty-five of the latter to every one of the former. Families earn great merit when sons become monks but as a Thai mother I would worry about how thin they become. Still, seeing orange-robed monks wandering about does create some calm and continuity in a bustling world. By feeding monks, donating to temples and worshipping at local wats, the Thais hope to gain merit to prevent or at least lessen the number, of rebirths. This gives them a point to their lives but will worship of the Buddha give way to worship of the box? More and more we realise that God, Buddha and other deities basically represent the whole idea of Creation, a personification of what is good. We bought ourselves a mini-Buddha each in one of the oldest wats of all, built 1296. One of the older monks blessed them for us.

M had films developed, seemed okay until he saw his fat black Buddha was missing. Film had been snarled in the machine so back we went. Humble apologies and a new film. 'Never mind,' I said, 'at least you have the skinny Buddha, there are plenty more fat ones around.' Mooched around the night market, loads of different stalls open all night, every night. Had to be very wary of pickpockets. Another big adventure tomorrow first trip in an Asian bus.

Monday the 13th

Wat a relief, only one wat today. Mind you, that involved a multi-hairpin trip up a mountain in a Calor gas type fuelled metal, windowless minibus with the driver clasping his hands together when passing shrines on some of the bends. Then three hundred steps up a dragon-headed staircase. All this to reach the Doi Suthep wat. At least we saw our first Buddhist monks in class. You can get some good views but Chiang Mai has its own LA smog and we couldn't detect even one of the three hundred wats. Wat a disappointment. We shared the minibus with three other farangs, a couple from Sydney (lived near Meadowbank where we took that long misguided boat trip to the singing bus driver) and a lass from Boston. All went for a *kao soi* lunch – crispy noodles and slightly hotted-up chicken, 25p each. Then all went to the University Folk Museum via ice cream shop where M tried coconut but found it a bit tasteless. Eventually found the museum as a helpful Thai followed us on his motorbike to make sure we were not getting lost. I did try to identify it by the Thai writing but all I led us to was the insectary. Saw enough insects last night in the night market – huge May bug jobs, scorpions, tarantulas and emperor moths with wings the size of your hands.

Museum all about the various hill tribes. Tried to identify the two little delinquents I photographed in the morning on the three hundred steps. One was carrying a baby all wrapped up on her back. They wanted 10 baht each for me to take their photo. The American girl had paid 10 but never really got the photo. I said 5 baht each and made them line up properly before I paid up. They tried to make faces but I said 'No money,' in my best Thai so then they co-operated very sweetly; as I left them Mother suddenly appeared, whipped the money and rearranged the baby for the next gullible farang. They were probably Meo from a nearby village. They live mainly above 1,000 metres with opium as their main cash crop. They are the main highland producers. Unfortunately, like the Maoris and the Aborigines they are beginning to experience a culture conflict, as are many of the hill tribes. Many have become opium addicts. We could have done with a sniff in the morning when we went to reserve our air-conditioned seats for tomorrow. First – we were sent to an actual bus until I pointed out *prung nii* – tomorrow. Then it was booth number one to number two to number three (clerk asleep, totally unwakeable) then lady came to rescue – over road to separate office. In Asia ticket buying is a journey in itself.

Martin from near Meadowbank was able to tell us a few bits of Thai etiquette. I was saying how a Thai gentleman would not let me have the spare seat beside him on the train. Apparently I had probably offended him by standing in the passage with my 'private parts' above his head. I should have crouched or not stood next to him. Also mean farangs who try to over-bargain are in the class of 'sticky-shits'. Still, we seem to be getting the hang of it all; being adventurous with food; organising our own bus rides for less than 100 baht compared with organised tours of over 800 baht. The only problem at the moment is M's camera, which seems to be giving him a load of topless wats. He'd be better with topless Thai females although they seem to be very slim all the way down. M's beard still provokes long looks and enquiries as to how old it is. Sometimes I have to pick a dry noodle out of it. Just as well it is not the clear or glass noodles as they are sometimes called, as I don't like to say what they look like.

Tuesday

Writing this in woven bamboo snack bar on the riverside at Tha Thon waiting for boat to Chiang Rai. Super new air-conditioned coach brought us here. Driver, plus hostess, plus the 'traffic abuse,' attendant, who shouts at anyone who seems to be getting in the way. We were not sure whether he had another purpose as the window was closed and the miscreant would not hear anyway. Actually he did load luggage so obviously all the driver does is drive. Pleasant route with views of really craggy sharp hills, hill tribe settlements, paddy fields, and so on. Should be an interesting river trip as we are only a few miles from the Burmese border and the boats have a guard with a gun, which they keep in a plastic bag most of the time.

Captain's Log

After mad loading of one hundred farangs on to loads of overgrown canoes, ten per boat, we set off at 1 p.m. Our boat is the first of a three convoy as our pilot knows the shallow sections. Still manage to hit gravel and if it is too shallow we have to disembark and walk. See wading fishermen, ballast collectors, washerwomen and little 'monk'ees swimming. By 1.20 one boat in convoy gone. By 1.40 second boat gone. Will we make it? Incongruous complicated television aerials over wooden huts hanging over the river. At 1.30, forgot, baling out rear end of boat. At 1.45 cameras out – suspension bridge. Engine slowed, waiting for lost boats? Revolution, sorry, mutiny – all sitting on one side of boat instead of in bottom, legs out. At 2.10 lost boats catch up. All out to hill tribe village. M persuaded to buy a necklace and bracelet, sort of fertility type. Never too late, I suppose. Everyone back in bottom of boat. Through rocks and boulders. Constant haze around us as burning and clearing season. Armed guard in boat up front, not really war, but because farangs collected together equal many bahts. Banana plants – one group of hill tribe use the yellowing of the banana plant as a signal to move on. Splashed by swimming natives. More rock dodging and bottom bumping. Wallowing water buffalo. Pass the Tourist Security Squad Border Patrol Outpost – couple of guns pointed. Shooting rapids, backs soaked. All out, walk 300 metres, rapids too fierce. At 4.15 one boat evacuated so we acquired two extra plus bike – even lower in water. Reckon we had the best navigator. The other two boats in the convoy rushed ahead, so we passed them with all their passengers out pushing the boats. Should have stayed in the line behind.

Yesterday we saw a unique line of bats pour out of a roof, at least five per second and still pouring after quarter of an hour. Well, how many bats was that? Four thousand, five hundred at least, quite a lot. Back from bats to boats. Nearly five hours later we arrived at Chiang Rai. Captain's log safely concluded, just bottoms a bit soggy and numb.

So now we are near infamous Golden Triangle, so called because it is encompassed by the borders of Burma, Laos and Thailand. The Golden is the lucrative opium trade. Still continues in valleys not frequented by the Thai army. Hill tribes can legally plant opium poppies for their own consumption but of course there are loopholes. Lots of tripeds waiting at Boat Stop to whip us off to various guest houses. Hard choice between the Porn and the Boonbundan; settled for the latter as we have had enough excitement for one day.

Wednesday

Air-conditioned Government Bus to Sukhothai. Very well-organised English-style Chinawat Hotel with two massive double beds, own shower and loo. Usual arrival amble around Sukhothai, smaller, less touristy so we managed photos of markets, overcrowded buses and strange loads on transport such as large clear poly bags of prawn crackers, shallots and a trussed live pig in a large basket. Sukhothai means the dawn of happiness. Guess we should be happy to arrive safely after a journey in which we saw an upturned sugar cane lorry and an upside-down yellow car 50 feet below a hairpin bend, plus the inevitable lookers-on. What a coincidence – bumped into Martin and Herma again from the singing bus driver region of Meadowbank in Sydney. They had changed their plans and a few seconds later and we would have missed them. This time I would not let them move until I had their address.

More fun over menus. Glass noodles have now become cellophane noodles. There is also cow tongue soup. They seem to have it in for the female of the species as we have also met wife sundae. That's got to be a bit of a boob. Sorry folks, but you have had a rest from wat jokes and you could be suffering from wat deprivation. M is eating things like brandy snaps filled with shrimps and ground pork. I am just looking at the electrics, frayed and knotted wires held on to the ceiling with metal cup hooks, from which swing paper lantern shades. As the electric fans rotate, revealing their innards of tangled wire we become a little concerned that we have not yet seen a fire station in the whole of Thailand. Today our bus attendant had to cool the air-conditioning unit by chucking buckets of water over it. Still, we're not worried, Thais seem to have charmed lives.

Thursday

Trip round very old Sukhothai. It was Thailand's first capital over seven hundred years ago. Very old walled city with three parallel moats between the city walls. This was the birthplace of the first Thai alphabet. Innumerable prangs – shrines that look like giant corn on the cobs. Wat Sri Chum had a sitting Buddha with an eleven metre leg span. You could climb narrow steps around the back of him and look out under his unhairy armpits to annoy those trying to take photos from below. Another prang was held up by thirty-six elephants sculptured in the base. The whole place had a real feeling of antiquity.

Late lunch and a 'let's flop on the bed' for a couple of hours. Evening walk along the river. Old boathouses still in use; kids fishing and damming the very murky water. Always waves and smiles and big hellos followed by the usual shrieks of laughter when we reply. Even more mirth if we say goodbye. Most of the Thai people are charming and very helpful but I supposed like any society there are the rougher ones. Some of the paintings in the wats are like video nasties with gods biting off women's heads and then sucking the blood out of the neck. M has a lovely photo of a dragon with a damsel hanging out of his mouth, nipples exposed. Advertisements for their videos are pretty lurid: voluptuous women, lustful men, saws, hatchets and blood everywhere. I actually caught M being shown an illustrated Thai porn book by our driver. Giggles galore when I pretended to be very disgusted with the pair of them.

Tried a few hours' kip before midnight bus to Udon Thani but really earplugs are a must in Thailand; if it's not vocal frivolities, music or loudspeakers then it's various animals, randy dogs or serenading cockerels. You can tell we are in north-east Thailand near the Vietnam border as there is a touch of the 'community' atmosphere. Loudspeakers through the towns give news and music and at 8 a.m. and 6 p.m. there is a total stoppage, traffic included, to stand for the national anthem. At 6 we watched them lower the flag outside the Government Offices. Tough luck if your barbecues on the pavement end up charred or if you are in the middle of the road. All stops for around three minutes and then all dashes on. Dashing on is something you learn when going on public buses but more on that tomorrow when I've recovered!

Friday

Day of the public bus. It seems that whole families own their own bus and have a franchise for certain runs at certain times. Makes life easier for farangs when changing buses as family touts accost you with 'Ware lu go?' If it's their run, your baggage is whipped off and you are gently whipped on to the bus. Dad does the driving while son number one minds the front door, son number two minds the back door. Number one does out the tickets, number two follows to hold the money. Farangs don't always receive tickets so I think there is a bit of a tax dodge there. They try to make the bus homely, not just by cramming on nearly a hundred passengers at one time but with the decor. The kitchen clock hangs at the front, plus a large decorated mirror for Dad to keep an eye on the passengers. There is always a stereo with huge speakers and lastly the little shrine. Useful if you need to pray for your safety, especially in the rush hour when buses compete with each other for passengers. Cut-throat overtaking takes place to reach the next stop first, passengers are hustled on and Dad drives off. How he doesn't lose his sons, goodness knows. As the bus is half a length on they have to catch up to leap on again. The best thing to do is to treat it all as entertainment. One bus had an old television with a large scenic photo stuck on it, presumably to take your mind off the journey. Trouble was that the windscreen behind it was cracked like mad so it was difficult to forget your possible fate. 'All good training for India,' says M.

'More like bad bussing,' I reply.

Visited Ban Chiang, a village of seven hundred families. A very old man has said that about two hundred years ago, four families immigrated there from Laos. Before that it was presumed nobody lived there until 1966. Steve Young, an American, tripped over the root of a banyan tree and happened to see fragments of pot sticking up in a circle around him. The locals had seen these before and even bits of skeleton but thought nothing of them. Excavations began and thermoluminescence tests by Pennsylvania University testify that the Ban Chiang pottery is around seven thousand years old. Its red on cream painting is similar to other early civilisations such as those in Turkey, America, Mexico and even Palestine. They buried articles and corpses in their graves in a similar way to the people of Eyenan, Palestine eight thousand years ago. The same type of green beads, copper bells and magnetic beads were used as mediums of exchange by the Red Indians, Maya and the Aztecs. Questions are now being asked as to who were these people of the red-on-cream culture in Thailand. They knew how to grow rice, weave, work in metals such as bronze, tool-making and other skills. Is it possible that the people from Ban Chiang went to America or across India to Asia Minor, or that nomads came from Asia Minor to Thailand to America? It just seems that Ban Chiang is the place the world forgot seven thousand years ago.

M reckons that with all these similar skills, these earlier cultures could have been taught by the survivors of Atlantis, whose fabled technology was very much the same. Anyway, it gave Ban Chiang an air of ancient mystery. The museum had a very interesting display of excavations and showed the

problems of analysis in the finds. There were skeletons and
infant burial bones in large pots. The village is a very quiet,
clean and peaceful place compared with the rest of the
Thailand we have seen. Apart from a few shops and the
inevitable televisions, it is as it was two hundred years ago.
The shops try to sell you original and fake pots. Don't
know why they bother as they are not allowed out of the
country. Had a ride in an open tuk-tuk with everyone
waving and saying hello. Felt like royalty. We are definitely
in an area where beards and red hair are seldom seen.

Saturday

Felt like a different kind of royalty when we went for the
bus to Phai Mai (pronounced Pee My). Touts were out but
this time there were two very keen lots in competition. One
lot took M by the bag and then another lot steered me in
another direction. I could see us going in two different
buses until we decided first come first served and anyway,
their bus looked newer. Usual home from home in the bus
and we have realised now that the bus may well be the
family base, at least if they have to stay overnight in bus
stations away from home.

Phai Mai had only four farangs and very little English
was spoken, although one place had tried with the menu –
noodles with cap fish and spicy fishes stomach, or fried poi
san. It gives you a good feeling of adventure to 'boldly go
where few farangs have boldly gone before'. Apologies to
Star Trek.

Saw some of the biggest and oldest stone sanctuaries
built by the Khmer in the eleventh century, influenced by
Indian civilisation. Later they were deserted and fell into
ruin, but looking at the crooked angles it could have been
an earthquake. The sanctuary included a hospital and
libraries as well as shrines. So aren't we fed up with

dilapidated old holy places? Well, this was the most holey of the lot. It was quite different, because the Thais, with their incredible 'we can make it whole again skills' are doing just that, but piles of old stones and mounds of dust later the result is hilarious. Irreverent, I know, but the place looks like a jigsaw gone all wrong. Even the door arch carvings are full of pieces that do not belong – half a god or half an elephant and anything else that more or less fits shape-wise but not picture-wise. Still, it is some undertaking when you look at, the muddle they have to work from. The main prang has been wholly restored and is most impressive when floodlit at night. We gave them an A+ grade for sheer endeavour and for making one old sanctuary more amusing. Then visited the largest banyan tree in Thailand, possibly in the world, spread over an acre.

Usual amusing evening stroll – I shall miss these. Hoped to have a quiet night but discovered that all-night markets do go on all night. M thinks we were also over something like a bottling plant turning out Cokes or Fantas all night and we had the largest and loudest chiming clock with a full set of bells on our landing. Comprehensive schools will seem like silent monasteries; not that the monasteries are so silent with televisions and:

> monablasters – one speaker radio in a monastery
> steryblaster – two speaker radio in a monastery

Sunday

In the end I gave up and woke up early to read the guide-book about yesterday's sanctuary. The English is unique. 'Ponds were used for rain water which was used "by the citizens of the town for providing which was poured on the lingams".' During the excavation of Prang Brahmadat (lucky Brahm) 'small stone lingams or phallie images were found'. For the ignorant amongst you, lingams are symbols of Shiva, one of the three main Hindu gods. I'm not too sure about the phallic images. The unusual aspect of it all was that it was a holy centre for Buddhism and Hinduism at the same time. Not that we can talk language-wise. Using my best Thai, or perhaps the worst, for our Sunday brekkie we ended up having omelette on rice, Coke for me and soda for M. That was the result of my Thai rendering of fried eggs, toast and tea! What would it have been if I had asked for bacon?

Then bus to Nakhon Ratchasima, or Korat as the Thais call it. Stayed at the Silly Hotel, sorry the Siri Hotel. Bus to town of Pakthongchai to see silk making. Very old looms at work, brilliant colours. Didn't buy anything as they only had very expensive 'seconds': £12 for shirts with grubby colours, caught threads and spotty bits. Spent ages selecting five shirts at 200 baht each (£5) and offered 750 baht as a bulk buy. Great consternation as each shirt was supposed to be 430 baht, short sleeves at that. The 200 baht ticket was on the wrong shelf and should have been with the scarves. Still, we had a good look round the village. Reckon the mozzies – or was it only one – have had a good look round me. The anti-itch cream works a bit but you tend to scratch in your sleep. They have even gone for the soles of my feet which are pretty tough from barefoot walking on hot stone around religious places. I think I'll have to wear pants in bed, although M says it could be worse if one got trapped.

Thought we had found a quiet place for the night at last. First of all a randy gecko decided to call in the women. Sounds like a bass drum cuckoo call. Then just as he was obviously satisfied we had thunder and lightning and rain such as I have never heard before. Just as well we had a double bed each to put luggage and shoes on, as we honestly thought we would be flooded. So there I was in sun hat and pants clearing the floor in the middle of the night.

The hat? I put it over my head to deflect the draught from the overhead fan, the noise and the light. Hence *Pink Hat and White Knickers.* So long as I wore them in bed I was assured of a better night's sleep so I could face any adventure the next day. That is how you survive the hazards of a world trip!

Monday

Thought we would have some eggs for breakfast to help to settle our unsettled stomachs. Nice soft boiled eggs and toast. Toast arrived, ten minutes later we decided the eggs would be hardboiled. Meanwhile we looked at their framed jigsaws of places in Europe, including one of Mad King Ludwig's schloss in Neustein, Austria, which contained 12,144 pieces and measured 7 feet by 5 feet. The eggs did arrive, in a glass with a teaspoon, each boiled for one minute. Very difficult to eat with a spoon so I drank mine. Glad I did it quickly before M drank his and remarked that it was like trying to drink 'hot snot'. 'Your mum will have a fit when she reads this,' I said, rolling around with laughter.

We did discuss later whether I should include this in the diary for printing but the only progress I made in the family discussion was that 'messy mucus' was not so effective. You were warned that this is a 'human' account.

Five hours on a very crowded train to Bangkok but at Korat Station, divine providence, or whatever, caused us to bump into Sue and Mick, who had just travelled seven thousand miles in India. They did love it despite the tales of horror and the warnings they gave us: take an abundance of loo rolls and trust nobody. Back to James Guest House; lovely welcome, felt like coming home. M and Mick had been up the corridor from Sue and I on the train and did not stop talking for five hours, in between teasing the fat little lady sellers trying to pass them with their large baskets.

Much to the amusement of the other Thais (who get fed up with the sellers anyway), our likely lads would hold her basket while she squeezed past. A few yards later she would realise she was a bottle short. Fierce accusations while they stood there like innocent lambs with everyone saying it wasn't our two. A couple of minutes and they would give in. Another rather drunk old girl offered herself to M for a few baht and kept touching him up in naughty places. Finally she was too much for surrounding self-respecting Thais, who pushed her into the section between the two carriages to sober up in the fresh air.

Tuesday

Very pleasant, homely day. Washing and packing for me. Indian planning for M. Tranquillity shattered by the checking in at Bangkok Airport. 'Cos we didn't phone seventy-two hours before they had sold our seats, plane was full; we had to stand by till 11, although we told them flight was confirmed at their brand new office in Cairns. Two nail-bitten hours later we were given seats but they've been sent a peeved letter because there were in fact ten empty seats behind us. Bit off, I said. (On 22nd May, two months later we did receive a creepy-crawly reply from Thai Airlines: 'Letters such as yours are an invaluable asset in allowing us to take measures as necessary with regard to the points raised in our efforts to improve and provide the best possible service at all times.' What a load of old Thai-wash. Almost as good as a Churchill war speech.

And so we move on to the Indian sub-continent where the best – or should we say the worst – is yet to come…

Agras in India

Wednesday

Time: 3 a.m. Chatty immigration official. Ventured forth to face 'over-helpful' taxi drivers, after M had a great carry-on changing money and I tried to suss out hotels. Our first experience of Indian bureaucracy, although we did not really realise it. Three-wheeler auto-rickshaw for 25 km. National holiday so very helpful driver found us a 150-rupee room, 25 rupees to the £. Same standard as a £2 Thai room so India seems more expensive. Had a little jet lag doze before we braved Delhi. Just as well as it was the Festival of Holi where they all chuck dye at each other.

First wander and first photo which seems to sum up the anomalies of India. It is of three cows, one scooter, one long-haired gent, and a photocopy shop all on one street corner. While M had a longer snooze I had read about what you can eat in India. Thanks to the Lonely Planet guides I found you could have cornflaks or flex, pouch eggs, porridge for breakfast; French onion soap, porn coactale, bum chicken, mashrooms and bamboo sooghts, chocolet padding, or leeches and cream. Dare I ask about this one fried children? We have learnt in a couple of hours that however firm you are in any request, you will have to reason your way out of innumerable better Indian alternatives.

From food to faith, after all, we must get the priorities

right. Eighty per cent are Hindu; Hinduism has firm roots before 1000 BC but there are probably more religions and sects in India than anywhere else on earth. They all enjoy each other's holidays. Good Friday is a national holiday. The Hindus have many gods, usually identifiable by their means of transport. Shiva, the creative god, rides on a bull and his matted hair is said to have Ganga, the goddess of the River Ganges in it. Makes a change from dandruff. Supposed to live in the Himalayas and devotes much time to smoking dope. Sorry, got it wrong. Brahma is the creator, Vishnu the preserver and Shiva the destroyer and reproducer. He needs the dope to help him to relax between his destroying and reproducing. The gods have goddess consorts so it all gets very complicated but basically all these different gods are pictorial representations of the characteristics of one god.

Buddhism was born in India but it is a philosophy rather than a religion based on the idea of karma. Your actions in one life will determine the kind of life you will have next time until everyone is enlightened enough to reach Buddhahood. Seems to be a more gentle outlook and one of more tolerance than Hinduism. Then there are the Muslims whose influence can be seen in art and architecture in India. Its followers had an extra task; they had to spread the word even if it meant using the sword.

The Sikhs practise tolerance and love of others rather than god worship and will offer shelter to anyone. With their uncut hair in a turban, their beards and upright bearing they stand out. All M needs is the turban. Apparently they have great mechanical skills, so is he a secret Sikh? In Thailand he took pictures of engines and generators doing different tasks. One is of a generator bouncing up and down on a rubber tyre to provide amplifier power for a pavement pop group. I'm sure it bounced in time to the music.

There are also a few million Jains who believe that the Universe is infinite and not created by a deity. Spiritual salvation is achieved through reverence for all life. This means vegetarianism and some Jains cover their mouths to avoid swallowing an insect. One of their sects rejects all material possessions, including clothes. They are 'sky-clad' monks who stay in their monasteries. Finally, apart from Jews and Christians, there are the Parsis. When M said, 'Look at the vultures over those buildings,' on the way in from the airport, I thought he was joking. Parsis believe in the purity of the elements so they leave their bodies in 'towers of silence' to be finished off by vultures. They believe in good thoughts, words and deeds. No wonder India is such a love it or hate it place, it is such a country of contrasts and extremes.

I have just read that if I want to visit the great Jami Masjid in old Delhi, the largest in India, and to go up one of its minarets I must be accompanied by the 'responsible male relatives'. Will M qualify? Our responsible male taxi driver gave us a few tips as foreign tourists, a step up from farangs. 'Never leave luggage alone. You go one way and luggage go the other.' Talking of going, the whole world seems to be on the go outside our fourth floor window of our Natraj Hotel. In the distance you can see the golden dome of some taj, skyscrapers and nearer, the shacky open dwellings intermingled with blocks of flats. Cows roam in abundance with the odd bull who wonders if he should spread his favours around. The doorless public urinal shaded by trees, sheds its 'shake a drop off clients'. A very large swarm of bees hangs from the nearest tree. All this occupies just half the window as the other half is obscured by a high, half-rotten old wooden cooling tower, so goodness what we are missing in that half. Which reminds me, yesterday on the way to the airport, we realised we needed 2 baht more for the 300 airport tax. We didn't want to cash any more notes and I could have kicked myself for spending 4 baht on two sachets of washing powder just before we left the hotel. Easy answer, find a farang with coins at the airport and sell him or her a sachet. It worked. Today checking M's bumbag, except that they are now tumbags, so that we can watch them, I found 80 baht in notes. In those two hours of anxious waiting we could have had a £2 ball.

First look round New Delhi. Patches of extreme poverty but obviously nowhere nearly as dense as Old Delhi. Enough to make you take stock and to feel humble. You have to try to harden yourself but the sight of a large, brown-eyed scruffy urchin is hard to resist, as you realise that but for the grace of God it is not your child having to go through life like that. We both feel there is no need to go gazing at poverty in Old Delhi just for the sake of it. We saw the cardboard community near the main mosque. We know it is there and unless there is a very large miracle it will be there for a long time to come. A very sobering thought.

Thursday

If we thought planning our trip round India was formidable, then the actual organising of it was even more formidable as we really met Indian bureaucracy head-on.

Getting money was a two-hour, four-clerk, six-form procedure. Buying the Indrail ticket was a three-hour, three-buildings (a good kilometre apart each time), three-currency procedure. It was pound to dollar to rupees on the receipt. Still the first-class Indrail Pass was a bargain as it gave us the ride, assured seats, meals, sleepers and overnight rest facilities on stations. At 4.30 we were able to see the outside of the Red Fort with its stone elephants and armed guards. Mind, there are armed guards at any excuse. All the banks have them by the door but we are not too sure if they have bullets in the guns. At one bank M noticed the muzzle was bent so the guard would probably have shot himself in the chest. Back to the sight-seeing. Went to the Jami Masjid but it was prayer time so we couldn't go in. I shall never know if M qualified as 'responsible male relatives'.

Bicycle rickshaw back to Connaught Place. Took twenty minutes through very run-down areas as well as some curious markets, some of them selling cow-pat fuel. Cows are everywhere, sometimes in a line trying to cross the road. Accosted by beggars. I seemed to be better at avoiding it by imagining myself on the school playground trying to ignore what goes on. M started by showing his empty pockets but after a day he's given that up. Made up for it a little by giving our bicycle rickshawers a bit extra because they really do work hard for their money. Some aspects you can admire while others drive you silly. As far as the Indians are concerned, everything is 'No Pwoblem', however desperate the situation.

Friday

Up for first train journey to Agra at 5 a.m. The rail efficiency was unbelievable, BR could learn from it. Computer lists for reservations everywhere. Aircraft seats, free newspapers and super free brekkie. Tea served in little Thermos pots, foot rests, the lot. I shan't mind our 26-hour journey at the weekend. Arrived Agra dead on 8.09 and were swept up by a young rickshaw lad, who was rather taken aback when we wanted to make our first stop at the leper ashram. We thought we had better go there first as we had no idea how long we would need there. The plan was to check up on various projects for which our little 82-year-old Ruby has been raising funds. We gave them £30 to be going on with and we were both wet-eyed. They welcomed us warmly as visitors before they knew about the money. We were people from outside taking an interest. The state of some of them can be left to the imagination but their eyes reflected love and determination. One hundred and ten of them clasped hands in gratitude and while M sorted out the finances, I asked some of them if I could take their photo. Not all of them have leprosy but the aim is to keep families together. There is still a stigma because even our friendly driver would not put a foot inside. Anyway that did it. They all wanted their photos taken for Ruby so I had to do it in relays but I think some sneaked in more than once and two lads peeped over the back of the ladies' photos.

We saw Ruby's candle-making machine with hundreds of candles half made and covered in dust. No funds to finish them. The problem is they are selling the candles and spending all the earnings rather than keeping some back for more raw materials. Great plans to build a weaving shed for six looms. Need £5,000. Later on M and I discussed the fact that they really need more business acumen otherwise these little or large projects are just one-offs. Anyway, at the time of writing I am confined to the Grand Hotel, Agra with Delhi belly, yes me, the one who normally needs gelignite. M is out to see if there is anyone at the local convent or hospital who can shed more light on it all, as the candles don't seem to be working any more. Sorry about the feeble joke but perhaps this one is better. We're not sure why, but loads of fellas keep trying to flog rawhide whips to M for the wife. Is that their concept of our society or is it there own norm? Our driver at this point was joined by a friend and they took us to Agra Fort, built between 1565 and 1573, with massive walls, 20 metres thick stretching 2.5 km and surrounded by a moat over 10 metres wide. Shah Jahan who built the Taj Mahal was imprisoned here by his son until his death seven years later. Sonny boy was fed up with Dad spending his inheritance on fancy buildings. When you read about the Taj later you may agree he had a point.

Then we were whisked off to a carpet factory and we fell for it. As it was our third anniversary of becoming acquainted we bought a Tree of Life carpet to start off our new home. The colours are beautiful, soft blues, greens, browns and pinks on an ivory background. Not for putting in front of a spitty coal fire. Fascinating work effort. Boss employs a thousand families; each family averages nine workers, including children. I was a little disturbed by this but we saw three kids, average age seven, tying wool knots under the direction of the designer, aged twelve! He knew exactly how to direct them and the process involves 440 knots to the square inch. Yet there was no pressure as they were chatting and laughing as they did their few hours a day together. Each family produces an average of two 9 feet by 12 feet carpets a year. We liked the whole relaxed and caring attitude of the boss and realised that at least he was keeping some of them from the dusty poverty of the cities. Next stop was a marble inlay workshop, where a ten-year-old was happily working out his five-year apprenticeship chipping out pattern spaces ready for semi-precious stone inlays. Process known as pietra dura which also covers the whole of the Taj. Nothing grabbed us here, not even the thousands of pieces of mother-of-pearl inlay of the Taj on black marble. The work seems infinitesimal and the reflections are extraordinary.

Silver jewellery and our second submission; this time for our four girls as the saris we have seen so far are absolutely lurid. All oranges and garish yellows but later we found out that these are the traditional spring colours and we would have to go in the rainy season for the blues, pinks and mauves. Helpful manager gave us a cup of tea and as he is having a house built he was able to tell M the average building costs, so that we could see that the ashram was not being cheated.

Last trade call was an antique brass and bronze specialist.

Quite a character who liked an intelligent argument. He could tell M was a judge of workmanship and showed him a carved silver plate which took one man two years to create. I've never seen work so fine. It had to be done under magnification and very sadly the creator is now blind. There were photos of Mrs Gandhi's visit to the shop with her admiring the plate. The chief then asked me what I thought about women's lib, after I had nagged him kindly to stop nattering and get on with the bill so that we could get to the Taj before dark. He was hoping for a good argument although he had already put an extra free box in our order. I replied that I felt women's lib had made many women rather unsettled and perhaps unhappy having to split themselves between families and careers. They have the freedom to choose one or other but should not want it all ways by combining both, unless the husband is prepared to split his roles. My sociology seemed to impress as he then went to tell us how seven years ago an English couple met and fell in love in his shop. The girl then explained that she could not have children so the young man said they would adopt. For the last six years they have come back to India to adopt a needy child. This time they have decided to stop at six. I finished the pressie shopping by buying several sets of wind chimes with camels, elephants, horses, and the words peace and love carved in brass. I shall have some fun deciding who should have which but it's peace for us.

Could do with a bit of peace at night, can't win on this. Paid £10 to stay at the Grand Hotel with its peaceful location. So what happens? I get Delhi belly and the local canine tart gets randy with vocal responses from all around. M says he is going to wake up every dog he sees asleep during the day.

We eventually reached the Taj Mahal at 5 p.m. We could see it was no good going before as you have to walk bare-foot on the marble and you'd burn your soles off in the midday sun. It is as fine as you could imagine, constructed by Shah Jahan in memory of his wife. He was heart broken when Mumtaz died after seventeen years of marriage, in childbirth, having already given him fourteen children. The whole lot stands on a raised marble platform in a large formal garden. The close-up detail is amazing. Semi-precious stones are inlaid flowers all over the marble and finely cut huge slabs of marble spread the light into the central chamber. A very strong echo with innumerable visitors makes it resound like a swimming pool. We saw the sun fade down and left two hours later with a wave of admiration for the design and the daily work force of twenty thousand which worked for twenty-two years. 154 million working days allowing for holidays!

Sadly in the twentieth century there is the threat of erosion by industrial pollution. Still, we had the unique experience of our third anniversary with a sunset over the Taj Mahal.

Fond farewells to our two little 'rickies'; you do really become attached to them. You seem to carry their faces for ever.

Saturday

M has returned having had tea and cakes with the Reverend Singh and his wife, very kind Methodists who gave him a helpful contact in Dehra Dun, where business projects are already organised for lepers. Now M has to reorganise the route. The train timetable is just about impossible with trains that leave at 9.31 and arrive at 9 without going overnight. Not helped by the fact that India has so many places you have to use a magnifying glass to read the map. Second cup of tea and biscuits, this time with another M Singh who would like to be an Anglican Reverend. M said he'd find out about sponsored courses in Britain while

Singh number two said he would try to check on what was going on in the ashram. His wife seemed interested in going there to teach the children so all in all M had a very good day's liaison work.

During his return M came across one elephant, one mongoose and a baboon. After a few more hair-raising rides we have come to the conclusion that travelling in India means going wherever you like, so long as you do not hit a policeman, or he'll hit you with his four-foot pole. I think a few of our rickies would have been pole-axed if we had not been sitting in the back. Just spent a night in the New Delhi Station first class waiting room, where Mata Hari on the door could also have done with a large pole. Twenty times an hour she has abuse from would-be trespassers but verbally she sees them off. Very sweet to us, making a space for us to sleep on the floor, so we have now done it, slept overnight on the floor of an Indian railway station.

Sunday

Embarked on the longest train journey – 2000 km. Delhi to New Jalpaiguri. Like having your own little house with convertible berth and seats. Very good conversations with well-educated Indians and in between we traced our route in guide books to find one fact about each place we passed.

Kanpur has a good zoo. Lucknow has one of the largest vaulted galleries in the world, 50 metres long and 15 metres high; built in 1784 as a famine relief project. Bob Geldof would approve. Allahabad: meeting point of the Ganges and Yamuna rivers, known as a sangam. It has great sin-washing powers but not so good for body washing.

At Patna the Ganges is nearly three times as wide. Some confusion as street names being changed in Patna, for example Gardiner Road is now Beer Chand Patel Marg! It has a beehive-shaped stone granary, 25 metres high built in

1786 to store surplus against possible famine. Varanasi is the home of the ghats and gnats, I would think. There are over one hundred ghats along the Ganges – steps where pilgrims make sin-cleansing dips. Two are burning-ghats for cremating bodies; no vultures here. Women bathe in saris, young men practise yoga, Brahmin priests tender pricey blessings, and beggars donate karma chances. Bodies wrapped in white cloth on bamboo stretchers or on taxi tops arrive for burning. Not a good idea to take photos of these unless you want a quick cremation. Also shrine of Sitala: goddess of smallpox and a Nepalese temple with erotic sculptures. Indians are definitely double-jointed, even now on the train we have four around us in Buddha positions. M and one are exchanging patience tactics but M is not in a Buddha position. I am now acquainting myself with some Indian vocabulary. Learnt that most of India lives on dhal, a thick lentil soup, sometimes tasty, sometimes 'dull' but usually lethal on the wind front.

Lunghi, a loin cloth wrapped around the thighs, becomes a dhoti if pulled up between the legs. Goondas are ruffians and even political parties have goonda gangs. Hypothecated sounds very painful but it means mortgaged, financially painful, I suppose. Peepul is a fig tree in case you thought otherwise. Sof are the aniseed seeds brought with your bill to help your digestion. Wallah is a person such as a taxi-wallah. Wonder if you can have a wally-wallah – person who drives you mad, like some of the Indian porters and shoe shiners who deserve one hundred per cent marks for their dogged persistence. Finally, yagna is religious self-mortification such as sitting in a cage full of snakes. I think we shall have some yagna when we go on our first Indian bus ride.

You are constantly aware of extremes in India, especially manners. Some have beautiful, courteous manners; others are just plain awful. In the toilet this morning one gentleman (mixed loos) made three others wait while I went ahead. Yet out on the railway line anybody does anything in front of anybody. Not a question of good education, as the lepers have next to no education but their manners are impeccable – almost embarrassing. It docs give you very mixed feelings about India, but perhaps that is part of its fascination. You could never call it a laid-back holiday because of the constant pressure for survival around you. Feelings of guilt and inadequacy well up because your life is good and help you might give is only a drop of clean water in an interminable sewer. So it may help you to grow as a person but it will haunt you for ever. Visual memories of the Grand Canyon, lakes in New Zealand, forests in Australia cannot erase these more recent memories or even alleviate them. You have to try to concentrate on the smiles of the lepers and to remember that hope is eternal.

Monday

Long night's sleep from 8 till 8. Just as well as M now has the Agras, a worse form of Delhi belly, and feels rather fragile. Scenery boring anyway. M may have the Agras but I am having the aggro with the railway bedding staff. Despite the fact that we are first class having to go second class we are having to pay 10 rupees for bedding. As the train is four hours late we are being badgered for another 5 rupees. A staring battle of the wills commences. Come back fourth year grots, all is forgiven. Along comes a very tatty first class inspector. Battle won, I hand over the 10 rupees, look simple and smile sweetly. M says I had better practise my best schoolmarm memsahib look for the future. In other words be a right madam. All right for him, lying in the disputed bedding, eyes shut. So that's the bedding department. Goodness knows what will happen when the catering department comes for its money. Having seen the kitchen I think it will be BOO in the future – bring our own. Still we could always go to the complaints cell in Delhi Station or is it for locking up complaining passengers like us? Shall we ever see Delhi again?

For more than an hour we have been sitting in a place called Rangapani, not on the map, not on the railway timetable and hundreds of soldiers and ordinary people up front milling around the engine. For the past few days trains have not been allowed past Jaipaiguri; is the ban moving up the line? What, a relief, moving at last, although rather slowly. Stopped again, only five hours late now. Arrived at last, M too poorly to care. Organised porter, taxi and hotel at Siliguri. No going on to Darjeeling today, even though the guidebooks say no tourists in their right minds stay in the dust hole of Siliguri. M has agreed he needs a doctor so he must be bad. Gone a horrid yellow but says he cannot be that bad as he is not hallucinating yet.

I feel a bit like Meryl Streep in *Out of Africa* having to sort out the natives on my own. Hotel Rajasthani manager and staff could not be kinder. One relief is that it cannot be appendix or gall bladder and we did have double quantity hepatitis jabs, never to be forgotten. Delightful doctor, superb English. M has throat infection, viral stomach and general fatigue. Manager will not let me out on my own to get the medicines and has made a little lad be available outside the door for whenever we need him. This is India at its best. M very poorly, can hardly swallow the medicine. Had to put up my first mosquito net over him as the windows are not wired. Looks even frailer with that over him, a sort of sleeping beauty under the misty gossamer cobwebs. Wait till he reads this lot!

Meanwhile I have done some advance reading on Nepal, if we ever reach there. Railway mutinies and landslides do not help. May have to indulge in a taxi, about £15 for 90 km to Darjeeling. Nepal sounds even more topsy-turvy than

India. A no-nod of the head means yes, and a yes-shake of the head – no. You must pass by with religious buildings on your right, so do you keep going round in fanatical circles or merely walk backwards at great risk? The 1982 life expectancy was only forty-six but that could be because there is only one doctor for every ninety-six thousand people. M had better recover soon as we haven't time to queue up. Just discovered that there was another goddess of smallpox called Hariti. She used to gobble up children until Buddha made her give up this nasty behaviour and stay near him. Seems Nepal has had its own share of nasty behaviour. Near Kathmandu at Kirtipur, King Prithvi met strong resistance when trying to unify Nepal two hundred years ago. He did win but lost many soldiers so he cut off all the men's noses in the town. It is said today that the males of Kirtipur have shorter noses than the rest of the Kathmandu valley.

Tuesday

M a bit better but not fit enough for a five hour Indian bus journey. Took all his energy to eat some toast and have a wash. I wandered down Siliguri 'High Street'; high in smell, fruit stalls, biscuit shops, chemists and material shops galore. Very narrow, very dusty and a question of dodging all kinds of transport. No real hassle although I did receive some lingering looks. Quiet, sleepy day except I had a few short chats with our very helpful receptionist and his friend. Both would like short-stay jobs in England so I took their names and details to see what may be possible. They asked why we had come to India. Like many Indians they were glad that we had come but were not sure why we were mad enough to do so. I explained that charity money was not reaching the needy so it was really a working holiday. Now trying to phone Ruby's friends, Lieutenant Colonel

Fred and Dolly Hamilton in Kalimpong, having found the number in the directory by accident under Bhutan government. Can only go there with a permit from Darjeeling, which you can only acquire if there is no local unrest. Queuing up in a supermarket will be nothing after this lot. Mind you, I do appreciate how lucky I am to have this very adventurous experience of setting out on trips to dusky destinations, while back home they slog away at their nine to five's. Still, I could do with some porridge and baked beans! Looks as if Nepal has some magnificent scenery to restore our spirits. From one place you can see eight out of the world's ten highest peaks, including Everest. Some of the hotels have 'hot and cold water running round the clock' and 'air-conditioned baths'. Apart from all these novelties Nepal contains the widest altitude variation of any country on earth, although it is only 800 km long and on average 150 km wide. There are the sea-level Terai lowlands and then Mount Everest at nearly 9,000 metres. Sandwiched between the two largest world population countries, India and China, it has many different cultures. Marriage patterns show this: illegal polygamy; Brahmins meet each other for first time on day of marriage; no widow remarriage; *rodighar* where people are brought together before considering marriage.

The whole country is going through a rapid social change as well as having to face many more tourists. They are even having a litter problem on the treks around Everest. Tourists earn more than the Gurkhas now. Although it was the birthplace of Buddha more than two thousand years ago, the Nepalese combine the Buddhist and Hindu religions in a unique way. In the future they may have to stand firm to keep their originality; since Nepal lies between India and China, many other nations have begun to poke their noses in. Hope they don't have them cut of India and China: roads; USSR: power plants and a cigarette factory; Swiss: cheese factory; Germany: restoration of ancient temples; USA: general aid. So what about the Japanese? Too busy down under pestering the Aussies. Dare I pester M to tell him that there are scores of erotic carvings in Nepal or is he too weak to take it? Many temples have erotic carvings because the goddess of lightning is a virgin and would not strike a temple with this sort of sexual behaviour, too shocking! The Nepalese Government has realised that mountaineering is a good source of income. Royalties have to be paid and the higher the peak, the higher the fee. Everest is fully booked for years to come. Another recent change has been the use of paper money. Earlier expeditions had to have porters just to carry half their weight in coins to pay the en route expenses. Managed a chat to the Hamiltons; hope to see them.

Wednesday

M seemed a bit better but weak. Decided to have a taxi to Darjeeling but just as I was about to order it, he was seized by terrible pain, back and front. Kept saying it was worse than his gallstones so we sent for the Doctor. A soulful humming seemed to keep his mind a little off the pain, I hope I shall never hear that sound again. The doc came in a long twenty minutes, having left a surgery full of patients. Gave M a jab and said it was amoebic dysentery. Change of medicines but still at 4 not even a drop of water kept down. Rameshwar, our saintly receptionist, called the doc again as it was three days now. The doc (guess his name – yep you've got it – Singh) did say we might have to put M into a 'very best nursing home'. I just cannot believe that this is really happening to us – how much more does he have to face? So we have had two months of fun but India was the charity bit. Why is it being made so difficult? Are we having our inner resources tested? What do I do for the best? Fly him home? I suppose the best is to be guided by the doctor. He has phoned for a second opinion. Give him tonight and if not much better then it's drip time. Did think we should have a 'jobbie' analysis done but then decided to wait as it would mean me, jar and rickshaw trying to find complicated way to the laboratories.

Still see the funny aspects like last night when he let his wind feel free under the mosquito net. M was not keen on the boomerang effect and then we wondered what would happen if we did a Jasper Carrott and tried to set a match to it. Decided the mozzie net would act like a gas mantle and we'd have a right little flare-up. Anyway, I was glad to be under my own net, protected from mosquitoes and other foul things that waft in the night. At 10 p.m. doc and Superior Doc arrive. One anti-puke injection. I am told not to worry, to phone at any time of the night. 'Do feel homely.'

Thursday

Things look better. Sipping Horlicks, see how biscuit breakfast works. Fond farewells to Rajasthani staff and firm promises to pop in on our return journey. Manager ordered taxi and was giving the driver a good telling-off because on the phone he quoted 350 rupees and on arrival, when he realised we were farengs, it went up to 400. M stood there looking frail and I said don't worry. Manager said okay but you pay him no more than 375 'cos he's a bad boy. Manager looked really touched when I blew him a kiss. A very honourable gentleman.

Arrived Darjeeling after three hours of the most tortuous road ever possible. Bend after bend, sheer drops, no barricades, cows, pigs, monkeys in the way apart from passing lorries, buses, Land Rovers galore. Like the Greyhound buses which go to Ayers Rock to die, Land Rovers take the road to Darjeeling. Consoled ourselves by convincing ourselves that the train track was even nearer the edge at times. The road and the track kept crossing each other. Obviously no train for weeks as rails very rusty and people camped on the line, in very superior tents under enormous sheets of black Polythene. M was shattered when we arrived. I don't know how he survived with his amoeba and vertigo. There was plenty to look at; cultivated terraces in every possible mountainscape inch and buildings perched in the other spare inches. Around DJ the villages do not 'nestle' in the mountains, they hang like spent teabags. Why should they nestle anyway? It is a tea area. Now and again you can see where some homes are gradually sliding down. How mothers cope with babies on open verandas I do not know. I suppose it is like everything else. 'No pwoblem'.

Quite a change in the temperature from steamy Siliguri and we had to put on winter clothes as well as raincoats. Staying in a hotel which was originally imperial mansions. Probably built over a century ago, it has the original paint and I'm surprised it has not slipped down the hill under a century of dust. The floor gets swept but only from one area to another; dustpans have not reached India, although photocopiers and videos have. Many towns have video halls but the only televisions we have seen have been those on the platforms on Delhi Station to keep travellers from rioting when the train is five hours late. In our room we have old prints, a Victorian fireplace and antique wardrobe. The hundred or so rooms would be an antique dealer's paradise. The quietest place we have visited since we set off nearly three months ago and the one with the most magnificent view – if it stops raining. So here we are, 2123 metres up overlooking the Himalayas. Actually it's jolly cold. I'm sitting by a barren fireplace with the bed cover around me. Think I'll be very Victorian and go to bed in my clothes. Cold-water bucket washes are very definitely out.

While M had a rest I went in great fear and trepidation to register at the Foreigners Registration Office. What a joke. Two woolly hatted gentlemen said 'Hello', looked at the passports on the outsides only and said 'Okay'. After all that carry-on at the London Visa Office nobody was bothered whether we had a permit or not.

Spent a whole £1 on two beautiful, round, smiling, cheeky Buddhas; one in camel bone to go round my neck, and one in wood for M as a get-well pressie. Makes me wonder if this is the way we should see God, with his tongue in his cheek, looking at us lot making a 'pig's ear' of it down here, or in India a 'cow's ear'. DJ is a fascinating place but it is sad to see it deteriorate with little hope of restoration. Even the tea production is in jeopardy because the one hundred-year-old plants are nearing the end of their lives and the soil is becoming too poor to encourage new plants; not that much replanting has been done as it means a loss of harvest. Definitely live for today in India. We decided to live for today and to ease our stomachs by indulging in omelettes for supper at Keventers Snack Bar. From their own farm they provide ham, bacon, cheese, eggs, and so on but more amazing there are three of them, Tibetan, in coats and woolly hats cooking away in a minute, windowless cupboard by the light of a candle. The omelettes were superb.

M is having a kip while I read ahead. I think he'd better have a couple of days here before we attempt Kalimpong, three hours or more on more torturous roads in a 'come here to die' Land Rover. Wait till I tell him we could stay in HL Dikshit Road or BL Dikshit Road. Can't work out the HL and BL; possibly high and base levels. Extremes again. Dare I try the electrics to make a cup of Horlicks before I die of Himalayan exposure? No worry about washing – just read a notice 'Actue Water Shortage'. Do they mean actual or acute or both? Shouldn't laugh, they do try. Speak Nepali up here so I must get the phrase book out and remember our reversed head signals. Lots of monasteries so it is an uphill task keeping them on your right and nobody else seems to bother. Have to come downhill some time! Submitted to a bit of Victorian bundling in bed; getting to know each other under the blankets with all your clothes on.

Friday

Writing may be strange as I am having to wear gloves. M laughed but he has verily given way to his thermal gloves while he reads in bed. Seems impossible that just 90 km away we were wickedly naked with a fan under a mozzie net. Spent the day on short walks as the altitude gets you after the sultry dust of the plains. All poetic now as reading a *Book of India* by B.N. Pandey. Really interesting snippets of life, history, philosophy and literature. Realise now that dreadful Delhi and terrible trains are only a small part of India. Mind you, at 8.30 a.m. there was a call at our door to see if we wanted a donkey for sightseeing. One ride and you'd be flea-ridden for life. Decided we'd stick to deceasing Land Rovers without the wildlife bonus. Talk about wildlife, whatever will people say when they hear I had to buy a hot water bottle in India?

Found the Baha'i Centre and had an interesting chat. This is an increasing ideology based on the unification of humanity with regard for the needs of others rather than an emphasis on any particular religion. Funny how within the space of a few hours you can find linked ideas. Reading some of Gandhi's words, you can see he was of similar thinking:

'I do not regard God as a person. Truth for me is God'.
'To find Truth completely is to realise oneself and one's destiny'.

His destiny, he felt, was 'to wipe every tear from every eye'. Although he was proud of his Hindu inheritance he included all religions within the fold of truth. 'A semi-starved nation can have neither religion, nor art nor organisation.' He could see that for millions life was 'an eternal vigil or an eternal trance'.

In those circumstances how can one believe in anything? A cardboard box in the dusty, sewage-lined gutters of Delhi is hardly the setting for pure spiritual thought; very much easier in a secluded monastery on the side of a beautiful mountain or lake. Cynical? Perhaps India is reinforcing my feelings. Does the religion really matter so long as we see humanity and nature as a divine creation which deserves our every respect.

Swami Vivekananda, a century ago, wrote that it is wholly impossible to have a universal religion just as there can never be a time when all faces will be the same. We should not wish that we should all think alike as there would then be no thought to think. People collect water in cups, jugs, buckets, tanks but the essence is still the same; water. Our minds are like these vessels and the divine comes in different shapes:

We have to learn yet that all religions under whatever name they may be called, have the same God, and he who derides any one of these derides his own God.

So he who derides another human or particle of nature without a very just cause, derides the divinity of Creation.

And yet your days will be full
And without regrets, if you can say:
'With light did I kindle my life
With my all have I loved.'

Tagore
1861–1941

And in the meantime my hot-water bottle is kindling my feet!

Saturday

Land Rover to Kalimpong; 50 km of dicing with death. We were at the front with yours truly by the door, held by a wobbly bolt. Was it just as well that much of the journey was in thick cloud? Stopped at Testa Bridge halfway for permit check. Land Rover parked on a slope. So what? The handbrake was a stone on a back wheel. Kept thinking, does it really matter which God you have so long as one of them goes with you? Arrived Kalimpong, bit of a scruff place even by Indian standards. Had a wander, found Fred and Dolly's bungalow, left them a note, and had a few minutes' refreshing quiet in their very English garden. Now comes the exciting bit – this place has a 6.30 curfew because being in a corner bounded by Sikkim, Bhutan, Nepal and India there are loads of arguments going on. Burnings, robberies and even rapes and pillages occur. At present water for only ten minutes a day, no phones at all and electricity now and again. Fred and Dolly popped in – really friendly, will collect us for the day tomorrow. They told us how the area has deteriorated rapidly in the last two years because nobody seems to take any responsibility. Certainly looks it. The 1940 buildings are crumbling with filth and rot. Human respect seems very low here; people spit in the street, chuck rubbish anywhere, including a black banana skin right in front of me. The Thais lived in the streets but they did try to keep it clean around them and always had beautiful manners.

M had a rest while I explored more. I was just saying that however hard I try, my India pendulum swings more to 'leave' it than 'love' it. I don't 'loathe' it because I feel sad that a great deal of potential is being lost... when Dolly and Fred appeared and reinforced my feelings. M is beginning to realise that we shall have to assess very carefully whether some of the causes are really worthy of support. We are supposed to give £100 towards a church for the lepers. Apparently they were given a part to sit in in the ordinary church but some started to drift to the main part. It's not that the Christians are being unchristian, but sometimes ex-lepers can develop secondary infections which they may not bother to have treated. Anyway Dolly has fourteen of us for lunch tomorrow including the pastor, the superintendent, some teachers and community workers, so we shall really see what goes on. Fred and Dolly must be made of solid patience. Fred is a Lieutenant Colonel and yet during a general transport strike he had to fill in forms and pay 5 rupees to use his Land Rover. If they, after forty years of being out here, want to go to Darjeeling they have to write a letter of request to the chief of police. Strikes are the 'in thing' and that's why there is no phone or water. The lekkie did come on at 6 and I was just saying that was probably because the Big Lekkie Chief had a naughty book to read, when it went off again. Must have been a picture strip version. Mind you, when it does come on that is about all you could see to read. Perhaps they all should learn Braille.

Sunday

Dolly and Fred took us to the boarding school church service. Seven hundred and fifty children, some from richer families, some on charity, gave us some beautiful singing. The Nepalese pastor preached a rather long sermon on the techniques of fishing, as used by the disciples. Even Dolly was fidgety. We could see the children below, well switched off, some reading magazines, playing pencil games and crawling along the bottom of the rows. The church is English style but one corner is cracking off and the stained glass is bending and slipping out. I asked Fred if it was lack of funds. 'Not at all, just sheer Indian inactivity.'

He and Dolly are on various committees for different homes and face endless frustration because the money is there but nobody will get things done. Dolly has in her time run the blind school and the boys orphanage. In both she had tatty old buildings pulled down and just prayed that enough money would appear. We had coffee with Elsie at the blind school and saw eight year-olds guide children of four and older. They all make their own beds and fold their own clothes as well as having communal chores.

One blind lad sorts out the washing.

'How?' I ask.

'By smell.'

Forty children and he knows their clean laundry by smell. They can also recognise people by their walk; Auntie So-and-So walks like an elephant; not always very complimentary. The youngest at four and a half was a real heartbreaker. Normally they do not take them so young but this little fellow's mum has another two younger than him and another on the way. You would expect a blind home to be in a flat area but this is on a steep hill with badly spaced steps but they cope. We were also taken round Scottish Jean's house where she has thirty-four girls from four to eighteen years. Her attitude is one of firm love. Her main problem is that the altitude gives them runny noses so various ones are Snot one and Snot two and so on. They all love her dearly and come to see her when they have families of their own. What happens when this dedicated generation can no longer do the job, Dolly dreads to think. Most of them devote around forty years of their lives to this work. In the last couple of years it has been made even more difficult by the political terrorists.

At lunch we met the local superintendent, who has to have a six-man armed bodyguard as well as ten around his home at night. I remarked that it was all a bit like Northern Ireland without the bombs, to be told they have them as well. Aliens are only allowed two nights in case they are spies. The stories are horrific so it is just as well we go early tomorrow. Dolly and Fred say you just have to take it a day at a time and go on living. One Indian lady told us how she reads in the evening with a candle under a rug tent in her bedroom, because if the gangs see a light on they come knocking for money or shoot at the house. One night Dolly and Fred were playing Scrabble which turned into Scramble as they heard shooting so they decided bed was the safest place. Their neighbours next day said they had spent the night under the bed. Sometimes someone's head is chopped off, put in a basket and dumped in the town square or on the counter at the police station. The bodies are never found and the post-mortems usually state 'excessive loss of blood.' What else can they say when there is no body?

Nevertheless there are still laughs to be had. It seems that the electricity cuts are due to an elephant knocking over a pole. We do wonder, when the electricity comes and goes, has the elephant still got its foot on the pole? The Indian lady who reads under a rug by candlelight also told me that the birth control programme is a dead loss except amongst the educated. M muttered something about dog control as we had had three or four hours of barking in the night. Earlier he said he'd kick any dog he saw, but I said he couldn't do that in India until he filled in a form of consent.

In the afternoon one of their friends brought a visiting high-ranking British army officer, his wife and four children. Even though he was on Army business they only had two nights like us. Normally they are based in Nepal so they were able to tell us the latest on the situation there. The Nepalese Government has been tardy in renewing a trade treaty with India, so the latter is cutting off supplies, especially petrol. Coach companies are being allowed ten litres of petrol per coach per day and as Nepal has no trains the buses have long queues. We had already begun to think that with all the delays due to amoebas and trains we would have to cut out Nepal anyway. The coincidences seem to accumulate, as we should have seen Dolly and Fred on Friday, gaily gone to Nepal and have been well and truly stuck. So we had a really lovely day with Dolly and Fred and all we gave them was some money for charity and three toilet rolls. Fred gets army issue loo rolls but he reckons they are 'squitty' little things. Ours were from Thailand so Fred asked if they were made from coconut matting. They had some from East Germany once and it was like sandpaper. Foreigners like ourselves are instantly recognisable by our bottle of mineral water and toilet roll! Funny how your whole existence can revolve around water of some kind. Invited Kay from Bethnal Green for a brew-up but it was awful, and ended up in my hot-water bottle because we had only a couple of inches of our water ration left.

Monday

So we have done it at last, over three hours in a real Indian bus from Kalimpong to Siliguri. Bit feeble as only thirty passengers instead of the usual one hundred with hangers-on crawling up the back. Some bad parts where half the road gone in recent landslides. Only other drama was a recently 'gone over to 200 feet down' tanker. M said it could not have had petrol in it as it would have become a funereal pyre; perhaps only water. No wonder the tea was so foul if they carry water in petrol tankers. Talking of tea, I asked Dolly which Darjeeling tea she used. Turns out they have a tea 'merchant' who works on a plantation, helps himself to 'surplus' and sells it half price. He comes round once a month, and as Dolly says, it is all a good game which you are expected to join. Some of the blind boys have been known to sneak out at midnight to climb next door's guava trees to help themselves; a very high dangerous pursuit for a sighted person by day.

Popped in to say goodbye to Rajasthani friends who were touched by us bothering. Didn't manage to see the doctor but left him a letter, inviting him to stay any time he wanted. After all, he only charged us £1.25 per visit even late at night. When we offered more his reply was: 'That is all I charge anybody, I cannot take any more.' The Consultant for his hour at 10 at night only charged £4.

Train was nearly two hours late in leaving but we chatted to other farengi on the platform. Found we were in the same berth section as before, as M recognised the crack in the window and the bent glassholder. Somewhat disconcerting as this was where he had begun to be so ill. Never thought I would spend my son's twenty-first birthday on an Indian bus, rickshaw and train. He very gallantly said he did not mind his Mum being away so long as she bought him a Tibetan prayer wheel; not that he will understand what the prayer is, any more than we understand the prayer flags.

My own understanding of where we are going is becoming confused. A twenty hour train journey, then eight hours to do a two hour bus ride to the next eight hour train journey. Eventually we should reach Naini Tal (pronounced Nanny). Near there is the Corbett National Park, named after Jim who lived there. Just read his *My India* with heart-warming stories of the people he lived with, like the Robin Hood sultana who never robbed the poor, never refused to give charity and paid small shopkeepers twice the price asked; or the case of Chadi who brought Kalu to court for pinching his wife, Tilni. Kalu agreed to pay Chadi 75 rupees. Then a malaria-worn woman appeared saying she was Kalu's wife and would die with nobody to support her. Tilni said she would support her and give her half of what Kalu gave her. Then Chadi returned the 75 rupees to Kalu, saying that with two women his need was greater. So why did Tilni leave such an honourable gentleman in the first place? He did not wash often enough and was mean with his money – one scruffy miser, but a man of justice. Kalu had his head screwed on as well as he refused to pay Chadi's original asking price of 100 rupees for Tilni. He knew this was what he had paid for her when she was 'new'. Even with experience wives depreciate and Tilni was only eighteen when all this was going on. So Indians live for today but with a strong sense of fair justice. It is not clothes and surroundings that matter but the soul of the person. That explains the dirt and deterioration and of course the heat and dust don't help.

Tuesday

Experienced a good share of heat and dust in our third class train between Kanpur and Lucknow. Were sandwiched with some commuter card players. One let his friend play instead of him so that he could shout English in my ear and move his able elbow round my various curves. M sat opposite, smiling sweetly. Anyway this chief inspector of weights and measures (I think he was sizing up my body) made me promise fervently that I would write to him from England. M said I always kept my promises and I muttered, 'You wait till we get off the train.'

Two of the inspector's companions told him off for

being an irritation to me but he insisted he was just being nice to English guests. He offered to teach me Hindu in two hours but I wondered how 'handy' it would be. He escorted us to the reservation office for the next train and was even prepared to watch over us until it left three hours later. I persuaded him he should go home to his worrying wife, so off he went somewhat reluctantly. Train to Haldwani.

Wednesday

M asked the Haldwani station master if he knew where Dr Kate Young's leper colony was. Turned out George was a personal friend of Kate – 'We often eat together' – so he organised a tempo and told him to report back that we were safely delivered.

Warm welcome by Kate, eighty and Amy, eighty-three, breakfast, chat and lovely lunch, prepared by their very faithful Indian boy. As we have £60 to give them M took out his solar calculator to convert it to rupees. Kate was fascinated and played with it for ages; it was just like magic to them both. Kate is the doctor, Amy the pharmacist. Between them they run local surgeries and keep an eye on four leper areas. Lately they have had to resort to flying in order to get around quicker. Whether it hastens the end of their lives is questionable. The trip from Leah to Srinagar used to take two days but it is only half an hour by plane. You pay for the reduced time in units of fear. The landing strip involves going up a mountain and the taking-off strip involves going down a mountain and leaping off. One time the pilot was lost and all they could see was snow peaks all around, not below. Then they heard over the radio 'You are in Afghanistan, get out.' Very helpful.

A man in front of Kate leapt up shouting 'I fear no death.' Not so reassuring for the rest of them until Kate shut him up; we're not sure how she did. The half-hour flight took nearly two hours.

Left Kate and Amy at 2 to catch the bus to Naini Tal in the foothills of the Himalayas: jolly big feet, I say. Another stirring journey in bus with signs to read like 'Shooting Boulders'. Quite an explosive area this, even the hotels have 'geysers in every room' – hot-water tap. Naini Tal is like Switzerland except for acres of washing on tin roofs held down by stones: the roofs, not the washing. Re washing we are wondering what kind of local hospital it is here with the name of G.B. Pant Hospital. Dolly was saying that an edict was delivered that all foreigners shall avail themselves of an Aids test at the Calcutta General Hospital. So on behalf of herself and another old girl of eighty-five, she went to the local DC and asked if it was really necessary for them to make the two-day journey. He looked and as politely as possible said he didn't think it was. They were after young men from the Middle East. The other old girl was mortally offended by the DC's implication.

Thursday

Had a bucket of hot water for 2 rupees and a proper wash. It's surprising what you can wash over a bucket. Took cable car up to Snow View, when we eventually found where it started. We had been told the view was fine but what a wonder it was; we saw the actual snowy peaks of the proper, highest ranges of the Himalayas, 150 miles away and 150 miles across the skyline. I counted fourteen mountain ranges between but there were more obscured by the haze. The peaks were more awe-inspiring because they suddenly appeared above the haze. We could hardly believe that at last we were seeing the real thing. Again I had the Grand Canyon, Australian desert feeling of eternity because they could never really belong to man to be spoiled. The

Grand Canyon is timeless; the Australian desert infinite; and the Himalayas invincible. For the geographically concerned what we saw was the Trishul-Nanda Devi Range, average 24,000 feet. This we worked out with the help of an ad hoc Indian map-readers' committee in situ plus a magnifying glass!

Sat down for midday snack in our sun hats, when along came two Indians plus camera. One Indian stood near us so we offered to move. 'No, no, he only take me.'

They must have thought we had no sense of direction because Indian number two in no way had number one in the photo, as he pointed the camera directly at us. We were a bit taken aback being at the receiving end of a native camera instead of the other way round. Laughed when we realised we had been a bit slow and should have put our hands out for 10 rupees, as the going rate is 5 per person per photo. Coming back round the lake we were accosted by an Indian to show us another Indian lying on a diving board. M thought that he was ill and moved towards him.

I yelled, 'Don't get involved, it's probably a con trick.'

At that point the prostrate sat up too quickly, too soon, and we moved on, keeping up our pace until there were more people around. So perhaps they wanted to abduct me to Bombay. Kate told us of many attempts to abduct young girls in her area; so much so that one retired gentleman sits all night in the station looking out.

Apropos stations we have noticed how much tidier the stations are up this way; pot plants and no litter. We could not see why as there is never a litter bin; but solved it this evening when we watched a cow devour a fruit juice carton in one go. Every platform seems to have its own garbage-consuming bovine and heaven help it if it tries to pinch a free chapatti from the refreshment stall; out comes the stick at the ready under the counter. Needless to say these cows do not produce milk and do not really contribute to the fragrance of the platform. There is a hurried moving of luggage and children as the four-legged, horned hoovers weave their way along. Back down to Government Tourist Rest House, 60 rupees and very posh, for the night at Kathgodam, pronounced Kathgodam, or Pussy Go To Hell as the British army call it. Up at Naini Tal, 35 km away, we froze with all our clothes and two thick rugs each and now we are back to nude and fan existence. Tried to work out why the fare down was less and then remembered how the Land Rover between Darjeeling and Kalimpong free-wheeled over 10 km of the route, or should one say 'three-wheeled' when chunks of the road were missing. Great how things go missing in India. Yesterday on the way up we had to pass a broken-down lorry on a bad bend. Today when we came down said lorry had been moved over and propped up because the front wheels, engine, exhaust and other essential parts were gone. Gone for repair or gone for ever, we shall never know.

Friday

What we thought was a quiet guest house turned out to have a Mosque at the back with the 5 a.m. chanting. We did see it last night but with its flashing fairy lights we thought it was a disco. Kate and Amy with Felix the chauffeur picked us up so that we could visit the leper colony with ours and Ruby's money. A very well-kept colony but being 4 km from anyone it is often raided by dacoits who steal their goats, utensils, blankets and even their clothes. Helped Kate and Amy give out medical supplies of antibiotics, vitamins, aspirin, soda mints, cough mixture, ointments, bandages and anti-malarials. Amy spends days counting out six week pill rations in little bags for twenty-four of them.

Had lunch at an Agricultural Good Shepherd Home for abandoned children and fit children of lepers. Entry age has gone down and down. Just before Christmas one mother dumped her newborn daughter on the doorstep a few minutes after her birth, unwashed. Boys and girls learn farming and English. Problem is finding teachers who will stay as it is out in the country. A recent arrival is Magwi, aged eleven, blind since she was four. She cannot speak and they wonder if she is almost deaf as well. Anyway Kate wrote a report which we are taking, plus photo, to Dehra dun Blind School. DD was not on original itinerary but now we have three reasons for going there, so just as well Nepal is off. I don't think I could have handled the no-yeses anyway.

Today's journey was 100 km each way through natural forest where wild animals roam. In some hotels you have to watch out for monkeys sneaking into your room and pinching things, especially washing left out to dry. One cyclist was chased by a leopard until a bit of downhill saved him. At the home there is a rogue elephant which comes down in the night for a nosh of grain. Seems strange to see monkeys playing at the side of the road, not in a cage. Passed a massive lake reservoir, took six years to build, mostly hand labour and it involved submerging fourteen villages with seven hundred and fifty families needing new homes and land. A very untouristy day full of interest. How many eighty-year-olds have a typical life like our Kate and Amy? They have been doing this work for fifty and thirty-five years respectively. We could see love and trust in the eyes of their patients.

Now in the train to some junction or other. Arrive there 10.20 p.m. and then 11.30 train to Desirable DD, according to Lonely Planet guide a place 'of very little interest', 'not a great place for hotels', 'rooms grubby and overpriced', 'a large menu of rather questionable food'. Carriage is full of horrid little flies and dearest M has turned off his little light so they are all after me.

The 11.30 train was wishful thinking. We watched the Barellie Nightlife until 2.45 a.m. The time passed with the help of a delightful Sikh by the name of Winky Arora who breeds Angora and Kashmir rabbits for their wool. At present has eight hundred, wants to go up to two thousand. Must tell our Jenny with her twenty that he has found a solution to mothers cannibalising newborns. Seems they get a bit keen consuming the afterbirth and bite their heads off. A bit of salt in their diet a few days before giving birth solves the prob. All this you can pick up on Barellie Junction in the early hours! Winky organised our berths and our 6-rupee taxi on arrival at DD. He had a wicked sense of humour, mostly at the expense of other Indians. Reckoned the wheel and line tappers were deaf and that was why there were so many derailments. We said we would ask at the blind school for him whether they'd be interested in wool spinning and then leave a message for him at his shop in Mussoorie. All this message work, who needs an Indian postal service?

Saturday

Visited Dr Agnes at the Leper Rehabilitation Centre and she confirmed our assessment that the Agra Colony would need properly trained leadership to do any business. Very difficult to find people to do this so better to raise funds for one loom for their own needs, blankets, curtains, and so on. Then on to the Sharp Memorial Blind School, where we saw Ruby's little Dywana and gave her 300 rupees. We wished Ruby could have seen her face. Was supposed to be 250 but we rounded it up and pressed the three 100-rupee notes into her hand. She has learnt to use a knitting machine and eventually after another year will probably complete one school uniform V-neck pullover per day. It seemed to be a very happy community so we shall be able to make a good report to Ruby and Dolly. Another good report to Kate, Amy and the farm home is that the principal has agreed to take on Magwi for a six-month trial. A really worthwhile day.

Sunday

Having gone for a street night market walk we got lost and worn out so we laid in until 7.30. Then decided to move on to Simla as Mussoorie was obviously Mistoorie. Had an eight-hour Indian bus ride of the usual nature, overtaking on bends, and so forth. Hordes of men surrounded us at Simla, some rally or other. They looked like loads of escapee extras from *Gandhi*. Rather disarming but our coolie assured us they were all on their way home. Posh Hotel Diplomat with supersonic view, real honeymoon stuff with pine trees, clusters of houses on the sleepy slopes, hills fading into the hazy horizon, and the odd, very distant glimpse of a snowy upper Himalaya. Ooooh, isn't it romantic? M has announced that we are beyond the foothills, past the ankle, almost at the crotch, and he can't wait to get to the peaks. Isn't he awful?

Monday

Awake by 8 a.m. Fried eggs and chips in bed. Laundryman came so we availed ourselves of his services, as after a very bumpy section on the road a young Indian lad gave us all a helping of rice pudding. I felt so sorry for the kid because he was so embarrassed and obviously feeling awful. Indian justice being what it is, he received a smart clip round the ear from the one person who was not a target, while those of us who were just brushed it off and fell about laughing. I wasn't going to record this bit but M says it's all part of the human pathos or some such rubbish. He now has achieved co-author status.

Chores in Simla, reservations, bank and then as we were both feeling weak, possibly due to altitude, old age or hunger, we decided to try out the last possible cause and have a good feed-up. Seemed to do the trick. Little rest and then off on the next exploration. Really interesting because we found a copy of Kipling's *Plain Tales From the Hills* which are all about this area. They were really boring when I had to read them for O level but now with maturity and our Indian experiences I can appreciate them much more. Kipling certainly has the Indian work ethic well summed up:

> Good work does not matter, because a man is judged by his worst output, and another man takes all the credit of his best as a rule. Bad work does not matter, because other men do worse, and incompetents hang on longer in India than anywhere else.

Still they do deserve many merit marks for trying with their English, especially at Simla, where we saw these two this morning:

> Beauty Parlor, for the Treatment of Acnay Problems, Dendruff and Pimple Skin. Also Bridle Make-up.

How about this for a Classic?

> By courtesy of the North Indian Railway, a true test for Mensa...
>
> No cancellation charges payable when onward reeservation is not confirmed up to 12 hours of the scheduled departure of a train in which reservations has been made for want of onward reservation from a station en route but the same has not been confirmed up to 40 hours before the scheduled departure of the train in which reservation has been made no cancellation fee shall be charged.

The exploration involved me setting foot at over 9,000 feet, the highest I have ever been on earth and guess what was there? The Jakhu Temple dedicated to the monkey god, Hanuman. Very appropriate as this is a real monkey area. One was really narked with M for trying to take its photo so we beat a hasty retreat. They swing on serious branches and jump from tree to tree over drops of several hundred feet. Despite barbed wire around TV aerials, we saw one swing round and round until the whole aerial was bent, sorry, M says he actually broke it off. Now he is the technical adviser.

Tuesday

From broken aerials to our first bus breakdown. Having decided to do 250 km in a semi-deluxe Indian bus for 40p more, it developed a puncture one hour out. Spent the next hour in the sun chatting to passengers, everyone is so laid back. Reached the Kulu Valley after seven hours, a long, bumpy journey despite the semi-de luxe. Kulu Valley is pretty, again like Switzerland, although the latter is a jolly sight easier to reach.

Wednesday

After our shaking-up we did not sleep very well as the stomachs go on churning for hours. One-hour ride to Katrain, smaller, pleasanter village. Best Indian bus driver we have had and of course for the shortest journey. Walked to Patlikul to see the Tibetan refugee children's village school. Ruby was there four years ago when there were 230 children, now there are 330 and major building work is going on to bring it up to 400, with extra dormitories and staff housing. One large block has been financed by one deceased Frenchman. So despite being refugees the children have a good start and then have further chances at

Darmsala. Ruby sponsors some children there and we met Tsering Dolma and her daughter and son and her second two month old baby son. She invited us to lunch on Sunday in her tiny one-room home. She teaches at the school and lives in a room smaller than the smallest English bedroom. Her husband works on security in Lhadak, home twice a year. Not easy for Tsering but the room is beautifully tidy and she is a very serene, loving and contented mother. There seems to be a great deal of foreign aid already and we seem to have been to help a little more to justify our fun and frolics of the two months before down under. We are now a little weary and actually beginning to look forward to going home. Tomorrow we go to sixteenth century Nagar Castle to stay in semi-luxury for three nights so we shall make the most of it to be strengthened for the journey home. Dear old UK will seem like Heaven.

Long walks around the Kulu Valley gave us an insight into their way of life. The Kulu people are lighter skinned and very friendly. A great deal of stone building to replace wooden shacks shows the increasing prosperity from farming chickens, apples and even woolly rabbits. Men wear the Kulu cap, a pillbox with a flap in the back in which they often stick flowers. Women wear lots of silver jewellery and long robes of homespun wool. They always have a cone-shaped basket on their backs, filled with wood, fodder or human or animal kids. There are also Tibetan refugees who work very hard in families running hotels and bazaars, or making roads. The women hack up large lumps of stone, men tar and level, children carry grit while babies play in the sand. It's a hard form of family survival. At the moment our survival consists of Horlicks, coconut cookies, bananas and oranges – the Indian safe diet. It does wonders for your waistline.

Thursday

Bus ride from Katrain to Patlikul, 2 km, cost half a rupee each. Land Rover to Nagar Castle. Panoramic views from old courtyard terrace over mountains and valleys. Thick, tiny, very old wooden doors into the bedrooms, which have the usual castle thick walls and small windows. The castle was the Raja's HQ until 1660 so it will be the oldest place we have slept in. Long, idyllic stroll up the hills at the back and saw Nicholas Roerich's house with over thirty of his very striking paintings of the mountains. Perilous tiny villages hang out from the mountains, miles from any road, with stockpiles of hay and wood all neatly piled around them. A tranquil place in summer, but vicious in winter.

Back to our sunny courtyard for M to start his Ruby Report. I've had a go at some little drawings and so far have managed a very unsymmetrical Taj Mahal and a one cow, two-man lawnmower with the cow far too large. Have decided they will have to be cartoons rather than artistic interpretations. After all the cow is more sacred than man. Supper in between power cuts which are euphemistically known as 'load-shedding'.

Friday

Another trek, really making the most of the scenery and the peace, reaching really isolated villages. The women smile, the men try a little English and the children chant 'Hello, photo, goodbye'.

Yesterday M tried to redirect the whole irrigation system of India by damming a downhill stream. I wondered what little ploy he would find today. Well, it was a 'Let's photo wild life' day which involved stalking birds, lizards and copulating butterflies in all sorts of positions: I mean M was in all sorts of positions trying to keep up with them. Give

him his due, he did catch a very gross spider in the bedroom in a large tumbler, which it filled completely. You
could hear it clunking inside. He threw it over the balcony
and it landed with an even larger clunk on a glass table
below; too dark to follow its ultimate fate. Apart from
power cuts we had another electrical problem. For the first
time the little pot boiler did not fit the socket, but, magic,
the general emporium had two way light socket for three
rupees. So M had another little project, organising a boil-up
erection on one bed and three tables. What an ingenious
fellow he is in times of dire need. What will he do if we run
out of loo roll having given some away?

Saturday

Beautiful sunny morning so off we went to find the
Murlidhar Krishna Temple. As usual we went the most
circuitous way and climbing up we were very warm. Then
we saw we could be enveloped in snow. Found the temple
and I chatted to some girls while M mended a cart for some
boys who were moving large lumps of stone. New steps are
being built up to the temple but what a hand labour of love
it is. Just back in time to miss the snow but watched it
cosily from the balcony. Then wrapped up for a last p.m.
walk. Played Poohsticks with orange pips till they formed a
dam. I won. Then who could chuck their biodegradable
peel furthest down the valley.

M won. Surprising what you can do with the inedible
parts of an orange. M is beginning to show signs of needing
to get back to get his teeth into something better than an
orange. Extra mural pursuits today include trying to fix an
Indian ballcock and making a Concorde dart to go over the
valley. Have just caught him trying to make a hot-air-
balloon with a poly bag over one of our emergency candles.
Result: dripping plastic and burning smell. What fun!

Sunday

Even more fun when every morning in India you are greeted by a different sound. Today it was the monotonous hoopo bird, whooping away. No buses or taxis so we hooped our luggage down a rough 4 km track before our lunch with Tsering. Proper Tibetan mumu with mutton inside steamed pastry cases and rice wine. Stayed a couple of hours chatting about her children, Ruby, and so on. Saw one classroom piled high with kids inside and out watching the Sunday video He-Man. Local bus ride of one hour to Kulu, very uneventful, really rather boring. Had a raging thirst as Tsering had given us proper Tibetan tea. It's made by mashing tea leaves with boiling water, straining and then adding butter, milk and salt.

Monday

Lazy start. No breakfast anywhere so bought puff pastry samosas and filled them with boiled eggs done in the boiler. Usual one-hour puncture on the bus and a right carry-on putting tyres on and off the roof. Even the bus inspector helped. Found out that long-distance buses carry their own mechanic but the driver had to do a fair bit like jumping up and down on the spanner to tighten the nuts. They earn their rupees the drivers, driving over ten hours on the most dangerous roads on earth. It's no wonder the tyres keep collapsing with treads coming off and patches on with bolts. Poor M goes green at the lack of mechanics.

Only other drama, apart from the usual hairpin, hairline, hair-raising overtaking, was the pylon cable. All out to watch thirty men on one side of the valley heave and ho to raise the cable, which happened to be resting in our way on the bridge. Little fellow with loud voice and a red and a green flag directed the operation. One cable up, then cover the others lying on the bridge with coils of rope and over we go. No wonder the power is so spasmodic, the cable is 'naff' before suspension. Back at Simla and met by the same deep, sparkling eyes of our first coolie plus his equally charming friend. They would not let us go to our planned Hotel Vishkrant, not clean enough for us. Led us to the Hotel Victory where we were shown a 250-rupee room. 'Too much' we said, all prepared to move on with our lads. The lads, however, told the manager to stop trying it on, they knew he had one hundred and fifty rooms. So he didn't get away with it and they went away with their 5 rupees each and wishing us all the best. Sad when you know you will probably never see their lovely faces again. I wonder what will happen to them in the years to come.

Tuesday

Last stage of journey by train. Remembered that yesterday before the perilous descent into Simla we stopped at a shrine. Some devotees came on the bus with what looked like polystyrene beans. Everyone, us excepted, ate a few, some donated rupees and prayers were offered, we suppose for a safe descent. When it comes to offerings, M has become real canny. Small begging girls try to stare you out like stubborn adolescents so M lets them try it on for quite a while and then gives them a peanut. We do submit to coins if it is a crippled or injured child. Beautiful ride in a twenty-seater railcar down the edges of the mountains from Simla to Kalka. Took four hours but we stopped halfway at a little model station for a cup of chai – tea to you. Then overnight train to Old Delhi; suburban very crowded train to New Delhi.

Breakfast, then went to Baha'i Movement HQ and had a lovely chat with people there. Then on with another very obliging coolie to the Baha'i Temple, shaped like a lotus, very simple and finely made. Paid for by different countries; United States the infrastructure; Germany the marble; which was sculpted by Italians. Also going to build schools, hospitals, old people's homes and orphanages around the temple. This is the nearest thing to a united world socially based religion. The Baha'is feel that words must be coupled with deeds. Thinking of welfare we had a count up of all the places we had liaised between in India: two schools for needy children, two orphanages, two blind schools and three leper colonies, and don't forget Winky's rabbits. We told our coolie what we had been doing and he insisted we should go to a new temple where very few non-Indians go. We were made very welcome, given a rose and sweet meats and blessed with holy water as well as receiving a red sign on our foreheads. A really spiritual end to our stay in India and we realised it was the feeling behind it all, not the actual religion, which mattered.

On the way back we visited the Qutab Minar Complex. The minar is a huge tower, 73 metres high tapering from a base 15 metres in diameter to just 2.5 metres at the top. It was started in 1193, and apart from a small lean it has worn well but has been closed to visitors since a stampede led to several deaths on a school trip. Nearby is an iron pillar 7 metres high erected in the fifth century and scientists have not yet discovered why the iron has never rusted in two thousand years. It is said if you can encircle the pillar with your hands behind you your wish will come true. We watched a few failures and decided we had everything we could want; just the world needs a lot more love. Our final round-the-world trip view was the magnificent outlook from the Government Houses down the Avenue Raj Path to India Gate, where they had all the millions of extras at 40 rupees a day for Gandhi's funeral in the film. The gate bears the names of ninety thousand Indian army soldiers, who perished in the wars before World War II. Also the

President's Residence which was used for viceroys before Independence. Mountbatten was the last and there were hordes of servants to keep the 340 rooms, as well as 418 gardeners, including 50 boys, whose only task was to act as bird scarers.

Now at Delhi Airport waiting for the 3.15 a.m. flight to Heathrow. Looking back I realise I have made a few omissions such as our singing Indian in the Simla railcar who could sing Cliff Richard's songs word perfect and beautifully in tune. A few more language tips such as a bathroom with 'gaysir', and who needs prunes when they can have 'purge' for breakfast. One that is now part of our own daily usage is 'shelf' meaning stale. Rarely did we find a packet of biscuits which did not have the flavour of the shelf it had frequented for years. M did a last bit of 'emporiuming' and has now returned from purchasing our last bottle of mineral water. He is playing 'I'm bored so I'll pretend I have boobies with the air pillow'. He has been the perfect travelling companion, never losing his cool, never panicking and always seeing the funny side. Even had a laugh on the way to the airport. Innumerable signs have the letter T missing, such as Hotel Diploma—, Dis—illery. M says the station chai-wallahs are pinching them to put over their tea stalls. Just discovered why the Delhi Airport tannoy system is more difficult to decipher than most. Each speaker has a family of sparrows in residence. Long nine-hour flight, and of course we had a loud-speaking gentleman of Northern European origin behind us, who seemed to require no sleep. On his way to Iceland, it was a pity we could not freeze his jaws up before he arrived there. Not very humane, I know, but really. Did have a few minutes' peace when he went to the 'oilet' but I think it just oiled his voice again.

M has just landed me in it by encouraging me to smile at what looks like a Japanese gentleman we had fun with on

142

the train down from Simla. It's not him and he's not Japanese and I feel a right nana. We had a jolly time with our train Japanese as we were all leaping about from seat to seat trying to take photos. At one point the train swung round, the kids in the back stopped their singing and the photographers amongst us all ended up in each other's seats and laps.

'Musical Chairs,' said M.

That did it. Everyone fell about laughing. The Japanese (who had come to see the Indian Electrical System of all things) and the Indians knew exactly what he meant.

For those of you who would like to know some of our new language when you see us again, here is a brief guide:

shelf flavour – out of date, stale food
sparrows in the tannoy – not very clear
Indian electrics – one hell of a mess

Soon, in M's words we shall have girdled the world. From the plane in the early hours of the morning we even had a clear view of the vast Russian Steppes. Seeing these remote expanses you realise how large the world is physically, but experiencing other cultures you realise that we small mortals are all in it together.

The Sequel

Or should I have called it the sickquell? Simon and Debbie met us and persuaded us to have a coffee so they could tell us their news.

As they queued up I said to M 'Wonder what they want to tell us – marriage, unemployment, pregnancy, eviction or what?'

Turned out it was the first after having had the last and then deciding to buy their own place. It was gorgeous to see family and friends after all our adventures, although M's amoebas decided to welcome him home and he had two stays in hospital on a drip to overcome his dehydration. At first we blamed the pints of orange juice we drank on the Thai plane, probably reconstituted with Bangkok klong water. Silly hospital sent him home too early as the runs had stopped. They failed to remember that he had nothing left to run on. Forty-eight hours later, collapsed veins and back in again; the GP was not amused. Neither was M, who having experienced the efficient Indian medical system became somewhat disillusioned with the NHS.

With family help we went house-hunting. Matthew suggested France or Northern Ireland. Was there a message there? Martin and Hayley found semi-derelicts with thatched roofs. Jo and Richard came out tops with 'potentials'. The word potential means 'hole-worthiness.' Charlotte has just given up hope now that her father can clear his throat like a true Indian. We have settled for East Sussex but I feel the travelling bug will always be with us, like our memories.

First Just Deserts in Arizona

Saturday, 23rd March, 1991

This time the warnings were beware the mozzies, snakes, mule whatsits and giardiasis. So where were we going this time? Down the Grand Canyon, of course. First three were pretty obvious, but the last is your canyon equivalent of Delhi belly but not life-threatening. It's caused by excreta so hence we were warned to beware the paths of the mules. So what? We survived the Indian amoebas after all, or just about!

So, with the Isle of Man solidly below us, I am perusing what is in store – mesas, Chacos, Hopis, craters, painted this, petrified that, prickly cacti and perilous anything you like. Despite the dangers, the names lure you on to Tonto Trail, Snake Gulch, Hot Na Naa Canyon, Jackass Creek, Death Hollow, Dirty Devil River, Upheaval Dome and Swazy's Leap. The last is a crumbling tree trunk over a 100-foot drop and if you do not make a supersonic dash over it you do not make it.

The 'No Mozzies Shall Enter Here,' tent has had a trial erection on the sitting-room floor; not that there will be much room for us if more than one mozzy gets in. A treat for the sleeping bags – they have never flown before. Lastly, the bread rolls – Freudian slip – bedrolls which are only as thick as a medium slice of bread. For just under £10 we have apparently purchased the height of camping bed luxury. I wait to feel how an overgrown piece of toast can give a night beyond all dreams.

The immigration homework has just arrived. They must think we are a plane of slow learners as we have six hours to fill it in. Even so M has very carefully put his birth date on the surname line. I think we are non-immigrants and if we accept unauthorised employment we are subject to deportation. Looks as if M will be deported out of the plane soon. Having very unaccustomedly consumed a whole half-bottle of wine 'cos it's free, he is now grooving away with his earphones. On my other side the young lad has 'wet himself' with his half-bottle and is bouncing about as well to stop himself from sticking to the seat.

I have just read an article that you are never too old to get fit. So how does one manage it in a week before the Grand Canyon descent? M wonders if it means press-ups in your coffin! Then guess what? We have just had a video of plane airobics before we land. My two muscly, macho male 'sit-besides' have chickened out of it, supposedly to give me more room to perform. Four-hour stopover in Minneapolis where I tried to formulate a space theory on how so many very fat people were able to fit on planes. Talk about an overlap job. Plane to Phoenix, another overlap job. Two people in our seats refused to move. Airport cop job soon put it right. Arrived Phoenix 10.30 p.m. their time. Collected hire car but it was two hours of solitary moonlight driving through eerie rocks and cacti before we found a truckers' motel, Jo's Motel, in Black Canyon City. This city had about fifty inhabitants, about a quarter the size of Punnetts Town!

Sunday, 24th March, 1991

Eight hours' sleep and my first American breakfast whaeeee! They sure know how to eat. Visited the Montezuma Castle built by the Sinagua Indians. It was five storeys up a rough cliff and they even had a lift system. So even in AD 1100 they had high-rise dwellings. Then on to Sedona to find ourselves a spiritual 'lift'. It seems that much of the New Age spiritual awakening is happening there. Every second shop is connected with some form of life and soul improvement. Immortality consultations explore your past and future lives. This helps you to find out what kind of Earthling you have been or are now – original, divine, animal, elemental or half and half. What is half and half? we asked. Mother Mary's private sessions cost $125, semi-private $85. What is semi-private, we asked. Nobody in Sedona had the answers.

M then did a very skilled piece of hairpin driving from Sedona to Flagstaff. Seems strange to think it was just over two years ago that we came here for the Grand Canyon on the start of our world trip. Thought we had a peace and quiet motel but we had not noticed the Santa Fe railway crossing. Every hour we had bells, hooters and eighty-odd wagons rumbling. M had great fun playing with over forty TV channels but we ended up with Sean Connery against Al Pacino. Also fun frolics on a queen size bed each!

Monday, 25th March, 1991

Breakfast at Denny's: a killer veggie omelette. They set a stop clock on the table when you order and if it does not come within a set time limit you have it for free. Never happened. A few very skilled reversed U-turns took us out of Flagstaff. Highway 89 to Sunset Crater, a Mars-like landscape of lava flows and cinder cones. Erupted in 1064 and spread over a fifty mile area.

A beautiful drive down to the red sandstone plains and the Wapatki Settlement Ruins. The Sinagua had to move from their original homes around Sunset Crater when they heard rumblings and felt the earth shake in their cornfields. They made it just in time before debris exploded out of the ground and rained down on their pit-houses. Less than two hundred years later they had all just vanished, possibly because of over-cultivation and drought. The settlement had one hundred rooms for as many families. The high-rise was achieved by ladders up the side from one roof to another. The 'front-doors' were a small hole in the roof and down another tall ladder. No vertigo sufferers amongst them. There was also an amphitheatre and a magnificent stone-lined ball court for the ancestors of today's baseball players. Nowadays the area is occupied by passing chip-munks, skunks, bobcats, coyotes, snakes and tourists. Tourists are few as there is still snow around. In fact, M had to mend a puncture lying out in the freezing wind on snow-covered lava. Makes a change from lying out on Swindon High Street where we had the last puncture.

Next stop was Tuba City to mend the tyre. It was like some distant outpost stuck out in the desert. Being in the centre of the Navajo Indian Reservation you see them riding around in old pick-up trucks full of junk, no petrol caps, just grubby old bits of cloth stuffed in the hole. I left M for a couple of minutes to find him being persuaded by the local Navajo wino to buy a pair of 'recycled off a lorry' jump leads for a mere $2. A beautiful sunset ride through the Painted Desert where strangely shaped mounds looked like water colour paintings. A dramatic loop drive up and through the red rugged rock of the Echo Cliffs brought us to the outskirts of Page. M was still having a chauvinistic chuckle about this sign when we entered Page. He had to sober up because we passed nine churches all next to each other on the same side of the road. Their names were an education in themselves but we were spiritually mind-boggled by the time we reached the Burger King, Pizza Hut and motel downtown area. In McDonald's the staff have certificates for degrees in hamburgerology, probably taken at the Oven University. Perhaps M will get a degree in international squareyology. Still, it is just as well as we need the weather forecast. There are snow, wind and tornado warnings for where we want 'to boldly go' next. Will anyone believe that we encountered snow ploughs in the Arizona Desert in April? A bit like us buying hot-water bottles in India.

Wednesday, 27th March, 1991

No it's not, as I have decided to rewrite Tuesday, 26th March so I have had to tear a page out.

Rain, during a rather pathetic McDonald's breakfast, turned to sleet to snow. We wanted to see the old Navajo rock homes around Shonto but after driving for two hours through a snow blizzard we managed just one visitors centre. We popped in for a half-hour film and came out to find the car covered in over three inches of snow. M used the tracks of a van in front to keep us on the road. Suddenly the snow vanished and the desert reappeared. Another ten minutes and visibility was reduced again, this time by a sandstorm. It was an eerie experience to see the weird rock forms on the edge of Monument Valley first through snow and then through the swirling 'dust devils' or mini-tornadoes. Then came the hail, so within half an hour we were assailed by winds of rain, sleet, snow, sand and hail. The car looked like a chocolate pudding with runny cream.

UTAH	COLORADO
ARIZONA	NEW MEXICO

We were nearly blown back to Punnetts Town as we stood on the platform marking the only spot in the US common to four states and I reckon it was common to all their winds as well. We felt like a couple of mud dancers. Unstuck ourselves from chocolate mud mobile to settle for an early room at Cortez, Colorado. While on mud and Colorado, we learnt that it was estimated that before the construction of the Glen Canyon Dam, in one day at high flood stage, the Colorado carried over two and a half million tons of rasped rock, sand and silt. Today, thanks to us it would have had a little less. Now we have a major tornado warning just to the east of us.

Wednesday, 27th March, 1991 (for real this time)

M phoned the Mesa Verde ranger who said it was clear but icy so we decided to brave the fifty-mile drive round. We had just gone ten miles up when the petrol dropped from half to empty. A lady ranger sold us three gallons from the ranger reserve, apologising profusely at having to charge us $1.50 instead of $1.30.

'It's $4 at home,' we said.

'Do you earn more over there?' she asked.

I told her my teacher's salary.

'How can you buy petrol at that price on that?'

Saw Cliff Palace, the largest cliff dwelling in North America. It was discovered in 1888 by two cowboys. At the opposite side of the Grand Canyon, through the blowing snow, they could distinguish something in the cliffs which looked like a magnificent city under an enormous sand-stone rock alcove. The people who lived there were called the Anasazi by the Navajo: 'ancient foreigners'. They only lived there for less than one hundred years and disappeared like the Sinagua. So despite advanced research there are many unanswered questions. Only wood used in the floors can be dated as between AD 1200 and 1300. Of course, this is prehistoric to the Americans! Fourteen storage rooms lie at the top directly under the rock arch, reached only by hanging ladders and large enough to hold five years' supply of food: your first American freezer. The slope in front below the dwellings was the trash heap. The heap is the archaeologists' dream with pottery, bone and stone tools, yucca fibre sandals, clothing, ashes, corn cobs, human waste and dead bodies. The last was not from disrespect but because there was nowhere else. The body was buried in a flexed position with knees drawn up to the chest and wrapped in a yucca fibre mat. Possessions were placed alongside for use in the next life. Strikes me as a cheap way of getting rid of grannies. Your overgrown yucca plant could also be used for containers and as a vegetable.

As families grew in size more rooms were added. An air ventilation system was very necessary in the large round *kivas* which were used for workshops, ceremonies and smoking. We did wish we had not asked how the Anasazi reached their homes down the sheer cliff face. Little niches form the hand and toe trails. Each notch would take no more than the tips of fingers or ends of toes. They must have been an adept breed to carry children and burdens on their backs on these trails. Some were coded so you had to start on the correct foot. Otherwise halfway up a cliff face you would have to cross feet and regain your balance. One mistake could be your last!

Descending the twelve miles from the Mesa Verde, M had to be careful not to make his last mistake on sharp bends with hidden ice. Second night at very cosy Sandy Canyon Motel; large TV, bathroom, shampoo, tissues and so on, plus the usual two queen beds: all for $19. Tomorrow's weather includes the prospect of a 'sloppy day with juicy winds'.

Thursday, 28th March, 1991

So the weather channel five got it wrong: clear blue skies

and sunshine. Fatal stop at a wholesale rock shop; the rocks and crystals were cheap and beautiful so we succumbed. Drove through miles of red canyons and weird shapes, just like this page!

Stopped at Mexican water trading post. What an education! M went to the loo and came out all of a doodah. Apparently there were some very specific slot machines. He kept guard while I quickly looked round the door but I couldn't take it all in with one flash. Back he went with pen and paper. Ten minutes later he reappeared with the following trade description of a screamer for sale in this machine: 'If she is a moaner this will make her a screamer. If she is a screamer this will get you arrested. Make a little go a long way.'

'No way,' I said, 'you're not having one of those.'

We should have realised that a mid-desert cafe with these words on the door would be a setting for trouble: 'No Bears, No Bare Feet, No Bare Backs, No Bare Bottoms'.

After all this excitement we had a practice trail walk, one mile down into the Chelly Canyon. Would we ever manage the many more miles into the Grand Canyon? Spent the night at Keams Canyon with wood-lined rooms and craggy rocks looming up behind. Supper in local cafe. Fascinating to watch the Navajo extended families eating out. They have large, round open, smiling faces and obviously adore children. Found a copy of the local Hopi newspaper. They seem to have been contaminated by American humour. Dr R.U. Hurt had a few novel suggestions: 'If your feet hurt while you jog then try putting a slice of lunch meat in each shoe. It will give all the extra support you need.'; 'When listening to Heavy Metal tapes you can avoid damage to your ears by sticking a raisin in each ear. This will decrease the decibel level by up to 15%.

Friday 29th March

We could have done with raisins in our ears as our most expensive $35 room turned out to be the noisiest with all night television, trucks revving up and down, and the howling of wolves, in other words local dogs. The plughole in the bath would not plug and the taps went in reverse.

We trickled our way through Hopi country. They have a small square inside the Navajo Territory for ten thousand of them. Passed through old Indian settlements on the First, Second and Third Mesas. Present-day Indians still live amongst the ruins but in modern prefab, mobile or small bungalow homes. Some have built on to the original several century-old dwellings using the latter as storage sheds for mounds of junk. They also have modern round hogans in the same pattern as centuries ago. Average diameter was 20 feet using legs 10 inches in diameter for the 8 feet high walls and pointed roof.

As M said, it took nearly half a forest. These days they are prefabricated, probably come in kits. Previously they were for family ceremonies, now they seem to be for the banishment of adolescents. Also passed a very essential firm called the Le Pew Septic Tank Emptier Company.

Quick stop at Little Colorado Canyon; a gorge with rocks stacked like pancakes or do I mean waffles? Just mastering that a biscuit is a squashed scone, a muffin is a well-risen scone and a cookie is a biscuit, so goodness knows what a bun is. The Americans sure know how to eat. No wonder they have two queen size beds in each room for the twenty stoners.

Arrived at the South Rim of the Grand Canyon. It still took our breath away and we recalled that very first impact of just over two years ago. So what is two years when you see billions of years below you. Whoops, snow and ice on the trail. Do we really want to do this?

Saturday, 30th March

Just as well we arrived a day early as we needed it to organise permits, lodgings at Phantom Ranch at the bottom of the Grand Canyon and crampons for the ice. Our luck was in as we were given two cancelled beds at the Ranch so we would not have to carry camping equipment. I was a little worried that M would rather be macho and camp but suddenly he became all for equality. Mooched around the rim and then went to An Evening With John Muir by actor and writer Lee Stetson. He certainly lived the part and it was an hour of beautiful thoughts and humour. Even the children were spellbound. Muir was the instigator of many parks being formed and wildernesses being preserved. His greatest love were the sequoia trees; hundreds of years old and not put on earth for us to turn into tables. Sadly for him he failed in his bid to stop the Raker Bill of 1913. This authorised the construction of a large dam and reservoir in Yosemite to pipe Sierra water to San Francisco. The natural cost was the destruction of the beautiful Hetchy Mountain valley which was flooded to a depth of 200 feet.

Sunday 31st March

Our last day in March was to be our first day of sheer madness. As one ranger said – the Grand Canyon trails are not classed as easy, slightly strenuous, and so on but as murderous, more murderous and even more murderous. The views going down were indescribable and worth the pain of seven miles of tortuous descent. The Canyon is actually one mile down vertically. We discovered that your muscles are okay until you stop. Most of us, whatever the age or the fitness, walked around like splayed geriatrics at the bottom. The Phantom Ranch was lovely with a really international atmosphere and a wilderness spirit amongst us all. We had ranch stew, delicious and tender. Then we heard that the day before a five-strong mule supply train had slipped over the edge. The front rider managed to jump off but the bodies had to be brought out by helicopter. Was it really mule stew? Actually they were trainee mules as they do three years of inanimate load-bearing before they qualify for humans. We watched the faces of those on mules. They were not a happy lot. How could they be? They could see even further over the ledges and had very little control on the perilous cornering and the intermittent stumbling. These mules are large horses not just 'little donkeys'.

An early night for a 5. a.m. start. It's ten miles up so we figured a mile an hour plus rests. As the stiffness sets in we wonder if we shall ever get out.

Monday 1st April

Easter and April Fool's Day – which will be the most appropriate?

Ranger gave us the latest telex weather report for the top. Snow blizzards or was he 'fooling' us? Coming down, my crampons and I parted company so I decided I had more control on my bum. We measured our progress in billions of years as we moved from one rock layer to the next. Going up we measured it in points of a mile. Yesterday's scenery was wide expanses of rock. Today's was steep overhangs, waterfalls and echoing gorges. The rocks range through deep shades of purple, orange and green to pale shades including blue. It has to be seen to be believed and eight hours later when we returned to the top we realised that every step of pain and fear had been worth it. We shall never experience the like again. We had descended a mile from the earth's crust to its core. The last four and a half miles brought us up 3000 feet and half of that was through ice. We collapsed into the car, M put his hand on my knee. 'Well done, gall,' he said.

One hundred and eighty hikers go down each day and in the last two years more than seven hundred and fifty have needed ranger assistance to get out. There are helicopter pads for real emergencies but this is a risk in itself. Full leather boots, flame resistant gloves, suits and crash helmets have to be worn. Last year one man was found face down dead from hypothermia and another was rescued in the summer, close to death. His body temperature had reached 109°. In both cases they were inadequately prepared. The steepness can be shown in one photo where the trail starts white with snow and ice, then orange mud to pale yellow sand. Muscle sore but spirits high we stayed at Valle, out in the desert but we felt that the Kaibab and Bright Angel trails were now ours.

Tuesday 2nd April

Woke up to find we were next to a Fred Flintstone's Centre with shops, playground and restaurant advertising Bedrock Breakfast. We didn't risk it. We were still rather stiff but loosened up after movement. Drove a couple of hours to Flagstaff. Stopped to fill, the car with gas. We had stiffened up again and I got the giggles as M doubled himself over the car clutching the pump. As I hobbled into the garage to pay, the chap leant out of his cash window to inform us that, 'You folks have just been down the Canyon. Never mind, in a year you'll have forgotten all about the pain.'

A year! We can't crawl off the plane like this in four days' time. So we decided to have a little two-hour trek round Walnut Canyon. It was small and tree lined except for rock outcrops which looked like walnut shells. I was pointing all this out with a couple of Americans listening to me intently, when I felt a proper walnut myself. The next sign pointed out the walnut trees which gave it the name and M in the know had let me ramble on verbally. Still I got my own back when M had five films printed at the Fast Foto. His desert panorama had twelve pictures and he had a devil of a job sorting them out in the right order horizontally. Little did he know they were numbered on the back until I told him. What fun! Supper at Sizzlers. What a place. You can fill up your salad and pudding plates as often as you like. Americans seem to eat out a lot *en famille* as it's so cheap. Good idea if Mum works full-time.

Read a bit more about the various Indian groups. Useful facts like yucca roots make good soap. Sinagua Tribe seemed to find it easier to lay a new floor rather than sweep it clean. One old cliff dwelling had ten floor layers of clay with rubbish in between each layer, even fag ends made of cane. Today in the cliff dwellings we saw the hand and finger prints where the Sinagua had pressed in the mortar over eight hundred years ago. Back to our Travel Lodge, only just opened so it was $28 instead of the future $40. For an average of £15 we have had two queen beds, bath, towels, flannels, cap, shoe cleaner, shampoo, tissues, glasses, ice bucket and mammoth tellies. M is now well ahead with his *Star Trek*. Will we ever be able to settle for 60p Bangkok brothels again?

Wednesday 3rd April

Left Flagstaff to see a very aged hole in the earth. About fifty thousand years ago an unbroken plain was shattered by a huge nickel-iron meteorite weighing millions of tons and travelling at nearly 43,000 miles per hour or 400 miles per second. Layers of rock were flipped over and blocks of rocks the size of houses were blasted out. Three hundred million tons of rock were displaced. For miles around trees were flattened and no living creature survived. Today

Meteor Crater is a gaping chasm 570 feet deep, 3 miles round and a mile across. It could engulf a sixty storey building and twenty football games could be played at the same time on the floor with ten million spectators round the sides. Excavation drills used to jam on the meteor debris.

New research methods show that probably about eighty per cent of the meteor was vapourised on impact, five per cent blasted out and ten per cent buried. The other five per cent you ask? Already lost by stripping in the Earth's atmosphere before it landed. It has made a perfect area for training Apollo astronauts. There is also a 1,504 lb meteorite found in the area which you can touch. Rather weird to feel the hard, cold, knobbly object which came from we know not where. On to Wilmslow and the Mayfair Motel with its 'All Queens' sign. Bit worrying at first until you realise it's the beds.

Spent the afternoon at Holbrook, an old Wild West town as all we have had is Indians so far. County courthouse was a good, old museum with an historic one-piece jail. It was shipped by rail from St Louis at a cost of $3,000 and looks like an overgrown piece of Meccano. Perhaps it was better to be hanged. A typical invitation was:

> You are hereby cordially invited to attend the hanging of one George Smiley, Murderer. His soul will be swung into eternity on December 8th, 1899 at 2 p.m. sharp. Latest improved methods in the art of scientific strangulation will be employed and everything possible will be done to make the proceedings cheerful and the execution a success.

The state governor did object to the idea of a hanging being a cheerful event so a few pointers on conduct were made – no flippant or unseemly language, no ribaldry nor anything that would 'tend to mar the solemnity of the occasion'. We did not see but we heard about the Bucket of Blood Saloon. It was one of the first rock structures in Holbrook after the 1888 earthquake wiped out the whole town. The notorious saloon was named for its violent brawls that stained its floors as well as its reputation.

Saw the Sante Fe railroad depot, where in the real cattle days sixty thousand head of cattle were shipped out on the Atlantic and Pacific Railroad. The town now has over twenty churches but the first one was a Methodist built by Judge Sapp in 1912. His bride refused to live in a town without a church. At times we have been a little confused by the time as the Navajo nation observed daylight savings time from 1st April. The rest of Arizona and the Hopis are on Mountain Standard Time. Hence, you can hopi from one to another in less than one hour. I doubt if we shall be hopping about with our luggage in the airport. We have bought enough rocks and crystals to fill our own crater. I've given up saying, 'Where shall we put them all?' but rather 'Where shall we pack them all?'

M wanted to take home half the Petrified Forest but settled for one large chunk, after much picking up and putting down of pieces. Now we shall be forever reminded that millions of years ago, when dinosaurs roamed, the forests were buried under a sea of mud, sand and volcanic ash. Cell by cell the trunk and bark turned to stone. The natural grain has remained but is made of marble-like silica dyed by many different colourful minerals.

Spent the night in another colourful motel. The room was vast and so were the plumbing problems. The shower was a cut-off pipe so we took it in turns to do a Dutch dyke job by holding a plastic tumbler over the hole. Still it was only £6 for the night.

Thursday 4th April

Drove on through the desert to Paysan City. Definitely one of the Navajo's more Naffaho towns: one long street and one tiny motel. Four-hour drive through dust and heat and certainly no 'lust in the dust'. Braved a small walk out in the brilliant sun to photograph each other holding up enormous cacti. Beautiful poppies and other bright flowers meant we saw the desert at its best. Found a travel lodge at Mesa, near Phoenix, with the help of the Dunkin Donuts Lady. Swimming pool all to ourselves, all lit up at night. I shall never forget the luxury. The outside temperature was 90° but the pool was even warmer. Never before have I perspired doing a gentle breaststroke and had to come out to cool off. What an amazing mixture of weather we have had in ten days.

Friday 5th April

Unbelievably our last day. Phoenix Desert Botanical Garden. Saw how the Sonoran desert dwellers used the cacti for everything: shelter, medicine, food, tools, shoes, containers, even creosote tea can treat illnesses and insects secrete lac on the stems which was used as waterproof sealer long before we bought it in tins. Queen of the Night produce tubers up to 75lb. Very good for the Sunday roast. Some of the desert plants take a long time to flower. The agave or century plant may take one hundred years before it produces its one flower often six foot high, and then the whole plant dies. Prickly pear jam is pretty good on crackers. The people found many ways to make life more bearable. They built shade structures, ramadas, and rested at midday. Water was kept cool in clay jars which allowed minute amounts of water to seep through the sides. This evaporated and cooled the water inside. Yucca brushes were used to spread water on walls and floors so a breeze would cool the air. Deserts did not just survive, they lived.

Phoenix travel lodge. Olympic pool but I had to share it with a couple of others and it was a little cooler. Went to the world's largest municipal park, South Mountain, thousands of acres.

Saturday 6th April

Having survived the twisty roads of South Mountain Park and watched the sun go down over Phoenix, we had our last very romantic 'Stuff in all you can' dinner at Sizzlers. Gosh, I shall miss all this: snow, sand, blizzards, rocks, cacti, views and colours. Awoke to reality at 5.58 a.m. M did his last bit of skilful driving to the airport. Got a $6 refund for puncture. Checked in and all went well until the rock bag set off the alarm. Out came all the rocks, very carefully wrapped in layer of loo paper, until M's large pointed crystal proved to be the offender. Still it caused much amusement and funny looks. Went to duty free to buy smokes for friends. More amusement as not being smokers we had no idea which brands were middle tar. Even more embarrassment when I asked, 'doesn't king size mean they're longer fags?'

Settled at Gate 2 to be told to move to Gate 13. Ominous delay. Extra fuel needed as very full load, or was it the rocks? Mind you, most of the Americans are pretty well loaded, weightwise. Another delay. Plane on the runway before us had a hydraulic problem so it had to be towed off. M wants to know why they cannot just shove it in the ditch as seems to be the usual way of dealing with 'clapped-out' vehicles over here. If we wait much more we shall need refuelling again.

Off we fly at last with M saying, 'It must be fully laden as we are taking a long time to get up.'

Now, a hostess has asked him if he is going to be sick.

'Not likely,' the show-off replies, at which point she whips out his sick bag and rushes off. Comes to it when they run out of 'motion discomfort bags' as they call them, at the start of the flight. Bit like the Grand Canyon 'Faecal' bags which you are supposed to carry on the trails as loo paper takes seven years to decompose. I reckon I shall have decomposed by the end of this flight. No sound on the video channel. The fellow two seats from me is reading a manual on 'stress'. The one next to me is moaning about not being in the smoking section. Captain's log on London's weather: 49°f plus rain. Horrors, no sun and have to wear tights.

Fun fact booklet on the Americans tells me that McDonald's served 154 million meals worldwide – this translated into a single file of people for 87,500 miles – more than three times round the earth. Also Americans purchase on average seventy thousand ironing boards per week. That is enough to cover six football fields. Need to iron out a few flight 13 problems up here. Two loos out of action; half cup of tea at breakfast as the water tanks are running out. At least we did not run out of runway and the two old airport pick-up faithfuls were there to meet us, Simon and Debbie. Their first words: 'So where are you going next?'

Second Lot of Just Deserts in Egypt

Arizona at Easter and Egypt at Christmas. Two lots of deserts, miles and cultures apart. No longer the luxury of hired cars and queen-size beds but the old round-the-world trip 'down to sand' standards of the public bus and four-foot double beds. Tried to learn a little bit of Arabic but it was made a little complicated by Linguaphone's free cassette being Russian, despite my large tick in the Arabic box. After reading Khalifa's account of Cairo buses I decided my Arabic might be short-lived anyway.

> During rush hours buses (7 a.m. to 8 p.m.) are crammed beyond capacity so passengers cling to the outside or sit on the roof or in windows. The city's traffic chaos reduces the speed of the buses so they never stop. Getting on and off is an art, a sport and a proof of one's spirit. Boarding is to take a running leap and to clutch at whatever one can, window or door openings, bumpers or fellow passengers, who often extend a helping hand. Getting off is the real challenge, requiring what one connoisseur calls the Flying Dismount!

For the first time ever at least we knew where we would be staying the night when we first arrived at Cairo. One of M's bridge cronies is Egyptian with a deceased brother, who left his flat to his housekeeper. £15 each half board, so a bit upmarket from your 65p Bangkok brothel.

No problems at departures, although we did wonder as we had one very large bag stuffed with cup-a-soups and empty ice cream cartons as these are what the Egyptians appreciate. The latter are used to store grain, seeds, rice and so on, against the marauding desert rats. One lad at school brought me a pile as tall as himself. At the gate I was given a total 'rub-down frisk' and my hand luggage was searched, while Sir M strolled through. Sphinx's Alive, I thought, what have I packed? Then I was informed I was a 'random'. Isn't that a sort of a loose woman?

The pilot has just told us our route. Left at Windsor Castle, right turn at Brighton, left at Lyons to Pisa, then not too sure. All depends on the Greek controllers. Talk about Thomas the Tank Engine and the Fat Controller.

New 767 plane with small personal televisions and Fantasia for Christmas. Having finished school less than twenty-four hours before it is hard to believe we are off. Cairo Airport not as bad as Delhi or Bangkok but many, very helpful, grabbing hands tried to steer us to clapped-out old cars, so we finally submitted and took our chance. Conned again. Paid for a 'limo' but it was more than fit for a metal dump. Paid £40 although the government has laid down £30. Breaking the law is no deterrent. No laws on the motorway either. Overtake on any side, lean on the horn, only brake when in the boot of the car in front. All this at over one hundred kmph, even in Cairo itself. Ignore all traffic lights and duck when going passed armed police. Time saved is well used trying to find the ultimate destination. Armed neighbourhood watch opposite the flats had no idea where they were. Big welcome of hugs from Wasilla.

If this is the quiet part of Cairo, then no comment. We can hear the 5 a.m. mosque calls, the horns and the braking of innumerable near crashes. Seven floors up we can witness the mounts and dismounts at the bus stop. Some would-be passengers run nearly half a mile before they give up the chase. The Grand Canyon had to be easier than this!

Sunday, 22nd December, 1991

Day of reconnaissance in Cairo as well as learning how to avoid early death crossing the road. The trick is to go with the flow but downstream from the locals so they act as buffers. Also tried to master enough Arabic to tell Wasilla that we cannot manage a seven-course breakfast. For supper we had mozaat which translated is substantial veal stew. M has decided to buy an overgrown shirt. I think he feels he will have more chance of being seen when he crosses the road. Now after an ad on the telly he is threatening to buy a tank at the military surplus store near Ramses Station. I am trying to write this while Wasilla is watching Egypt's version of *Neighbours* except that the costumes are very much fancier. Coffee with Buffalo milk, very pleasant. Fallallahlam: heavens above, this *Neighbours* is cloak-and-dagger stuff. One robed fella has just been thrown off the ramparts of some desert fort. Makes *Dallas* seem quite tame.

Living in Cairo is anything but tame. The flat is clean and very spacious with large shuttered windows and balconies. Beyond the front door the communal areas are as scruffy as Battersea high-rise and as we came back this evening we saw definite signs of concrete fatigue on the corners. On top of some of the blocks of flats it looks as if the chunks of concrete which have dropped off the sides have been put up there out of the way. There is not much room for spare concrete on the streets. The cars are parked one after the other, bumpers hooked on each other. There must be some secret way of parking in Cairo. Now *Neigh-*

bours has come to the money bag and bribery bit, with a portion of head-slicing thrown in. M is waiting for the harem bit but I think it will be disappointing for him as it is in black and white with waves of desert sand blowing across.

Mind you, I did wonder if I was being sized for a harem when I had my bottom pinched at the *Registration Office* this morning. Wasilla made it dramatically clear that I should have given him a good old smack. Not likely when there are armed guards every ten metres down the corridors. They even have guards in the subways and each guard can see the next one on. How to keep you national service busy and your unemployment figures down for £2 a month pocket money.

Tomorrow we start on our discovery of the birth of the Egyptian civilisation over five thousand years ago. It was as if, after half a million years of semi-conscious existence, man in the course of two hundred years became fully aware of himself and his surroundings. Why was Egypt one of the first centres of such civilisation? The Nile. It was long and totally predictable. At the same time each year it flooded and fertilised the same areas. It ran due north and south so that the sun made a complete arc over it. The sun died at night and when a man died he was said to have gone west. So it is not a good idea to tell a young Egyptian to go west.

Monday, 23rd December

Shay, laban, aysh, gebna, bayed, krema, wa morabba for breakfast, all without looking it up. (Tea, milk, bread, cheese, sesame seed paste, cream and jam.) Perhaps dollops of fig jam will work some internal wonders. Off to the Cairo Museum after a chat to local Abdel Halim who was quite amazed that we could walk our way round Cairo without taxis or guides. The museum is incredible with all the exhibits arranged chronologically. Only one minute at each exhibit and it would take more than nine months to see everything.

The treasures of Tutankhamun incorporated tons of beautiful gold and very fine inlay work of precious stones. This was a modest tomb, so goodness knows what the others must have lost in wealth looted from them. Five gilded wooden shrines fitted inside each other and held the gold sarcophagus at their centre. The largest is the size of a fair-sized sitting room. His bed was covered with sheet gold with string stretched across the frame. Boxes of seeds and even soil for his long journey have survived over three thousand years.

In 1981 Sadat closed the Mummy Room to visitors but a very friendly guard unlocked the mummy of Ramses II for me to have a quick look. Can't say I saw very much but it was obviously a great honour and no baksheesh expected. Also the large limestone slab where corpses were mummified with a drain for the 'juices' to flow out. Liver, stomach, lungs and intestines were placed in four canopic jars in the burial chambers. Young Tut's were of highly decorated alabaster. The mummification was to ensure the survival of the *ka* or spirit contained in the pharaoh. From the various inscriptions and papyrus scrolls it is obvious that the ancient Egyptians were very visual and concerned with the simple elements of everyday life. Even today words are still a problem. One exhibit 'Delphins on his head warn of the approach of hastile serpents'.

There was a genuine feeling of humanity in the old small sculptures of ordinary people at work. Animals were also important. When a house was on fire the first essential was to save the cats, handing them from one person to another, while the house burned down. All of this greatly pleased Reshpu, the god of burning, as it kept him in business. Sensible lot these Egyptians, I decided, as we watched people in small boats cooking and washing up. Plenty of ready water if the boat went on fire and easy fishing for their supper.

Next stop was the Cairo Tower on Gezira Island. Must admit that apart from a few palm trees it could have been the Thames Embankment on the Nile. Obviously Cairo's answer to the Post Office Tower with its revolving restaurant. We had our 80p tea and cakes on the top but no revolutions. Probably only turned on for the romantic dinners. The tower being fifty metres higher than the tallest pyramid, you could just see the Giza Pyramids 6 km away in the haze and dust. Although it was winter there was still sand blowing from the desert. Periodically you had an extra free crunch with your bread and nuts. Good walk along the Nile to Dr Ragab's Papyrus Museum. Largest floating museum in the world and free but it was really a large houseboat exhibition plus shop. Saw how papyrus proper is made with strong warnings not to buy fake banana skin or sugar beet papyrus as it rots. On the way home we were swept up by a shopkeeper who just happened to sell essences. One free, very strong cup of tea later M succumbed to purchasing frankincense and myrrh. Just because it is Christmas I suppose he thinks he is a wise man. (Since coming home he has used the former to massage ailing backs with great success.)

Tuesday 24th December

This is ridiculous. Freezing cold, keen wind and pouring rain, it could be Christmas in London. On go the vests, T-shirts, pullovers, raincoats, hats and scarves, plus gloves to confront not the dustbath but the mudbath of Cairo. Metro to old Coptic monastery. Intricate wood carvings on ceilings, windows and stairs. Much amused by ten young girls trying to remove the muddy waters from the tiled courtyards using old jumpers and dresses while Mata Hari (escaped from the first-class waiting room of Delhi Station) supervised from the doorway. Giggling at M and his beard, they were not paying very much attention to her. Tried to find the 'Hanging Church' which was built on top of one of the old fortress gatehouses with its nave suspended over the passage. However, like many other old 'non-maintained' Egyptian buildings it may be the 'Fallen Church'. Found the Convent of St George which had a small room for the chain-wrapping ceremony. The chains symbolise the persecution of St George during the time of the Romans. A nun oversees the wrapping and says the requisite prayers. They will gladly wrap you in chains for free so long as they can practise their English. What a pity that they were shut for lunch. We did enter the Church of Saint Barbara. She was beaten to death by her father for trying to convert him to Christianity. Nearby stand the remains of the Ben Ezra Synagogue in whose grounds it is said are buried the remains of the Prophet Jeremiah. A spring also marks the spot where Pharaoh's daughter found Moses and where Mary drew water to wash the feet of Jesus. Quite a Biblical 'hot spot'.

Bargained for a cheap taxi which took us through miles of pottery kilns and the Cairo municipal rubbish tip, although there is still plenty in the streets and gardens. Then through the very uncanny City of the Dead, a vast Mameluke necropolis inhabited by several thousands of Cairenes, dead and alive (squatting families who have taken over the tombs). On Fridays and holidays families picnic on top of the tombs to pay their respects to the dead, who have been there since the twelfth Century: the dead not the picnickers!

At last we reached the Citadel but not until we had been the round of the tomb of Muhammad Ali. He was not too keen on the Marmalades so on March 1st, 1811, he treated

470 of their leaders to a day of feasting and revelry. At the end they were escorted down a very narrow lane. Ali's troops sealed both ends and all but one were massacred from the wall above. What a waste of a good dinner! We reckoned that his body was chopped up for several tombs as we kept having offers to see it in different places. Somewhat disrespectfully, I kept thinking of the boxer. We think the real Ali mosque was in the Citadel, whose domed roof can be seen from all over Cairo. This houses an enormous mausoleum with outsize chandeliers. Many stately rooms as the Citadel was home to most of Egypt's rulers for about seven hundred years. Not what I would call homely. Another view of the Pyramids and M suggested that we could walk home through Old Cairo. No problem, just winding, crowded, flooded, muddy ramshackle streets plus sheet rain, thunder, lightning and hail. Perhaps I should never have joked about snow on the Pyramids for Christmas. Many strange looks from old and young. Obviously your average foreigner goes by taxi.

We were soaked but we really felt we had come to know Cairo, mostly in our feet. Passed the Southern Gate where the last Mameluke sultan was hanged three times. He survived the first two attempts before the rope held. Have just read that we are lucky to survive our mosque visits. Insufficient baksheesh could mean a 'lock-in'. Observed the Mosque of Al-Hakim. Bit of a Caligula. No free movement for women, Jews and Christians. Decapitations for people he disliked. Rode round Cairo at night on a donkey called Moon, then disappeared in the nearby hills, believed murdered by his sister, whom he was about to marry. Strong women then. Shagarat's husband died but the son was a bit of a wimp so she killed him. Then she married a Mameluke leader but he took a second wife. Just deserts for him. Second wife not amused, beat Shagarat to death with several other women to help her using wooden clogs. Then her body was hung from the side of the Citadel as food for the dogs. Not that things have improved. We have just seen an Arabic TV advert where the wife is beating up her husband for what reason we are not sure. Yet in those cruel times, when Christian Europe was locking up its insane, Islam was providing enlightened medical care including delicate surgery such as cataract removal.

Christmas Day

Drier but just as chilly. Wasilla gave me my usual guided tour of the fridge to help me with my Arabic. There was the usual large portion of hugs and kisses when I got it right. Ordinary Egyptians try to live by the Koran – be kind to others and good will come to you. Today we met it more than ever. In the minibus to Giza we met two students and had a long discussion on religion, seeing it was Christmas. General agreement that all religions are the same and that all humanity comes from one Spirit. At Giza we all had mint tea in a local cafe and M had a go at one puff of a *shessa* (water pipe). Then one large choke. I wasn't sure if he was being drowned or smothered to death. Our lad made sure we got a deal for one horse and one camel plus guide to go round the Pyramids. M braved the camel first. First sight of the Sphinx. A little disappointing, smaller than we expected although 50 metres long and 22 metres high. Carved from one solid piece of limestone it was engulfed by sand for several hundred years. The Turks also used it for target practice so its nose and beard fell off. Now negotiations are in hand to have them returned from the British Museum. Take out shares in superglue!

The Pyramids were more impressive and we were able to make the very steep climb inside the largest, Cheops. This ascending passage is 1.3 metres high and 1 metre wide, length 100 metres and you climb at an angle of over 45°.

The way the massive blocks are butted is astonishing. You cannot get a penknife blade between them. In the Great Chamber the roof is formed of nine huge slabs of granite, totalling over 400 tons. There are even shafts for air as you are right in the centre of the Great Pyramid. The whole construction was one of total co-operation. It was 146 metres high on completion in 2690 BC. After forty-five centuries it is only 9 metres less. Two million, three hundred thousand limestone blocks were used, averaging two and a half million tons in weight, which would make the total approximately five and three quarter million tons. Massive earth ramps were used as scaffolding and it took twenty years to raise the Great Pyramid. Masons, mathematicians, surveyors, stone cutters, as well as one hundred thousand labourers completed the mammoth task. The Great Pyramid is estimated as weighing over 6 million tons, or thirty times the Empire State Building. Was this enormous bulk raised to cover the body of a single human? Even today it is the heaviest stone building in the world. Different theories on their existence range from a meditation centre, irrigation pump for the Nile, a mathematical or astronomical knowledge source or even an Atlantis time capsule. It is almost a global crystal ball. A back-breaking exercise for whatever purpose. The blocks had to be placed to the nearest millimetre to prevent excess pressure at any one point, or the whole lot would have collapsed.

My turn on the camel and I did not collapse even when we galloped. Somewhat bumpy as the poor animal kept stumbling on large stones and broken glass. My posterior very definitely had parts which had never been reached before. Still what an experience to ride and see over miles of desert sand while those at home consumed Christmas turkey and pud.

Sensibly we had agreed a set price so we were not taken on too long a scenic route for more baksheesh. Two hours was plenty if you wanted to do anything at all physical again before next Christmas. But the biggest challenge was yet to come. The big bus back to Cairo. Started well by easily mounting a static, empty bus. We were shown where to sit. Joined by several Egyptians, much smiling. Panic. Bus no go. Bus broken. Mad dash to bus number two, involving adept dodging of deep puddles and on coming traffic. I was terrified but we managed to jump on second bus at a slow run. Took us quarter of an hour to move down the passage to jump off at the other end. There must have been more than one hundred people in that forty seater bus but at least they are friendly enough to help you by giving you a gentle push towards your eventual dismount. Friendliness is the essence here.

Hordes of schoolchildren practise their English on us 'Hello, how are you, what is your name, you Engleesh, wellcom.'

They reel them off like tables so you have no time to answer. You end up repeating the answers like they do, with giggles all round.

Tea and cakes at Groppi's. M fancied the name. With innumerable lights and decorations it was Cairo's answer to an old-fashioned Lyons Corner House without the orchestra; all this for less than one pound sterling each. So much for English. I think my Arabic is on the up. I have understood Wasilla's suggestion that M should massage my hitherto unreachable parts to ease the ever-increasing stiffness. After all, I rode the camel twice his distance and some at a gallop. Just do not get the wrong idea; there is absolutely nothing erotic about riding a camel, I can assure you. Also managed to establish that Wasilla will be away tomorrow evening and that we shall be off to Luxor for a few days. She has left supper for me to have a cook-up in Cairo. Not many British women have that opportunity. Also Fort Knox instructions about locking our wardrobe, key under the mattress; locking the bedroom, key under the television. And now for tonight's useful Egyptian fact. Did you know that Napoleon reckoned there was enough stone in the three largest pyramids to build a 3-metre wall around France? Probably have to be a 2-metre one as many of the blocks have been recycled into Cairo's old mosques.

Talking of maths, some of the calculations on the building of the Pyramids are amazing in themselves. Herodotus claimed that the Pyramid took a hundred thousand men only twenty years to build. It does seem likely that the building took place when the Nile was flooded so it was a form of unemployment benefit when agricultural work was impossible. So here is the maths: 2,300,000 blocks, divided by twenty years, divided by 365.242 days, divided again by twelve hours. That equals almost one large block every two minutes. In every minute gap there is a layer of cement so strong that the stones often break before the cement does. All with just ropes, levers, ramps, sleds and rollers; so the work must have gone on unabated without strikes, sandstorms and no modern arc lights either.

Boxing Day

A spot of Islamic art culture to start the day. 'Bit boring,' as the kids would say. Somewhat repetitive and dull. More excitement as we descended into the Suk or Grand Bazaar. I had imagined loads of arches or tents with loads of leather, brass, cotton, and so on but the whole thing has become horribly Westernised with the worst plastic 'tat' possible. Most of the traders accepted 'plastic' as well. Next to no hand- or tailor-made goods; nearly all labelled from China or Taiwan. We bought a few typical souvenirs to disperse at home. Managed to avoid some major 'cons' such as a hollow gold pyramid for more than a solid one further down the street.

No public transport today as M very skilfully walked us everywhere. Tonight a big treat – a taxi to the station to catch the Wagon Lits. No, we didn't as they wanted 80p so we walked to the metro for a 10p fare instead. Have to economise now and again. Wagon Lits very efficient but expensive, over £30 each. Comfy armchairs by day, towels, soap even venetian blinds and a posh dinner included. Bedtime reading on mummification. Who needs Stephen King when you can learn how the brain was extracted by being broken up and removed through the nose. Great users of human parts, the Egyptians. I decided not to use the public laundry as the washing procedure may be okay but the ironing consists of a fellow taking a mouthful of water and spitting it out as a fine mist over your clothes. Down go your steam iron shares. Ironing is done to perfection using spit and a massive two-handed hotplate heated over glowing coals.

I have given up the idea of sending postcards – very expensive, garish colours, faded, out of focus, grubby or torn. Anyway, by camel express they apparently take nearly a month to arrive anywhere foreign, if at all. Just discovered we could actually earn money in television ads. They are always on the lookout for white faces to dress up as cowboys leaping on and off camels near the Pyramids. M is not too keen. I am not sure if it is the dressing up or leaping bit that deters him. We could go dancing and singing in the 'club car' of the train but he has chickened out of that as well. Still, we have boldly eaten many Egyptian delights such as *ful* with beans like a thick soup plus eggs, meat and onions. Certainly contributes to the desert breezes. Last night we had *molochiya* soup, delicious, slimy green, made by stewing a spinach-like veg, rice and garlic in meat broth. All this and figgy jam for breakfast, as well as our afternoon *shay* and *kak*, tea and cakes. Tea is served in glasses with half a bucket of sugar if you do not say 'No' quickly enough. You can sit for hours just watching men, women, children, animals (dead and alive). Three white faces appear at the end of the street. At breakneck speed Al the Cafe owner puts out table and chairs to ensnare the unsuspecting tourist victims. It did work with us but not with this lot. Then follows a truckload of pigs heads, all laid out in rows, snouts outwards. Finally a child with large basket on head containing over six live ducks.

Cairo is a city of contrasts. Less than 1 km from a high class antique store there are mud-brick houses where goats wander through living rooms and water comes from spigots down the street. Round the corner from the Hilton Shopping Arcade donkey carts hustle by laden with gigantic cauliflowers, garlic, carrots, and other vegetables. Yesterday I nearly fell foul of the law when my misguided horse helped himself to some prime carrots from a passing cart. I'd forgotten from my donkey-on-the-beach days that you have to pull from left to right.

Friday 27 December

Up at 5.30 a.m. Ample breakfast so we kept half for our lunch. Not much sleep because although the carriage was made by Messerschmit, I think they must have used recycled planes. The whole thing rattled although the ceiling quietened down a bit after I had kicked it from my upper bunk. Scooped up at Luxor Station by Hotel Sinai tout. New hotel wanting recognition so there was loads of creeping and crawling. Only £6 a night for the two of us. Pretty basic but hot and cold shower and three beds. Lots of free cups of tea.

Strolled along to Karnak Temple. Full of mammoth pillars, coming out like mushrooms at the top. Apparently fifty people can stand on top of each one. We'll take their word for it. The temple was started in 2000 BC as Egypt's main centre for worship. For fifteen hundred years it was built, dismantled, stored, enlarged and decorated. The whole site could hold ten Christian cathedrals and there are over 130 of the massive pillars each over 20 metres high and 15 metres in circumference. We recognised many James Bond backgrounds, so where 007 has trod, so have we. Millions of miles of engravings all over every pillar and wall. Apparently the workers used to live nearby for years and work in shifts. A very fine engraving shows the goddess Sekhmet, the spreader of terror, as a strangely beautiful, bare-breasted and lioness-headed creature. A match for any man!

Back to the Sinai Hotel. Confusion over room but 'Magic Man', as he calls himself, eventually evacuated a poor Egyptian so we could have a balcony. 'You will put me in your book.' He used to be a teacher of history but got fed up with the rigid system and being told to smarten up. He really is a scruff. He gave us strict instructions on how to organise ourselves and how not to be cheated by Egyptians.

Saturday 28 December

Mohammed from the hotel escorted us on the ferry across the Nile to the West Bank. Then we bargained for a day's service with Nubio, his brother, and the family taxi. Everyone seems to be related to everyone else round here.

The tombs were splendid and many of the reliefs and vivid colours could have been done yesterday. Again they are a feat of prime organisation. Artists were given a section and told what to draw. Master artists vetted and improved the outlines if necessary before cutting. Then the masters prescribed the colours. A film of beaten egg white was applied as a final protection. The Valley of the Kings is certainly a place of death as nothing can grow in the sandstone cliffs, which are deep and scorching. You can just imagine the excitement when new tombs were found. Many had deep pits to keep out thieves but not with much success. The tombs were designed to resemble the underworld with long rock-hewn corridors or a series of pillared halls. Tuthmosis I was the first Pharaoh to have his tomb cut in 1495 BC and now over sixty-two tombs have been excavated in the Valley of the Kings alone. At least the guards can no longer plunge you into the dark for more baksheesh. Fluorescents have arrived; fortunately in tasteful pale but warm orange shades.

Tutankhamun's was closed. Its discovery was touch and go, as Howard Carter excavated thousands of tons of rubble for six seasons. His last attempt was under some workers' huts and there it was; just before his money ran out. The mummified body of the young Prince has been left intact. The tomb of Ramses VI goes 83 metres into the mountain. It was built for Ram V but Ram VI decided to save himself time and money by taking it over. The unusual ceiling shows the goddess Nut twice, stretched across the morning and evening sky. She swallows the sun in the evening and gives birth to it in the morning. The tomb of Amenhotep II goes down ninety steps. The huge burial chamber is mostly intact with stars all over the ceiling and the wall like one painted scroll. His mummy, plus twelve others were found in 1898 and he still had a garland of flowers round his neck.

The temple of Hatshepsut was next. This is a series of three large pillared terraces cut into the face of the Theban mountain. It had a sphinx-lined causeway and gardens on the terraces. However, Tuthmosis III, who got fed up waiting twenty years to succeed her, had, within weeks of her death, obliterated or covered her image wherever he could find it. Bit of a sulkpot he was. Fancy doing that to your Mum's portraits.

The Ramesseum was built by Ram II to glorify himself

for all eternity. It was a massive temple but apart from a few pillars it is now scattered around in large lumps. One such marble lump is the head of Ram II which was part of a whole body 17.5 metres high weighing 1000 tons. The whole thing was brought by boat from Aswan. How on earth did they stop it from sinking? M has gone all poetic:

They broke up old Ramoses
So now it's hard to discloses
His nose from his toeses!

The next stop was totally unscheduled. The taxi coughed and died in the middle of what we thought was nowhere. In a trice Nubio plus M plus locals were in the bonnet. I was besieged by children offering me the family buffalo to photograph for baksheesh. M was fascinated by the method of adjusting the car timing. The distributor was unscrewed and innumerable twists later, when it sounded right, the job was done without any need for your modern stroboscope. Not that it seemed to do much good. M wondered if there were any leads at all under the layers of tape. The engine was probably held together by sand.

So we soldiered on to the Valley of the Queens ready for what we have called the Ali Baba Campaign. Tomb 55, the Amunherkhepshep was the scene of the 1991 Battle between the Italian coach group (about fifty) and the Ali Baba English coach Group (about forty) and ourselves and a few other loose English. All this to get past El Guard of the tomb. As the tomb was being improved by the Italian Government of course they won and were allowed in first in tens. Then Ali Baba summoned his lot which we had tried to join to keep the numbers even. Coalition no go. Ali Baba said, 'You must behave the system.' So we did our best. People came out somewhat glazed and we began to wonder whether it was worth the wait. Eventually El Guard smiled benignly and let us in. The benign smile evaporated when he realised there was no baksheesh. The wait was worth it as the 4000 year colours were as clear as ever and it was rather touching to see the nine year old prince being led by Ram II to Anubis, the jackal-headed god, who then takes him to the Passage of the Dead. Amun's mother was pregnant when he died. She aborted the baby and a five-month mummified foetus can still be seen in a glass case. You still feel that it all happened a short time ago.

A few more splutters and the taxi made it to the ferry. Small boys on the ferry tried to sell us scarabs big and scarabs small. I managed to beat mine down from £20 to £3, but M using *Money Programme* techniques, acquired a better one for £2. I think his moustache helps because he is always being greeted with 'Welcome moustache', 'Happy New Year, moustache', 'How much, moustache?'

You'd never believe it but I must be the only tourist in Egypt to be constipated. So between the ferry and the Hotel I consumed a kilo of fresh figs. Supper at El Hussan's but the two little waiters were run off their feet dealing with over fifty of us. M was all brave and tried *Kufta*. Turned out to be tomb-shaped beefburgers. Anyway, as I write this M has finished his kufta half an hour ago and my pizza having been bandied about from table to table has gone back to the kitchen. My famished wailing is to no avail. M reckons they have gone down the Nile to catch the anchovies. I think the tourist bureau had better have a go slow on recommending the El Hassle. However, when it finally arrived, it was lovely so I have just asked M if he fancies a cup of tea.

'What, next week?' he replies.

Long stroll through the Night Bazaar. Much better than the Khaw el Khalily in Cairo. Loads of fun in the statuette shops as M has made a drawing of his favourite god Tarawet. So to avoid any purchasing he produces this as the one he really wants, knowing full well it is a bit uncommon and they hopefully will not have it. Five or more frantic Egyptians scour the shelves in every shop. Then his bluff was blown. A little old man who had been following us called 'Monsieur.'

Fatal move, we turned round.

'I know very special shop, you get what you want.'

'No, no, no,' we say.

'Only a minute,' he say.

So what do we do? We follow.

Shop one, no good.

'You try one more.'

'No, no, no,' we say again.

You've guessed. We follow again.

This time we have the shop of a very fine, young Egyptian with a beautiful artistic face and his craftsman's hands engrained with dust and nicks where his tools had slipped.

'If you wait five minutes, I fetch one from my home.' So why did we wait yet again? Even I was keen to see what he would produce and whether M would be put on the 'pyramid' as they say. Two Tarawets later he returned, small, medium. We conferred and then the ultimate. The drawer under the counter was slowly unlocked and lovingly revealed was a superb basalt figure of Tarawet, ten inches high and around a stone in weight. The young sculptor had done just one as a trial from the original tomb drawings. He had not shown us it at first because it was much more expensive. However he could see that we both appreciated fine work and we think he was being selective about who bought his special creation.

So we took a part of the creative spirit of our young artist and I still remember his dark and deep soulful eyes. From then M had to carry our Tarawet around as we dare not leave him. That will teach M to play bluff in future!

Sunday, 29th December

Gluttons for punishment. Slow-food breakfast at El Not-Quite-so-Hassled. Seems to be the only place with a reasonable loo. Bus to Temple of Hathor at Dendara. A copy of the other temples by the Greeks and Romans, so relatively young, only two thousand years. Hathor was the goddess of pleasure, love, beauty and light, despite having the head of a cow. Still has much of its large solid block stone roof. The engravings and colours are still well preserved except in parts of the lower half, which were buried in the sand until a couple of centuries ago. Hathor would be pleased with the pleasure her temple gives now, although she seems to have had a mixed-up life herself. She was the wet nurse of Horus before becoming his mate. Dendera was the ritual place where Hathor gave birth to Ihy, the child of Horus. The temple stands at the edge of the desert where green pastures of the Nile give way to the sands of the desert.

The views were spectacular with the sudden change from emerald to gold.

Horse and carriage back to the bus and the now nightly adventure walk dodging, 'You see me, big bargains, velly cheap', and so on.

M this time after uncut crystals, was caught again by the brother of the jeweller's brother-in-law or something like that. This time M had to go through the alternative healing test, how with what, and so on. Passed by gem shop owner, Ahmed who has been doing healing and meditation for fifteen years. He has to keep quiet about it but was obviously delighted to chat to someone else who knew what it was all about. Gave M some useful tips, such as holding then putting amber chips in a flame and sniffing the aroma. Three times a month for heart problems. He gave M some amber pieces and chose him one crystal. I suggested one that had a slight chip in it so that we would not be taking the best. Psychic Ahmed said, 'Not that one,' and made M have a perfect one.

We promised to send back Bach flower remedy info as he knew nothing about them. In Egypt healing is done by touch and Ahmed was surprised that we are not allowed to touch patients. He would like to help more Egyptians but they do not believe in it. Advised me to drink cartons of milk to relieve my bung-ups. Ahmed is married to a very pale Norwegian lady. They have a dark-skinned son, aged five who is bilingual in Arabic and Norwegian, and a very pale blonde, blue-eyed daughter aged two. What a culture contrast, from the cold of Norway to the heat of Egypt. Amazing what our chance encounters bring.

M was proper poorly in the night, Pharaoh was having his revenge. So he had a quiet day while I did routine chores like the bank, shopping and cancelling our hired bikes. I sat in the salubrious roof garden. Magic Man appeared to tell me I no need pay for 'bisikillies'. Had a chat to the young housekeeper. Mother dead. She works in the hotel as well as studying French, English, philosophy, geography and history at home. Wants to be an officer in the Army so many of these young people, however poor, still have their high ambitions for which they are prepared to work very hard.

M still a bit weak so I went round Luxor Museum on my own, which seemed very strange. Shopping for our train journey. Just imagine me next week bargaining for bananas in Sainsbury's. At the checkout: 'These are a bit black: £1 too much, I pay 80p.' However would the computer system cope! M a little stronger so struggled to El Less Hassle next door to El Big Hassle. Passed Ahmed on the way who suggested pure lemon juice to sort out M's innards. Still on milk for mine. Talk about opposites. The town was all lit up for New Year plus an Egyptian Father

Christmas being pestered by long-shirted children outside the cake shop. M just made it back so I paid the hotel bill. Managed to slip some extra to Mohammed for all his kindness. I did it under the counter while Magic Man was assuring me that I would give him a good write-up in next year's Lonely Planet guide. As I went up the stairs, Mohammed blew me a kiss and looked quite sad. It always makes me think about how things will be for them in the years to come. He earns less than £10 a month and is shouted at non-stop. All he wants is a little home and a wife. However can he do it? It seems that many of the hotel owners worked in Saudi Arabia for fifteen to twenty years and came back with enough to buy homes, cars and half-built hotels, which they furnish with the discarded furniture of the rich.

The little bike boy is in trouble. He was hammering clips to hold up the flashing fairy lights when his hammer missed and cracked the wall-size mirror in the hall. Whoops! M better but tired. I felt sad that he had missed a whole day but philosophical as ever he said 'Perhaps I wasn't meant to go to the tombs in the Valley of the Nobles.'

I think he's worried he might have had a murky past life there. I reckon I might have been a sun priestess as sunsets always reach my soul wherever we are. Tonight's over the feluccas in the Nile brought another not-to-be-forgotten glow in my heart.

Tuesday, 31st December

That was Monday. This is Tuesday, the last day of 1991, a great year. Taxi ordered for 8 a.m. No sign by 8.10 so we walked, luggage and all, through the market. The taxi would never have got through. We should have realised when they were laying out their 'dinasaur-sized cauliflowers' yesterday evening. They have to spend all the night before on rugs on the lumpy, dusty road to secure a pitch. The cauli stalks are wrist size. It would take ten of ours to make one of theirs. You buy your poultry super-fresh, alive and wriggling. No need for poly bags; just carry them by the legs.

Found our reserved seats in a non-smoker but ninety per cent were already puffing. So we did our 'no smoking, what is this?' performance to be informed very politely that the rule only applies once the train is moving. Hilarious conversation with a young Egyptian in front of us. We were not too sure how much to believe. Four wives; Luxor, Cairo, Scotland and Switzerland. Was I Scottish, as I look like his wife in Glasgow? M was asked in great confidence how many other wives he possessed. We explained it was illegal and you had to be divorced first. A very expensive business as ex-wife receives half your worldly goods. Four wives know their place and do what they are told because they respect him. Much astonishment when M related that he is a student with four children, four grandchildren and that I support him. I'm not certain who thought who was telling the most 'porkies' but Muslims are not supposed to be embroiled with 'porkies' anyway.

Major stop at Asyut. Out come the fags and the bisqwat sellers. Packets are shoved under your nose lest you sleep and miss a truly golden bargain opportunity. Episode two from our friend in the front. At one time he was the oriental toyboy for a lady over fifty at the Savoy Hotel. Stop press. He has let it out that he is in the army. A Shakespearean soldier! I suppose he is entitled to his fantasies as a descendant of the ancient pharaoh kingdom of Thebes. For seven centuries the city had nearly one million people, most of them contributing to the splendour of the temples and tombs. Not that modern daily life yields totally to the ancient. It brings in the tourists but the fellahin work the fields as they have done for centuries. People continue their business in the streets quite unaware of foreigners tripping over them or over the payments which are eighteen inches high. That is to stop the Egyptians parking their cars on the pavements. You would need a monthful of evenings to cover the whole bazaar full of fake antiquities, overgrown shirts, brass by the ton and miles of lurid, crumbly banana papyrus scrolls. With great pride we were told by many that Luxor would soon have tarmac on all the roads. Goodbye to the challenge of avoiding mini-floods created by the Luxorites trying to keep the desert sands at bay.

From the train we have been able to see how countless irrigation schemes keep the Nile valley green. There is a salt problem as the high dams for electricity have almost eliminated the flooding process which used to remove the salt and lay down new mud. New towns are being built on nearby higher desert plains so that less farmland is used. Ichmail from the seat in front then sat beside me for what M termed Auntie Patricia advice. As a woman what did I think of his chances with a 39-year-old lady from Holland? A month before they spent four days (nights?) together and since then she has phoned around ten times. I suggested he should consider the fact that she may want to marry him, so he should not lead her up the desert. He wants to marry her as she is a mature lady who makes him feel warm. Philosophy on love and need: 'You can need someone because you are lonely and there is nothing better around, but you may not love them. I pointed out I could survive without M but I just happened to love him. Anyway, our young man felt that if he had a good chance he would be a gigolo no longer. M mentioned Aids but no problem as he always wears four condoms at once as one just breaks – called Tops in Egypt. Once the word Tops was spoken every Egyptian head turned to look at us. M was dead useless at the fatherly advice as he was rendered speechless with

186

trying to hide his laughter. He did manage to mutter helpful items like 'going Dutch', 'Dutch courage' and 'Dutch caps'.

As we pulled into Cairo and dismantled our luggage another Egyptian gentleman came over, saying he recognised us from the hotel in Luxor. He asked if we needed any help. He was going back to the army as well. I think they were all coming back a day early so that they could live it up for the New Year. He squeezed my hand and wished us all the best with real sincerity. Wasilla was also sincerely pleased to see us as she had missed our company. She was horrified that I had paid so much for my fruit and I gathered from my slow comprehension of her Arabic that some traders take naughty advantage of tourists. We did not tell her about our train conversations!

Wednesday 1st January 1992

Talking of naughty advantages, we wandered around old Cairo again and several little lads at various times pinched my bottom or groped the top of my leg. All good Egyptian fun but they were very quick to escape M's ready hand. In between all this excitement we visited the Sultan Hassan Mosque built by the Marmalades (Marmelukes really), with stones which historians reckon were pinched from the Pyramids. It was a theological school but the imposing interior is without any fancy decor to make it easier to concentrate on praying. Over the way is the Rifai Mosque, a bit more elaborate but dark, probably so that nobody could really tell whether you were praying or what you were up to. King Farouk and the Shah of Iran buried here. The latter's casket was paraded through Cairo in 1980 with President Sadat, the Shah's family and Richard Nixon leading the cortège.

Through the large local market full of nattering women

and clucking chickens in baskets. Egyptians never seem to hurry and if you stop just to look around, within a couple of seconds someone will ask if you need any help. If you want a bus they don't just point but take you there and see you on to the correct bus. We are getting the hang of the numbers now: 0 is 5; backward 7 is 2; backward 3 is 4; proper 7 is 6 and the big V is 7; upside-down big V is 8; 1 and 9 are the same. A dot is 0 so heaven knows what happens about your decimals. Now I have it, they use a comma for the point. After all this we hope you get the point! Today we needed bus 54 so all we had to do was to look for 0 backward 3. Don't think I'll progress into advanced Arabic maths. M is good at the numbers so between us we could run a 'get by in Arabic with M an' Pat' course.

Had to use my Arabic to its limits. Enter pharmacy. Explain in Arabic *emsaak*, wiggle my bottom and hold my stomach.

'Ah, you are in the constipation, no pwoblem.'

Shuffled out with twelve red bullets for fifty pastries.

Treated ourselves to a New Year's afternoon tea at the Nile Hilton. For £1.50 each we had tea and cake and read the *Egyptian Gazette*, only fifty pastries. Bought it as day one of 1992 and it has a bit about everything all over the world making it a historical souvenir. Then appeared our two Ali Baba allies from Luxor, Petrina and Andre. Despite their Russian and French names they came from North England. More tea and chat as very wet and windy outside. Their paper had the case of the very pregnant Egyptian lady who decided her time of deliverance was at hand. She boarded the bus for the hospital and found herself 'distracted from the matter in hand' by a fancy gold watch on the wrist of the gentleman beside her. She tried to pickpocket it but was caught. All the passengers dismounted to escort labouring lady to the police station. Charges were put off until after arrival of baby. Rather laboured singing now on the telly as we have Egypt's *Opportunity Knocks. Neighbours* has not been on for a couple of nights so I think they have all met their final episode over the parapets.

Taken for a bit of a financial ride in the Anderson Museum. It cost us £1.50 but only half open so we were round it in half an hour. Poor do compared with the Egyptian Museum for £3, which needs nine months. Still, at least I could photo the view from a harem window and we saw the intricately carved mashrabiyya screens, which allowed the women to observe the goings-on of the men without being seen.

M is greatly amused by the 'come-on' sex advertising by slinky women for all the fattening foods possible. Read that Sahar Hamdi, belly dancer, has underestimated her profits by half a million pounds as a tax dodge. *Neighbours* is back, actually called *Andalusian Guy*. For someone like Wasilla, who has never had the chance to learn to read or write, the black and white, periodically snowstormed television is a godsend. We hope she will use our money for a new colour one but being a real softie she will probably spread it through her family.

We eventually reached the largest mosque in the world, Ibn Tulun. Built in 876 and Tulun used to keep his whole army and horses at the ready in the courtyard. Ascended my first minaret. M waited gallantly below in case I was blown off.

Thursday, 2nd January, 1992

Metro to Halwan at the end of the line. Half an hour of passing through Cairo's highly condensed dwellings. People live under arches or ruins. Others in new but totally jammed blocks of flats. As I type this on 12th October we have just had the news of an earthquake in Cairo, killing nearly four hundred people. M reckoned a density of one thousand persons per acre so what hope would there be? Taxi to Saquara Pyramids and Tombs. In the twenty-seventh century BC the Step Pyramid of King Zoser was the largest stone structure. It started as a flat mastaba bench type structure but Imhotep added to it five times. Nearby are the oldest examples of tourist grafitti. The vandalism of twelfth-century admiring Thebans is now protected under glass. In front is the serdab. This is a stone block which contains a slightly tilted wooden box with two holes drilled in it. Looked through for an eerie glimpse of life-size Zoser's stony face gazing up to the stars. Serdabs were used to draw the Pharaoh's ka to the outside world. The real one is in the Egyptian Museum.

The Unas pyramid is a big mound because for the first time the interior became more important. The texts inside are the earliest examples of pharaonic tomb writing. The last pyramid in the area, Sekhemket, was abandoned when it was three metres high. You cannot go inside in case there is a cave-in. There are also subterranean galleries where twenty-five sacred Apis bulls were mummified and placed in granite coffins weighing up to 70 tons each. In 1851 the famous archaeologist Mariette wrote of this discovery:

> The finger marks of the Egyptian who had inserted the last stone in the wall, built to conceal the door-way, were still recognisable on the lime. There were also the marks of naked feet imprinted on the sand which lay in one corner of the tomb chamber, un-disturbed for thirty-seven centuries.

One tomb had some interesting surgical scenes including toe removal and circumcisions.

The thrill of our day was the Persian Tombs. Few go down these as the entrance is covered by a wooden hut and you have to find the caretaker. You have to go 25 metres and 120 steps down a vertical iron spiral staircase. In this deepest burial chamber in the world there are three tombs with very small but very clear and colourful wall drawings. One was an admiral and the other a court physician. I was able to lie in the body-shaped sarcophagus. The tombs were deep to deter grave robbers but that failed because thieves cut the present spiral entrance passage. As Dahshur is now a military zone we had to view the Bent Pyramid from afar. It represents the design change from step to smooth pyramid. A few technological hitches here as halfway up the angle of the slope outside changes from 52° to 43°. Possibly the initial angle was too steep to be stable as the Red Pyramid next door is a constant 43.5°. At Giza they cracked it. The problem; not the Pyramid!

As it was freezing and Wasilla was away for the night, we retreated home early. En route we had an 18p Madonnaburger for the hell of it. Not really a McDonald's but the boss has pinched the idea as near as he dare. He justifies the name by having photos of Madonna everywhere and Madonna music all the time. We have had some varied music today, including Boney M and 'Show Me a Motion'. The Arabic laxatives did work a treat! Two beautifully cooked-by-charcoal burgers, chips and orange juice cost £1.50 for the two. Three cooks for about fifteen customers fan away like mad to boost the heat and the smoke! I'm not sure which is worse, the Madonna smoke pit or the heavy layer of smoke lying over Cairo. Countless factory chimneys belch it out night and day. Perhaps the next T-shirty, jeans and trainer generation will sort it out. They are the only hope for Egypt. M has just said that with some buildings at an angle of 10°, millions would perish if there was a Rift Valley earthquake. Unbelievable, 16 inches of snow in Jerusalem, floods in Alexandria and Cairo well below normal temperature. I was only joking about snow on the Pyramids. Actually, many thinking Egyptians reckon that Jesus must have been born in the spring because any shepherds out on the hills at that time of year would not have been wise shepherds. They and most of their flock would not have survived. Regardless of religion most Egyptians make merry at Christmas and New Year.

Friday, 3rd January, 1992

Rainy and cold. Pyramids or museum? Pyramids and the weather cleared up. Good wander round and for a few baksheesh, because we were on our own, we were shown some of the smaller, more gentle tombs. Much of the area is still under sand, unexplored. One tomb had a row of statues to show the whole family with a child at one end grabbing the hand of the next one. Another had statues of the person at different stages in his life and they even showed the changes in his face. We kept being trapped by robed escorts trying to show us different items. I think number one trapper must have passed a message: 'Look out for Musstash, very hopeful.' They probably use the Pyramids for echoes. Being Friday we could hear the chants from nearby mosques as they echoed round the tombs.

Finally we visited the Bark Museum. Not a load of mummified dogs but a very ancient barque. The Cheops Boat is the most ancient vessel found in perfect condition anywhere in the world. Forty-two massive limestone blocks covered the boat pit and on 28th January, 1955 the last block was removed and the contents revealed for the first time in four thousand five hundred years. The boat had been built and then taken apart and stored in thirteen special layers in the pit. Some researchers believe it was a solar boat for use by the deceased pharaoh on his eternal journey. Others think it may have been used to carry the dead pharaoh down the Nile before burial. There is evidence it was used in water. The lengths of Lebanese cedar wood boards are around 45 metres. The ten oars are 7 metres thick. No nails were used. Ropes bound the parts in a most intricate manner in a system which is completely unknown today. The larger wooden blocks carried hieratic signs, which indicates that the ancient Egyptians believed that instructions were very necessary for the Boat to be reconstructed in the afterlife:-

Right front   right back
left front   left back

Every piece was PVA treated to prevent any damage occurring from exposure after its long life in the hermetically sealed pit. After the discovery of the boat the museum was built over the original pit. There are walkways so you can see it from above and below. The glass is double-glazed with each pane 8 cm thick and a further 8 cm air space. This is to insulate the interior from external desert dust, heat and tourist noise. The air-conditioning controls temperature and humidity. A double door system prepares the visitor for the transition from the heat of the Giza desert to the cool of the museum. It gave us a chance to warm up! No artificial lighting as it could affect the very ancient wood. It took nearly thirty years to build and the Museum itself is shaped like a boat nestling at the foot of the pyramid. There is still some of the original matting used to cover the Royal Cabin against the heat of the sun. To see this fine boat, made so many years ago, was an awe-inspiring event. The complicated technology of today cannot compare with the pure harmony created so long ago. Inwardly most of us like to feel that we are part of something eternal; that some part of us is immortal. That part of those ancient boatbuilders is still with us. Their beliefs were the core of their existence and nearly five thousand years on we too can believe in the ultimate.

Saturday 4th January, 1992

Our ultimate day in Egypt. The time has flown by. Last weekend we felt we had been ages in the Land of the Pharaohs and still had ages left. Morning with Dr Nagib and wife so they could go to duty free and buy goodies on our passports. Tea and cake with them in very posh cafe. Last stroll across the Nile for last visit to Egyptian Museum. This time it meant a great deal more as we had seen where these 'goodies' had been for so long. Closed at 4 p.m. so at 3.55 sharp the guards start to clap you towards the door. Clapping with them we slowly withdrew.

Back to Wasilla for the last time. She used up all our carton and cup-a-soup space on goodies for us and her relations in UK. With a large hug and a 'I love you Madam Pat'. I was presented with her very old, bone china, gold-rimmed coffee cups; all because I made the effort to learn a bit of Arabic so that we could communicate. I just wish I had tried a bit harder.

Wasilla up at 5 a.m. to make sure we were up. Little night doorman had fetched a taxi. Wasilla insisted on coming with us. Tears from both of us as running through our minds was the question – shall we ever meet again?

'Welcome to my taxi,' said our driver. Our Christmas weather may have been chilly but the human warmth gave us an Egyptian Christmas never to be forgotten.

Alaska All The Way!

1992

Under the sweltering sun of Britain's hottest summer in years, we packed our woolly hats, gloves, scarves and thermal long-johns 'No shorts,' wailed I to M, 'for ten whole days.'

Usual reply: 'No problem, put them over your long-johns.'

Having booked up months before on a teacher exchange to Alaska, how were we to know that our usual system of 'escape the cold' was to be totally reversed? Our perennial readers will know that we have been on Alaskan shores before but that was a bit of a cheat. It was the skinny south peninsular bit opposite Canada and not what one would call Alaska proper. This time we were to venture into the sub-arctic, north of Anchorage. Quite a coincidence that in the hot, crowded city of Cairo we were looked after with TLC for ten days by our landlady, Wasilla. Now by kind courtesy of Wayne and Judy Bredburg we were to spend ten days in the cooler, less populated town of Wasilla. Same name but culturally and environmentally almost poles apart.

So we received the usual dire warnings with special reference to bears – no deodorant, suffocate your toothpaste and hang up your grub. One bear sighting and I shall be hanging in the tree, never mind the grub. Apparently you should just stand and chat to them or if it makes you feel safer lie down foetal-wise and then you'll probably be licked to death. M reckoned it could be no worse than our school trip to Euro Disney with fifty adolescents in various stages of hormonal displacement. Bears would be pretty tame and less adrenalin-arousing than the sullen looks, heaving bosoms and thrusting posteriors (M's description) of the female love bite brigade in the back row of the coach. At least this time we would be a mere minibus load of mature members of the teaching profession, apart from the stowaway, M.

Having changed planes at Minneapolis, we did wonder whether that would be our last contact with civilisation, as our rattling, snorting and very definitely ageing 170-seater, 757 struggled to take off. Then we had our first touch of wilderness ways, no silver service on the plane (cutlery to you). It brought out the pioneer spirit as passengers improvised with foil tops, nail files, plastic cups, chopstick pens and fingers. We arrived at Anchorage at 11 p.m. and we were met by hosts complete with flags, badges and hugs. Wayne and Judy drove us back to their lovely home by the lake and we sank into our seven foot square bed, Twenty-four and a half hours from the UK.

The first day we acclimatised with Judy and Wayne, in other words, a great deal of vocal interaction between Judy and I, with Michael in his element helping Wayne to build his shed to house his four-wheel drive vehicle. Later we were welcomed with speeches by local dignitaries and our first salmon bake. Salmon are everywhere, basking in innumerable and indescribable vessels in various stages of marination, glazing, drying or smoking. Another fish treat is whale fin buried in the tundra for ten days and then eaten in a fermented stew. Recent problem of Eskimos consuming stink-flipper with a can of beer and then dropping dead.

All this from Dennis on the four-hour trail to Denali

Park, in a luxurious three-piece suite with a panoramic view in his 34-foot long motorhome. Now in the permafrost zone with vast ranges of mountains all around and a mere 200 miles from the Arctic Circle.

So we followed the amazing Alaska Parks Highway running from Anchorage to Fairbanks through spooky creeks with names like Hurricane and Slime. It seemed strange to see road signs with names previously seen on the very top of illuminated globes. We had time to learn the significance of other names such as the Lower 48: the rest of the US. Although many Alaskans do originate from there, they do seem to be a little disdainful about the outsiders, as they call them. We also discovered that when Judy said she would sort us out a sack lunch for Denali, she really meant it. We did wonder if she meant it to last for the whole ten days. All this was punctuated by Dennis's bear-raising tales, such as people feeding them by hand and the inevitable consequences. Mile after mile passed by with spectacular autumn tinted giant mountains and glacial plains.

With less than half a dozen main roads in the whole vast state (one-third the area of the entire US) there is very little fear of getting lost on the roads. However, we did wonder how they managed to construct the Alcan Highway in 1942. That one-lane road crossed 1,500 miles of mountains, rivers and forests, as well as bottomless marshes, known as muskegs. Eight months of hardship and heroism it took. Machinery snapped, ice jams rammed pilings, overflowing streams ripped out bridges while muskegs consumed trucks and bulldozers. It took 11,500 troops, 500 civilians and 11,000 pieces of equipment. Hitherto sleepy villages woke up to armies of military engineers and their whole life style changed. Nowadays new bypasses have eliminated much of the old excitement and challenge. Between Mile 234 and Mile 275 over 132 curves have been straightened out. One of the original kinks was due to an old trapper offering the men a bottle of Scotch if they brought the road a little nearer to his cabin – and they did. Another part followed the path of a rutting moose and became known as the Junkyard for American Cars.

As we drove cosily along it was hard to imagine that the Alcan men would drive for thirty-six hours in the back of a GI truck in a constant -30° temperature. One soldier's feet froze in the open truck and they had to be amputated there and then. In fact, many of the men ended up wandering and lost in the wild.

At least with our knowledgeable Sybil, we knew we were safe. She took us as far as cars can go into the park, while the others half-drowned themselves on rafts in torrential rain. We even had a Christmas Day tea and cookies celebration at the Princess Hotel. At Denali they observe Christmas on 25th August because of the abominable snow-binding weather in December. There are four seasons up there – winter, June, July and August. So we had lit-up trees and decorations but no snow. Interesting that everything has to sprout, grow and reproduce in a short three months. Ended the day with an Alaskan log cabin fun night, all paid for by our hosts. This was a melodrama performed by the waiters and waitresses with everyone joining in and a great deal of 'wahooing' and waving of red-checked napkins. They were professional performers from all over the US and really worked hard for a rousing evening. Finally crashed out in our log cabin while others stumbled to motorhomes, hoping to find the right one for the night.

Saturday

Having got this far, I think it is time to have overcome the jet lag and record the specific days. Not that I can guarantee that this magnificent organisation will last as I may become literally carried away. Anyway, they found the right moto-rhomes but crossed communication lines resulted in a not quite so right start. Result was that motorhomes went one way, park buses went another and poor Carol, our host leader, was left to travel the first half on her own. As our native host leader's name was Amanda Grange, the tannoy at the Denali Visitors' Center referred to us as the Grange Party. That did it. Stowaway M adjusted it to the Grange Hill Mob. After careful explanation to our Alaskan friends that it was a UK television programme about a school, the name stuck. We did begin to feel sorry for our leaders trying to organise a minibus load of teachers. None of us wondered why Amanda slunk off to Juneau for a couple of days and left Carol to continue to do a wonderful job with us and for us.

So we reached the Eielson Visitors' Center and prayed for Mount McKinley to come out of the cloud, which it did, at the foot and the top. It has been seen only fifteen times this season and we nearly missed our sighting because of the bear drama below. Mummy bear and her twins were blueberry grazing towards the centre so we were told to stay on the viewing platform. Meanwhile beyond the bears we could see three figures coming up the hill, unaware of the three furry browsers just over the top. Lady Warden – minus gun I may add – waved her arms in a semi-circular motion so that they would make a wide 'bearth'. It was not wide enough, as shown by the bears taking an inquisitive look in their direction. Bears moved, trekkers moved alternately until half an hour later three bored bears moved off in a different direction. One of our respectfully regarded head teachers was a trifle disappointed that there was not a little bit of blood for the video. We did wonder if the three trekker miscreants would have preferred to have been 'bear cordon bleu' than experience the lady warden's ticking-off.

On through Sable Pass, one of the last refuges for the

magnificent grizzly, which managed to survive the Ice Age. Nearby at East Fork River, Adolph Murie carried out his study of wolves in 1939. He focused primarily on one wolf den and for three years, armed with notepad, binoculars and bedroll, he perched above the den and watched the wolves come and go, often round the clock. To determine their diet he analysed 1,174 wolf 'poos' (current in-word with the grandchildren). He found that the wolf played a valuable role in culling animals with weaker genes – moose, caribou, and so on.

Next thrill for us was to watch the golden eagles riding the thermals in Polychrome Pass. The pass was formed during the Ice Age. About ten thousand years ago the glaciers retreated leaving a wake of chaotic wasteland of rock and rubble. Chocolate brown meltwater flowed everywhere and PP thundered with breaking ice and crashing boulders. These 'erratics', often over 500 feet high and weighing thousands of tons, sit like solitary misfits on the open plains. On a clear sunny day it is hard to imagine the winter when only dog sled patrols can go through. I think we shall have trouble getting through departures as M keeps slipping in rock samples for his Young Farmers to see.

'Must have my conglomerates,' he says.

'Whatever turns you on,' reply I.

Sunday

Church Service with Wayne and Judy at the Lutheran church. Wayne was a bit naughty before we even started. He warned me to give him a dig if he fell asleep. I didn't dare look at him. There is a very close-knit community between the church and the school, where everyone is genuinely concerned about everyone else. M became well involved with preparations of pigs for the Alaska State Fair in his role as a Young Farmers' leader. Wayne cajoled him into playing hookey from school visits so that he could help him to shave, wash and oil the pigs. In the afternoon we cruised round Big Lake in Carol's very luxurious mobile boat home. This was another chance to hear about life in Alaska direct from the horses' mouths – or should I say bears'.

Like fishing tales, I think Alaskan tales grow in size with each telling. We heard about big Kodiak brownies (not cakes); bears which stand nine feet tall with claws like pitchforks. Intelligent and agile they can easily outrun a man and will quite happily eat black bears for tea. High-powered bullets have been known to ricochet off their skulls. Locals carry beer cans with pebbles so that the bears are given advance warning of their presence.

Monday

This was the day of the school visit and we saw nearly all of them in the Mat-Su district, which covers an area the size of England. The schools concentrate on positive rewards and there are signs on every possible wall with words of wisdom such as: 'Hard work is the yeast that raises the dough' or 'Everyone smiles in the same language'. There is 'zero tolerancy' regarding drugs, alcohol and gangs. It seems to work although it may be helped by the general feeling of well-being and the immediate access to wide open spaces, even in winter. During the latter you can plug your vehicle into electric heaters in the car parks while you do your shopping. There are less privileged students and the new Job Corps Center has dormitories as well as a block for one-parent families. Students aged between sixteen and twenty-four can receive vocational training in subjects such as the Culinary Arts, Wastewater Treatment and even Heavy Equipment Operations. Success is measured on them obtaining a job and *all* teachers keep a lookout for these jobs.

Actually we all had to have a bit of training in the language of the Alaskan. 'Sourdough' appears everywhere as it seems to be used to name food, people and places. Originally it was a longlife yeast but it applies to anyone ancient enough to have used the stuff. Sourdoughs are the miseries who stay in Alaska because they do not have the dough to leave. Sourdough should be tough outside and tender inside. If they are not they are best used to shingle roofs.

Tuesday

Wayne organised us with a flight on Bill Bear's float plane so we both skived a school visit. We were given a safety talk including how to find food stores in the floats if we happened to be stranded on a 'glaysher'. With his thirty-three years of experience he gave us a silk-smooth take-off from the lake. It did seem strange to see your bedroom window at close range from the air. This was an unforgettable experience, flying over glaciers, seeing great chunks of ice adrift and the incredible radiant turquoise of the compacted glacial ice. It really puts your lifespan into perspective when you consider that the ice crags below you were compacted over ten thousand years ago. In the words of William Brown Alaska's 'immense and ceaseless grandeur numbs the mind, glazes the eye and plagues the writer who would describe it'. We were somewhat numbed by the last twenty minutes of our trip, as our fellow French lady flyer was struck by a severe attack of mal au vent. We wondered if she were about to have a heart attack and Bill radioed about the possibility of landing on a different lake so that an ambulance could be waiting. Anyway she just made it back but we were not heartened with Bill's verdict of beaver fever: a digestive killer. Fortunately she was out of earshot when all this was under discussion.

After all this excitement we embarked upon the Alaska state fair. Hours of fun we had seeing the biggest of everything and this is not a tall tale. Massive cabbages weigh in at 98 1b and mammoth guinea pigs weigh in at 10 1b. Further thrills were provided by racing pigs as well as speedy scaling and sawing lumberjacks. M was suitably impressed by the flashing 6-foot handsaws. The judges were also impressed by the pigs, and much to the joy of Wayne and M they claimed first, second and third overall best. W and M were like pigs with infinite tails and there were 'Wahoos' all round and a celebration barbecue, not pork.

UK animal rights would have a prairie day in Alaska. Giant steer are advertised as '10,000 Burgers on the Hoof'. Quivering gerbils are used for gamblers' rat races. Pigs used for steeplechasing happily dash round for their cookie awards. However, huntin', shootin' and fishin' have strict rules. One moose a year or you lose your gun permit, your four-wheel licence and cop a heavy fine. Three salmon a day or give 'em away. M and W will be coppin' heavy punishment before long. Judy and I try not to laugh as they wander back hours late from some exploit, pockets crammed with weird freebies. They lose all sense of time or responsibility unless it concerns Young Farmers, pigs or workshop gadgets – a real pair of Just Williams.

Wednesday

Ultra-early start for Kenai Fjords. Fabulous trip of five hours by steamer with an 'all you "sea" food' lunch. For various geological reasons the mountains are slipping into the sea and the original alpine valleys filled with glacial ice are now deep fjords. Many of the former mountain peaks have become wave-beaten islands and stacks. The Alaskan

Good Friday Earthquake of 1964 showed that the forces are still at work. With its epicentre in Prince William Sound the earthquake heaved up the gulf floor as much as 50 feet, lowering, lifting and shaking the land for 550 miles around. The ground shook like jelly and ports went out with the shock waves. One 30-foot wave was aflame from ruptured tankers spilling and igniting oil. In this earthquake the Pacific Plate slammed seawards 66 feet. The shoreline dropped 6-feet in one day. Yet there is still a mountain backdrop, one mile high, mantled by the 35 by 20 mile Harding Ice field.

Several glaciers creep down from the ice field like giant bulldozers. Nunataks or lonely peaks rise from this frozen Ice Age tomb. They 'cave' icebergs into the fjords and the boom can sometimes be heard twenty miles away. We were lucky to see the brilliant blue, 150-foot-high jagged edge of the Exit Glacier. You have to be careful, however, as the odd tourist has had bodily parts speedily detached by falling ice blocks; one even lost his head! It seems that glaciers can move twenty feet a day without making a sound. Another fact, icy from the Alaskan know-alls, is that the Columbia Glacier is 3,800 feet thick in places and is so big that Washington, DC could fit in it.

Fifty miles round Resurrection Bay on a rainy, misty day was dramatic. The photos of low grey clouds, black mountains and murky sea may not be colourful, but as Wayne said, they sure will be awesome. Animals spotted were puffins scurrying to and from precarious rock perches, sea otters basking on their backs in the water and the gregarious, endangered stellar seals all clumped and jabbering on an isolated rock.

Our leader had her work cut out keeping us from being in danger. She implored constantly that it would 'greatly enhance my comfort zone' if we would move away from various precipices.

We were what the Alaskans would call a potluck group but we moulded into a good stew. There will be a good stew soon, as I am writing this during aerobics time on the return flight. In an hour we land at Minneapolis for a further stew in 83°F.

'Bring out arms from the chest,' we are instructed.

'Whose arms?' our lot demand.

One member is not taking part and the rest complain because she has not brought an excuse note from her Mum.

Thursday

Day in Anchorage, where the excellent museum gave us the chance to study the culture and history of Alaska. The guide or docent (never found out why they have that name – clues welcome) was another fast-laner, who pumped us with facts, probably to show us that oil is not the only commodity they pump in Alaska. So here comes the major 'Did You Know' section without which no diary is complete. Alaskan igloos were not dwellings but outside freezers. A German shepherd dog has sixty thousand hairs to the square inch but a sea otter has around a million, give or take a hair or two. Caribou have hollow hairs to provide better insulation.

Stopped off at Eklutna Village to see one of Alaska's oldest buildings, the 1830 Russian Orthodox church. No wonder they go mad over Bodiam Castle. Colourful decorated spirit houses cover the many graves near the church. Despite the cold, Alaska was inhabited long before that. Around Anchorage was a summer fish camp for the Dena'ina Indians. Digs show that the area was settled around six thousand years ago. Later on, gold brought Euro-American settlers who lived a 'frigid' life in tents while their homes were built. Oil has lured new settlers from the outside and the Wasilla District has four hundred new pupils each year.

Friday

Last day and we visited Mr Dingle's prize cabbage patch. There we stood, fifteen of us, for nearly an hour in the pouring rain, admiring a row of overgrown cabbages. Apparently many are consumed by moose and we were hoping it would be 'mad moose and Englishmen out in the early rain'. A few UK teachers were beginning to ask if moose really did exist in Alaska, apart from the stuffed one in Anchorage Museum. It's always last winter, last month, even yesterday but never today. Mind you, September is the one permitted hunting month so perhaps they had gone into hiding. Wayne told us that if the family moose ration of one is shot early in the morning, you do not have to go to school until the afternoon. All Terrain Vehicles troop the roads bearing folded moose or caribou corpses. Culling is essential for their well-being as well as helping the freezer supplies of human residents.

Farewell lunch at the old Colony Inn with the lady mayor. This was followed by afternoon tea with Education Superintendent Norm, with his ready wit and amazing 'my mother-in-law is a mud wrestler' patter. He hopes to write scripts when he retires and one is now under consideration by Robert Redford.

Our final visits included a reindeer and musk ox farm. The latter is the only one of its type in the world. The musk ox were real characters with appropriate names such as Joe Montana, a bit of a lad; and Gilda, a bit of a madam. They can be a rough lot, even butting each other at 70 mph with the noise being heard over a mile away. Yet their wool is as soft as cashmere. Similarly, the beauty of the wilderness belies its harsh existence. Salmon, for instance, have a hard time. They hatch in fresh water and go to sea, the pinks immediately and the kings in about two years. They roam for two to five years and thousands of miles and finally return to their home streams to spawn and die. It seems hard to realise that the hyperactive leaping salmon we saw in the fjords would later be like those we saw struggling to spawn and die in the rivers. Their rotting bodies provide food for the next generation although out of a hundred eggs, maybe only two complete the cycle as adults.

In winter Alaska is a hard place for humans. Minus 60°F can crack engines. Places like Kodiak lie in perpetual rain or mist. In Yakutat the Tlingits have no words for blue sky; 10 feet of rain falls each year, 15 inches in a day. Winds of 120 mph can produce waves of 100 feet and can even influence the winter weather of Europe. So why do they stay? After nine days we could see why. There is a challenge and a magic which hooks you. As we took off from Anchorage we knew we had been hooked.

No Hot Dinars in Jordan or Petrified in Petra or Knickers Round your Knee

So here we are in our Royal Jordanian airbus on our first guided tour ever. Will we manage to listen and do what we are told for six whole days? You will see. Jules Verne away!

Very interesting screen in the plane that shows us on the map where we have reached, speed, altitude and outside air temp. Bit concerned that we were 190 feet up while we were still on the ground but then realised that it was 190 feet above sea level. Even more concerned when the outside temp reached -58°. Will the engines freeze up?

So why the titles this time? Number one is due to the NatWest Bank failing to find us Dinars in time to go away. Having ordered them two weeks in advance I went to collect said Dinars. Great deal of form fumbling, blame passed to post office for non-delivery.

'Piffle,' said I, 'you never ordered them in the first place.'

Blame now passed to World Travel Service for not looking hard enough.

'Great, no hot dinners for us in Jordan,' whereupon I am informed, 'No pwoblem'.

Where have I heard that one before?

'US dollars will do and we'll waive the commission.'

'Think so too,' I reply as I stride out with $296 in my hot hand.

Next incident was the leaky lorry in front of us on the way to Gatwick. Suddenly we were assailed by the spewlike contents of the aforesaid lorry – smelly offal and relinquished guts from the local chicken factory. M reckoned the heavy rain had gone into the lorry and watered down the innards. Anyway, after ploughing through that lot sheep's eyes will seem very tame. Whoops, now we are going by Budapest, Bucharest and the Bosporus on to the Black Sea. Quite a B— of a journey all to avoid the no-fly zone over Yugoslavia.

Land at Amman to find we are in the Bedouin group so we have to follow the Bs everywhere. Thank goodness we are not in the Corinthians; they look a bit ancient and stuffy. Still it's better than being in the groups going to Damascus; Dam 1 and Dam 2. Kalib is our guide, very experienced, trained with the Department of Antiquities, thirteen years experience and a sense of humour. I bet he's met some weirdos. Bedouin group seem pretty sane, ninety per cent teachers. One possible weirdo, slightly balding, bearded, follows me around!

Arrive at Amra Hotel, very posh Hilton type, half a quarry load of marble everywhere. Crash out after admiring full moon over the jebels of Amman. Hills not Jezebels. Original Amman was on seven hills like Rome, now more like twenty-two.

Tuesday, 6th April

Writing this on the desert Highway which runs north–south through Jordan. Think this machine is going out of direction. Wouldn't like to break down on this road unless camels make good mechanics. Camel photo stop but they tend to stride out haughtily into the desert before you are ready for that Lawrence of Arabia shot. Enough to give you the Hump! I suppose at a value of £1,000 each for transport, milk, racing and ultimately meat, they are quite a bargain at the price and entitled to be snobbish.

Back to Tuesday and our DIY day round Amman. Supposedly easy to find tourist office on Third Circus. Quite a circus with ten men in the archives department all telling me where to go. M outside with a much more helpful taxi driver who guided us to the ministry of tourism. Not what we want, we thought, but one superb book, map and posters later, we came out to find our helpful driver ready to take us to the Citadel. Very cross he was that we had been overcharged for our first ride. 'B—foreign taxi drivers,' he said, so we just kept quiet.

Wandered round the 'being restored' Temple of Hercules. Gang of workers plus one crane, trying to work out which way round to place newly made pillar alongside old one. Nowhere near the same as the old Roman one so we think the final result will be more like the 'Templus Horrendus'. Strolled down the hill to the amphitheatre and bazaar. Ammaners very fascinated by M's beard and binoculars. Kids wanted to grab both but there always seemed to be an adult at hand to rescue us if necessary.

Wednesday 7th April

Serves me right for not keeping up to date. Having decided to soak in Jordan life and leave the write-up until we had a few hours in the Dead Sea, I managed to soak the diary as well. 'Out a bit further,' yelled the bearded official Dead Sea photographer, who had let me try first and had no idea how difficult it is to move around in the Dead Sea without rolling around. Down went paper and pen and up they bobbed again. So now I write on salt pudding paper with a ready-salted pen.

So on Wednesday the Bedouins set off for Mount Nemo. A very fine view and supposedly the place to where Moses climbed at the end of his life. One thing for sure, the Bible has far more meaning when you see the holy places yourself.

On to Kerak Castle used during the Crusades. Stuck out on a mountain ridge there were many nasty goings-on or chuckings-over from here. Apparently the enemy captives were thrown over with wooden boxes on their heads so that they suffered as much as possible by not losing consciousness before they hit the bottom. There would be a great deal more of the castle today if the locals had not purloined large lumps to build their homes. Many of the nomadic Bedouin are becoming wealthier by selling land and then moving into concrete. Westernisation is everywhere in the form of poly bags, coke bottles, and so on.

Shades of India with a perilous drive over the mountains to Petra. No need for sleeping policemen to slow down traffic; dead donkeys do just as well. Not sure whether swooping vultures are fixing their beady eyes on the latter or just hovering in the hope of fresher tourist-fallen-over-the-edge meat.

Kalid is trying to teach us Arabic numbers by repetition but it is hard work for him. In between he tells us corny jokes. 'What is Jordan going to contribute to the new world order?' in a very posh voice.

'What?' we chant.

'Mensa,' he chuckles.

'Ah, ha,' we chorus, 'knowledge.'

'No, no, very good lamb stew,' comes the enlightened reply.

M and the other Bedouin delinquents are a bit naughty at times. They add comments to Kalid's attempts to make us more observant. 'And there we see an Arab trying to do up his flies.'

Thursday 8th April

Up at dawn to ride down the 2 km of narrow, twisting lane or siq, through the towering rock cleft to the red ruins of Petra. Very few people, the echoing of the hooves, the early light and the sudden view of the ruins was an unforgettable experience. Words cannot justify it so I shall not even try but just carry the memory with me. It beats the first glimpses of Ayers Rock, the Pyramids, Chichén Itzá and even the Taj Mahal. The physical and technical skills that must have been used to carve the intricate facades and to dig out the massive chambers in the solid rock face are quite unbelievable. We wandered all over and at the end of the day there was my little Arab horse boy waiting with a big smile and the horse of course. He wanted to practise his English and it turned out I was the same age as his mother but I looked younger. They don't need Open University degrees in psychology on how to earn a bigger tip.

Petra was built by the Nabataeans before the Romans arrived. That's about all your history as my older readers have said too much history gets boring. Being a pottery trading centre there were piles of old pottery shards over a thousand years old everywhere. Kalib showed us how to dig around and help ourselves. The local Bedouin were selling larger pieces they had found, some of which were even better than the ones in the museums. M found a piece of broken handle and ten minutes further along found another bit. Later on as we laid out our spoils on the bed we discovered that the two pieces fitted exactly. Almost as good as Kalib, who has a specialist collection of decorated oil lamps and found a missing piece two years after the first find. Many of his are bedroom ones with acrobatic Arabs.

Friday 9th April

Wander round Little Petra – a smaller valley of carved facades, tombs and dwellings, some still occupied by the Bedouin in winter. Then on to the oldest village in the world, Beida, traced back to 6000 BC.

Afternoon – second ride down the siq but not quite so dramatic because of more sun, crowds and dust. The memory of yesterday's ride will still linger. Just as well we are travelling now. Next year our Hotel Forum will have a hundred more rooms and six other new hotels are being built. Kalid told us of plans to pave the siq; less dust but less romantic. Three hundred and fifty horses do four return trips a day but these are to be reduced to two hundred by natural wastage.

There was definite natural wastage from our figures as we sweated our way up innumerable 'gradients and stepses', ref. Kalid, to the gigantic monastery carved out of the top mountain. Once again very impressive and a little beyond that we saw one of the most impressive views on earth – across to the Great Rift Valley with sheer cliffs of rugged volcanic rock as a dark contrast in the foreground. A bit windy in all respects, what with the natural elements of the weather and the man-made elements of the various types of beans consumed by certain Bedouin group men at breakfast. Is this why Kalid keeps informing us that phosfart and tourism are Jordan's largest exports? Kalid led us in another Arabic number lesson but his efforts this time were reinforced by a 100 mile echo round the Rift Valley.

Saturday 10th April

Down to the Dead Sea the Bedouin group went in a coach, and as you know the diary was nearly drowned. Further biblical arousal when we saw the gleaming pinprick blobs of three minarets on the top of the distant mountains – Jerusalem, and tomorrow is Easter Day.

M used the binoculars to look across the Dead Sea to the caves where the Scrolls were found, or so he thinks. We were advised not to go outside the hotel grounds as it is a sensitive military area. Few days later we read that West Bank closures were tighter for Easter. We do seem to land in tricky places! After the eventful 'float' we sunned and chatted. Ninety per cent teachers in the party, a few of which managed to drown their national curriculum folders in the Dead Sea. So do you know that the Dead Sea is the lowest point on earth? Now you can pass level 3, attainment target 5.

Sunday, 11th April, Easter Day

Farewell Dead Sea through hectares of fruit cultivation to return to Amman. Realise how strange the passage of time can be. Feel we have been away from Amman for fourteen not four days. Lovely day re-wandering through Amman and its three small, but excellent museums, only 25p each. Costumes, Bedouin tents, Dead Sea Scroll containers, and so on. A photographer's paradise from the oldest statue in existence (seven thousand years) with its flat figure of a person apart from a cheeky little bottom, to the curled-up bones and skull of a child buried in a pot under the floor of the house so it could stay with the family. However some of the explanations were a little mystifying. Sack: 'Goat and sheep skin bags used to store food and grain. There is somebody who leaves the hair on the skin and others take it out of the sack. But about coloured after taking out the hair by the dyes.' It is almost as good as Kalid's sun rising in the 'yeast', which is more than can be said for the rising of yeastless Jordanian bread, but at 5p a loaf, what can you expect? Nevertheless, I wish I could speak Arabic a fraction as well as Kalid speaks English.

We were relieved to see that the newly erected pillar at the Temple of Horrendous was now properly in position and being shaped to fit. Talking of being shaped to fit, I slipped down a gradient and gouged my knee. No bandages so I resorted to a clean pair of bikini knickers tied round the wound – hence 'Knickers Round Your Knee' – travellers' tip of the month.

Monday 12th April

After last night's fun supper we were all a little low at breakfast. M wore his total sheikh outfit to the supper and I think the other males in the party wish they had indulged in less than £10 worth of fancy dress. I was a little worried what Kalid and the waiters would think but they all laughed and vied with each other to show him how to do the headdress properly. Since then he has scared the wits out of his daughter at the airport, also his mother at her front door, the Young Farmers at Punnetts Town Hall, the grandchildren at Wellington Country Park. I just hope he does not carry out his threat to 'do' Tunbridge Wells Shopping Centre. The trouble is he is beginning to enjoy wearing a long shirt and paunches about quite naturally in it.

Usual breakfast debate about how to melt the butter. Gets cruder every day. It comes in little packs, kept cold by floating in cold water. M started it all by melting it on the coffee pot. I found friction between the hands was a good method so I dare not say what the next suggestion was. What a sad day. No more of Kalid's mixed-up left and rights, no more of his hysterical sights but plenty of hysterics when we arrived at the airport. Until then the Bedouin group had been on very good behaviour. The Nabataeans were first on the coach, older and wiser, of course. Then we had the last attempt by Kalid to test us on our Arabic numbers. Useless we were but much better at the new world lamb stew joke. The Nabataeans were a bit 'put out' as their courier's best joke was 'Have you had a good breakfast/lunch/dinner?'

'Yes.'

'Then you can push the coach.'

Talk about indigestible jokes.

Airport official boarded coach to give last instructions before 'Magic Carpet with wings' – Kalid. Official commanded: 'You will put boarding pass on page with Jordan stamp in passport. You will collect boarding pass when your name is called out. You will identify luggage and weceeve label. You will put label in safe place, not in your passport, not in your boarding card.' By now the Bedouin were giggly and fidgety and making Heil Hitler signs. The Nabataeans were not amused. Glares descended upon the errant Bedouin. Total crack-up as we were then told 'The Menses [sounds like a female complaint] will go through the menses security. The womenses will go through the womenses security. [An even worse female complaint.] The bagses will go through the bagses security.' Did he mean the tarts in the party? 'Where do the gayses go?' we chorused amidst the scornful looks of the Nabataeans.

The final shot was: 'Suppose you can't make up your mind?'

At the time of typing this up I am beginning to worry if M can make up his mind regarding his identity. His latest threat is to enter the Women's Institute at Rushlake Green in his shriek outfit, sorry his sheikh outfit.

The last act of general confusion was the name-calling. To try to restore sanity, Kalid took over. First call 'Clark'. Problem? Yes. Three sets of Clarks in the Bedouin group not even counting the Basso-Clarks. 'Initials,' we yell.

'R.J.' wails Kalid.

'No R.J.s,' we chant.

So one decisive M Clark moved forward to help our Kalid, who by now was beginning to feel like an antiquity himself. Turned out the initials meant Royal Jordanian.

Back at school the kids have relished little finger tips of Dead Sea water. Just as well no bacteria can survive in it! They have felt the salt soggy diary, laughed at the photo of Mrs B floating with her homework in the Dead Sea and tried to sink all sorts of objects in the Dead Sea water. They have been impressed by the photos of the distant minarets of Jerusalem, touched by the remains of the child in the pot under the family floor and amazed by Miss in her harem outfit. So we spread our fun around!

Mix-up in Mexico or No Chickening at Chichén Itzá 1992–1993

Not sure what day it is

Twenty-four hours of planes and transits (Houston) and we made it for our first night in Cancun on the Yucatan Peninsula of Mexico. Hotel Plaza Kokai (cock-eye) after what seemed to be the most cock-eyed trip from an airport ever. M reckoned we went round the same fountain three or four times at ten-minute intervals. Temp 80° and Christmas trees all over seems really strange – heat, fairy lights and tannoyed – 'We wish you a Merry Christmas'. Shades of India, at the bus station but we found the right queue for bus to Mérida. Cancún was much too civilised for us. Acclimatised for the day until evening bus departure. Took us nearly the whole day to find the correct bus queue. Departure okay but half hour out and bus broke down. Bus mended in the dark. The trip of 340 km finally took six hours despite suicidal efforts on part of driver to catch up time with perilous overtaking. Not a good idea to have front row seats, especially at night, when you miss oncoming vehicle lights with points of a second to spare.

Nearly midnight check-in at Hotel Dolores Alba. Old, built round a beautiful and peaceful tree-filled courtyard with large wooden gates. Perhaps it was a monastery or nunnery at one time. Now very bravely sitting on Re-staurante Los Alemendros awaiting our latest culinary adventure. M has settled for a *Poc-Chuc*; not too hot, he hopes. They certainly seem to be 'chuccing' it about. I'm on *pollo pibil* – chicken in banana leaves. After 'mutilated' eggs for breakfast I'm playing safe. M's has arrived, still sizzling on a cast-iron plate. Mine has a pile of what looks like black mashed potato, or as M defines it, 'fresh bear poo'. All wrong: Mexican mushy beans.

Sorted it out; Tuesday, 22nd December

First Mayan adventure. See-Saw collected us for trip to Uxmal. Just as well we cannot see-saw ourselves into the future. Those Maya were some builders although they never used the wheel on proper carts, only on toys; they had no beasts of burden and no metal tools. So between AD 600 and AD 900 they left their mark of elliptical pyramids and other fine buildings on the Yucatán landscape for mad Englishmen and some women to climb in the midday sun. Not helped when the Englishwoman has size eight feet to climb steps four inches in width, 180 of them at an angle of 60; a total height of 40 metres. Guide ran up the steps so you were led to believe that it was fairly simple until you were a third of the way up and looked down. Guide insisted that you looked at the isosceles shapes of the Maya, all connected to the cult of the rattlesnake. When the latter shedded its skin it was time to prepare the soil for planting. My skin was certainly rattling by the time we reached the top of the Uxmal Pyramid.

'The rain gods or Chacs were also very important. Natural rock wells or *cenotes* were used to cast virgins and captives to appease the dear old Chacs. Earliest date of Mayan building seems to be around AD 569 – date on a door lintel. Experts reckon that Uxmal was rebuilt around five times. How anyone knows anything is amazing. The unexcavated parts show how the jungle has covered all the ruins. Plants and trees have trailed and penetrated the pyramids. Nevertheless, the elliptical shapes can still be seen. They must have had some very complicated and accurate mathematical planning.

A clever chronological lot, those Maya. Their calendar based on a long count from 10th August, 3114 BC was more accurate than its European counterpart. Patterns on buildings show an awareness of a 52-week cycle. Their calendar was actually accurate to one ten-thousandth of a day so they were more precise than we are today. With their system they could predict the revolution of Venus with an error of one day in six thousand years. The long count is supposed to end on 24th December, 2012 – twenty years from now almost to the day. Make the most of it, folks!

A cruel lot as well, those Maya. According to See-Saw, the Mayan equivalent of basketball 'compounded' (we think he meant 'consisted of') a stone ring, eight metres high, through which players, heavily padded with leather, had to hit a hard rubber ball. The game went on for hours and winners were awarded precious stones, jewellery, clothes and even houses from the spectators. And the losers? They ended up in what one might call a barbecue pit, because they would fight to the death. Hands were not allowed to be used.

Quick trip to Kabal, another Mayan site with acres still to be excavated. Includes the ornated Puuc-designed Codz-Pop Temple. Sounds like a fizzy drink. The west facade 'compounded' two hundred and fifty masks each with small pits for burning incense or oil. It must have glowed like a Chinese lantern for miles around in the jungle. In the steaming heat of the midday jungle sun we had to keep our wits about us to keep up with See-Saw. Having had our speedy 'compounding' on the facades we then had to rush round to see the 'backsides'. We did admire our See-Saw for his 3 Es: energy, English and enthusiasm. Definitely a Mayan descendant.

Through small towns back to Mérida. Saw women with what looked like hammocks round their shoulders but they were outsize shawls ready for instant use when the sun goes down. Many still live in the old palapa huts, made with tall, thin sapling trees placed close together to form the walls and topped with a palapa roof. Families sleep in hammocks, and if it is cold a fire is lit below. Watch out for blisters on the posteriors! It's not a hot botty job as far as M is concerned but a rather hot snotty job with a streaming cold. Still he made it to a Chinese cellar for a well-filling mein followed by a nut search in the supermarket. I stood outside with the bags otherwise you have the hassle of the 'left shopping baggage'. Watched small boys stocking shelves and packing bags at a speed of light. Oh dear, no nuts. Will have to settle for Sainsbury's from home! Seems a long way off as I sit on my rocker (not off it for once) in the quiet leafy courtyard, receiving multinational smiles.

Wednesday, 23 December

Ye Mayan Gods, 8.20 a.m. and breakfast ends at 9. Mad rush but hunger is a great spur so we make it. Must confess that I am not being very good at keeping this diary so I shall have to make some reminder notes. Do Paul Theroux and Eric Newby have this trouble? I wonder. I shall need a good smooth bus ride to catch up, but not much chance of that in Mexico. Museum of Anthropology is a good induction into the more gory aspects of Mayan culture. Contemporary Mayan blame the arrival of the Toltecs for the nasty bits. Sunbathing and M is having trouble with his bits, as the towel is too short. Ten minutes' peace after decision made to keep toes on the towel. What a wimp!

Now he is in a hammock wondering how on earth they make babies in them. No problem as we recall last night's family with ten children under ten and all beautiful look-alikes.

Now back to the gore! The ancient Mayan concept of beauty was pretty barbaric. Teeth were filed and what was left implanted with precious stones, such as turquoise; no injections of course. Another torture was to tie babies and small children to boards like a press to flatten their skulls as another sign of beauty.

How I shall ever get this diary done, I do not know. I have now been invited into a double hammock to see how they hold. Now M is thinking of ways to save money as yesterday I bought a panama hat for £6 and today I left it on the bus. Can we cadge a lift to the ruins? Can we find a jungle way in to avoid paying? I give up, I'll just move on to Christmas Eve.

Thursday, 24th December

If there is no more diary then the hammock did not hold and we broke every bone on the concrete floor. We survived. Joined Jean and Freda (our age plus) doing VSO in Guatemala. Did our local bus bit to the Loltun Caves – five hours' travel for one and half hours round the caves. Worth it for their vastness. One part is as large as a cathedral. The Maya held religious ceremonies here. At various points you can see carvings of serpents gripping human heads because this symbolised the entrance to the underworld. From one of the chambers you can look up to the open skies partially covered by jungle, very eerie. The fossil of a Mastodon was found here. All very impressive. Equally impressive was our hitched 8 km lift back to the bus station. Half a minute of touting and we were leaping amongst locals and oil drums for an open-air, breezy ride in a pick-up truck. Wonderful fun as we descended the Puuc Hills (aptly named) and waved to everyone on the way.

Christmas Eve shopping; limited ourselves to the 50p shop. I received a mini-hairbrush, while I gave M a long-handled, spring-loaded nut retriever. I shall have to watch out that he does not try to retrieve my spare parts. Special dinner in the Mérida Square with Jean and Freda. Persuasive Mexican gentlemen tried to sell us double-size hammocks and flashing yo-yos so we succumbed to a cut-price panama hat each.

Forgot to mention that we had dinner in the Grand Hotel yesterday. Soft music, palm-filled courtyard and very cheap. Shall I ever have such balmy evening romance again?

Christmas Day, Friday

In a muddle of a bus station we managed to track down the Chichén Itzá bus. Superb Dolores Alba Hotel with round pool and hammocks (already described and tested). Only £7 a night each and very reasonable meals. Near to Chichén Itzá Pyramids. Extensive and impressive but not so dramatic or steep as the Uxmal Pyramid. Definitely a climb for chickens, not that the Maya or Toltecs were chickens. Devotion to gods often meant self-mutilation, like drawing a rope through your tongue. Or it meant being quite nasty to your captives according to rank, ranging from torture, dismemberment, decapitation or having your heart torn out. Four attendants restrained the captive while the still-beating heart was extricated. Then it was barbecue time. How do we know all this? From engravings on large stone slabs or *stellae*.

Walked back 4 km in the heat and reflected on last year's Christmas Pyramids in Egypt. Anoraks across the desert last year; T-shirts and shorts across the jungle this year. Next year?

Saturday, Boxing Day

Once more the public bus but not until 10.30 a.m. so we had a solar cook-up and a swim. M was making any excuse not to swim as it felt cold. The last was 'There's a dead snake swimming in it.'

I tried to work out the logic of it until I saw a worm-sized baby snake floating on top. I lovingly rescued it – the snake, not M, of course – and wrapped it in a leaf to dry out on the window sill. A good piece of scary evidence to take home. Unfortunately, it was obviously a good snack for local cockroaches, termites or maggots or whatever. Not a scale left!

A two-hour wait to change buses at Valladolid. Armed with map I attempted to find the main square with cathedral. Failed. M then had a go but was back in a few minutes – too hot. We watched four hunky Mexican men putting up flashing, musical fairy lights round a statue of Mary in the bus station waiting room. Half an hour later and they were still in a muddle. Fortunately the bus arrived before we were driven mad by high-pitched electronic 'Jingle Bells'. It's amazing how you can communicate 'This music is a painful experience' to people from other lands without saying one word.

Very crowded bus so M and I ended up with a four- and seven-year-old respectively on our knees. Mother was standing very proudly and pregnantly further down with two more small children. She was totally oblivious to our two trying to remove the stuffing from the seats in front to see how far they could throw it out of the window. I tried 'naughty' in several languages but a better game followed: how many bits could blow into M's beard. M finally won by tickling them under the armpits as they reached out for a reload of ammunition. All this in a bus with ninety people and baggage. We saw one old girl loading what looked like bags of concrete under the bus.

American buses come to Mexico to die a slow and painful death by bump and load. There are sleeping policemen bumps in every village and they are killers of buses and passengers. Every bus has a crucifix at the front with various extras. The more decorations the nearer the bus is to its grave. One crucifix had flashing lights; probably to take your eyes away from the very cracked windscreen. Another had a large bouquet of plastic flowers to draw your attention from the capsizing door and perforated seats. At least we didn't have the local priest blessing us and the bus as they did in the Himalayas. Eventually we arrived safely if rather sweatily at the Tulum Crossroads Motel. Two beds, cold water and no furniture for £5 each a night. Not a bargain. Still, the moonlight walk by the Caribbean was free and very memorable.

Sunday 27th December

Another 5.30 a.m. start, up for 6 a.m. bus to Coba, and this is supposed to be a holiday. 'Gotta have your culture,' says M as we watch the sunrise over the bus stop.

Breakfast in a reed cafe overlooking the early morning mist over the lake at Coba. It was worth it. Coba opened at 8 and we were at the top of the highest Mayan pyramid by 8.30, all alone, looking over thousands of square miles of jungle. Takes a bit of deep thought to really believe that you are in the middle of Mexican jungle while everyone at home is recovering from Christmas. Talking of home, archaeologists believe that Coba was home to forty thousand Maya and that it contains six thousand five hundred structures of which only a very small number have been excavated since 1973. They are also baffled by the network of sacbeob which ran out for over 100 km around; 3 metres high and 10 metres across. Sacbeob: stone-paved avenues.

All very fascinating so long as you can survive the mozzies. Definitely an ants paradise – thorn ants, which live in small thorns; huge termite nests hanging in the trees; leaf ants leaving 2 to 3 km trails about a foot wide.

Avoided a three-hour wait for the bus by offering to show Pierre and Tina from Denmark the way to Tulum; all of which meant we were able to explore two sites in one day and that being a Sunday meant it was free. Tulum means City of the Dawn and if dawn means renewal you certainly have it here. The ruins are small but the setting makes up for it. The crooked old buildings hug to the rocks and sandy beach, lapped by the cool blue waters of the Caribbean. The ramparts are 7 metres in thickness so methinks it was a fortress. They contain an interior walk-way from which Tulum's defenders could throw spears or chuck rocks at invaders. Another early night for a 6.30 a.m. start.

Monday 28th December

Last public bus journey of the holiday. Fairly new bus, very civilised and very boring, Perhaps just as well as the one-hour boat trip over to the Caribbean island of Cozumel was anything but smooth. We had to do our last-minute-Michael-Palin-wait-for-us rushing-down-the-dock-bit just as they were pulling up the plank. A 200-seater boat, no cars, so not very large. The waves were massive and we saw very little horizon on either side for the whole hour. Just as well we caught that boat, as there would have been no room at any inn later on. We had the second last 'accommodations' of the whole island. New hotel, own pool, two minutes from the sea, five minuters from the traffic-free centre for just £7 each a night and breakfast for £2. Who says Caribbean holidays are expensive? Found out we could have half-price scooter hire plus free brekkie at posh hotel.

The catch? We are bait for time share, but as our friendly Mexican said, 'you eat breakfast, listen to the garbage, take scooter for day and say 'We tink about it.'

With clever planning you could do this every day.

Wandered along the beach, spotting bright, blue fish in rock pools. Just as well we were not spotted by the navy in their no-go area. We did wonder why it was so deserted. Chicken with *mole* for supper. Mole is a dark brown, slightly spicy sauce over sort of cannelloni chicken rolls with melted cheese. Okay but too much mole.

M is shaking the bed trying to get his pen to work for his intellectual word puzzles. He's wasted a load of it trying to draw Mayan faces on my bodily pyramids. That's the trouble with these naked siestas. Not a piece in peace.

Tuesday, 29th December

Taxi collected us for our free breakfast. Timeshare salespiel from Moya, ex-Teddington, Middlesex, six years ago married Mexican diver. With the best of motives we paid 4,836,048 pesos as deposit on what we thought would be a boon for family, investment and retirement. Turned out to be a con so the less mentioned about it, the better! Less mentioned about my snorkelling, even better. What a damp loss. The water kept coming in. Still, the scootering was wonderful; round the Island, with sun, wind, sea and sand around you and through you. Another never to be forgotten exhilarating adventure. M was ever so skilful at driving, except when we endeavoured to go down a one-way street the wrong way and the Mexican policeman was waving to us very friendly, or was it frantically?

Wednesday, 30th December

Michael writes: 'M here as Pat is totally aneabreated after consuming her free margarita with our meal. It is a leathal

227

mixture of tequila, controw and lime juice with salt around the rim of the glass. Apparently the locals use this as an anesthetick as it totally parlyses the legs.' Spelling unexpurgated. Reckon M was as gone as I was.

Scootered to San Francisco Beach. Brain still half in the margarita clouds so I hoped I would not fall off. Back to reality as we scootered through a tropical rainstorm. M enjoyed his snorkelling but not his supper – Mexican mixed grill. Ghastly, tough meat looked like fried socks and probably tasted the same. Manager not very concerned so no tip. You'd think they would try a bit harder with over eighty other 'caffs' in competition.

Thursday 31st December

Last day of 1992, up with the lark, pedal bikes hired by 8 a.m. Only 20 km to be done today in high 80s temp! Don't ever be fooled by scientific theories that hot air rises and cycling is cooler in the heat. About as old Mexican hat as the claim that chillies are not hot either. M swam around a lagoon looking at weirdo marine life and purposely sunken statues. Like skiers, divers spend hours comparing narrow escapes from ravenous rays, preying puffers, oglin' octopuses, shooting sharks and greedy gropers. Old Cousteau has a lot to answer for. Sheltered in ice cream parlour from more rain.

Last romantic dinner together in La Mission; looks like a converted church. Every half-hour the Boss put the clock to 11.55 so that at 12 we could pretend it was New Year!

'No need to spend big money on a New Year's Dinner,' he said.

Helpfully he warned us to visit a supermarket on the way home for tomorrow's breakfast as nowhere would be open.

'Not body stand up!' he declared.

Friday, 1st January, 1993

One keen cafe open for breakfast. Sat with fun American couple. She taught biology to fourteen to eighteen year olds. Horrified to hear that our less able have to keep up science and a foreign language until sixteen. Less able in her area do basic skills in the morning and are paid in the afternoon to do work around the school or in local firms. No work; no pay.

Last wander round to take photos of hideous pottery in shop windows. Being shut we wouldn't be caught. Also the nativity scene in the square with its animals totally out of proportion; camel twice the size of elephant but latter quarter size of wise men and shepherds somewhere in between. Cozumel Airport size of average Safeway. Walk out quickly to plane between downpours, otherwise soggy seats. Beautiful view of Caribbean and the Yucatán Peninsula. Four hours at Houston. Watched planes being filled with food and petrol at one end and loos being emptied at the other. Like gigantic human beings!

Read how during the spring and autumn equinoxes, a series of triangles on the great Chichén Itzá Pyramid, on the north stairs, becomes an undulating serpent as the shadows fall on it. It seems to go up in March and down in September. This amazing display lasts three hours and twenty-two minutes. In addition there is another pyramid inside the Great Pyramid. When opened there was a brilliant red jaguar throne with inlaid eyes and spots of shimmering jade. M actually braved the sweltering inside to make it to the top throne room. I've also forgotten the echo in the ball game court. A conversation at one end can be heard 135 metres away at the other end.

Interesting conversation with a young lad from Fleet. Failed English O level. Did an OU degree and now sets oil rigs at £1,000 a day and in great demand. What does this prove? What does anything prove? It's 1993 and we have had another unusual Christmas learning about the world, its people and places.

South Africa Safari or Khaki up the Kruger!

A year having passed since our last major trip, we decided to be really organised well in advance for South Africa. A month before, clothes were laid out on the spare bed, the local charity shops having been divested of much of their stock. Not that I can ever go in Age Concern again after M declared that being a pensioner I should have a discount on my purchases. That was after he had tried on every hat in the shop.

Then came panic number one. According to the words of the Lonely Planet travel guide one should wear mellow-coloured items on safari, so as not to upset the wildlife. Hence a large tub of khaki dye was purchased. An even larger tub of boiling, burbling, bile-coloured brew was concocted and the Age Concern relics were cast therein – clothes, not geriatrics! Whoops, B and V being close on the keyboard it should read 'vile-coloured brew'. Left the brew to mulch, wondering whether the clothes would become real relics in the process of the lethal dye. Returned ten minutes later to stir them a little to find that a hole in the large tub had enabled the fortunately environmental dye to cascade down the garden, leaving a soggy pile of mouldy-looking clothes. We just had to hope that our treks would be in pale green scrub. To rub salt in my wounded pride I remembered that I had not added my kilogram of salt to set the dye colour, so we would probably end up a sweaty off-green as well. A week later, recounting the saga of the leaky, pukey brew at the Women's Institute, Colette, an ex-Kenya resident, said 'Oh, we used to go in the game reserves in any colour. It doesn't bother the animals at all.'

Farewells to son and daughter-in-law. Strange, however often we travel, I still feel that lump of emotion as I watch those I love go off into the distance. Quick but bumpy ride in a creaky Sabrina plane to Brussels. Freudian slip, I mean a Sabena plane but it did curve around a lot. M was dispersed three rows before me so he escaped the smoker with BO right behind me. Ten minutes to gallop from one end of Brussels Airport to the other for the ten-hour flight to Johannesburg. Then there was an hour's delay in loading, a Noah's ark affair with us being ticked off on a tatty aircraft seating plan. Row in front of smokers this time so Sabena not winning any brownie points. Usual musical chairs after take-off while separated co-travellers tried to co-travel again. Then the inevitable 'Is there a doctor on board? If so, please can he make himself visible.' Lady collapsed outside the loo; not enough room for a good old stretched collapse inside the loo.

Not much room either for the self-barricaded dozen-plus strikers in the Imperial Car Hire office at Joburg Airport. 'Some start this,' we muttered, but a very helpful gentleman guided us to uniformed staff in the car park. Wielding clipboards with lengthy lists, they were trying to allocate cars like they did in ancient times, minus computers. So that was the start of the first day, together with low clouds, a cool breeze and the threat of rain. We wondered if we were really in South Africa in the height of summer, or whether it was all a big con and we were still in England.

Usual highly efficient post-landing driving by M took us to Pretoria in less than an hour. We decided to avoid Joburg after seeing the headlines in the plane newspaper: Johannesburg squatters riot with guns.

Settled ourselves in Hotel Formule 1. These are spring-ing up everywhere. They are superior versions of the Hong Kong cabinet hotels. The rooms are assembled like Lego blocks held together with Meccano inside. Even the small television is suspended on an outsize piece of red Meccano rod. All this plus brekkie for £10 each. Early night, partly to catch up on sleep and partly to prepare for 4 a.m. wildlife viewing sessions. With these early starts I do not envisage much wildlife between M and I on this holiday. Whoops, wrong again.

Friday 9th December

Charted our way along to the tourist office in Pretoria after our breakfast in the Formule I Star Trek control dining room. We sat on our swivel stools near a ten-slice super-sonic toaster, with a mind of its own, ejecting half-done toast everywhere. Spock'd soon sort that out! Was it a coincidence that the manager of the hotel was a Mr de Kerk? Was it another coincidence that there was not another tourist in the tourist office or had the news of our arrival arrived before us? We do tend to leave a wave of unusual happenings... snow in Egypt, floods in Jordan, terrorists in Mexico and last year we even managed to arouse a hitherto dormant volcano in Chile. Yes, we had done it already; mid-summer and there was snow on the mountains behind Cape Town.

By 8 a.m. we were on our way and all went well until we found that we had strayed off the main N1 road and were on a parallel side road, which led us through a township called Hammanskraal, not marked on our map. There was a great deal of inter-crowd activity but it was not until later, when we picked up our Hitcher With No Name, that we learnt that it was in fact inter-taxi warfare. We had wondered why we had seen several burnt-out vehicle shells. Our Hitcher With No Name waved to us at the turn-off from Pietersburg to Tzaneen (the T is silent). His car was out of action and the taxi bus was probably burnt. Despite having an hour of his company we never found out his name. A civil engineer but his politics were anything but civil and definitely unprintable. He gave us several wildlife warnings; elephants in particular, just keep moving and the same for hippos. Cheap but posh hotel at Znaneen, although we did become somewhat weary of hearing the Christmas Carol tape on a constant loop. We reckoned that this lot of employees would be barricading themselves in, not for a pay rise, but to have the wretched tape turned off, as there was still another two weeks to Christmas.

Saturday 10th December

Thanks to the offending tape and the sound of jingle bells at 5.30 a.m. we were away on the road to the Kruger Park by 8 a.m. Entered the Northern Punda Maria Gate and embarked on our first day of wildlife spotting. The park is the size of Wales, so readers need to realise that seeing the animals living in their own wide habitat is not always so easy as wandering around a small safari park. Still, our first morning included impala, zebras, baboons, all crossing the road.

I never realised how exciting it would be to see the animals wandering around totally at ease in their habitat. We are the vulnerable observers, locked in our camp cages each night. Do the animals say to one another, 'There goes another man in a can.' First tropical thunderstorm and we were on the highest viewing point looking 360° for hundreds of miles. Lightning all around, rain lashing down plus great claps of thunder which shook the car. Vulnerability set in as I imagined the worst nightmare of being stranded in the rain and elephants coming towards us. Who needs *Jurassic Park*? Piles of steaming poo, glistening pools of wee and decapitated trees inform you that they are out there.

First bushveld night at Sirheni. Six of us in all with no shops, solar power and a fence between us and the predators. Large, basking, innocent-looking crocs were visible from our thatched roof dwelling, as well as very large footprints just on the other side of the fence. M has a wonderful time with the large binoculars. By the time I have managed to focus in everything has moved on but I did see the crocs' yellow marks and the waterbuck with target marks on their bottoms. Too much potty training probably. M is very conscientiously marking them all off in his 'Kruger Park I Spy Book'. Meanwhile I read the 'I Spy Records' of the camp, such as sixteen hyenas seen at a kill, bull elephant closed the road to the camp by pushing two trees across. Warden had to saw them up at 4 a.m. Fell asleep wondering what was in store for us.

Sunday 11th December

This was probably the most terrifying day of my life. I think I used up all my safari adrenalin allowance in two sets of less than five minutes. Left the Sirheni Camp at 5 a.m. and were beginning to wonder why we had spent all that money to come here as nothing much seemed to be happening. Then we spotted the backside of elephant number one just in front of us as we turned the corner. Driver M was not too sure whether to be more alarmed by me or the elephant. 'Keep the engine running, the book says,' gasped I into his left ear. Then number two elephant appeared on the other side of the road, nearer, full frontal and we were between them. Seeing them in a zoo is one thing, but big, dark, loose and coming towards you, ears aflapping madly, is quite another. M was his usual calm self but to put it emphatically I was s... scared. My stomach just churned, cramped and gurgled and the calmer M remained the worse I became. 'No panic,' he kept saying, 'they don't care about us.' However, photos taken, he did start to reverse back and then turn.

Later, when we had plucked up the courage to retrace our journey, we found that their tracks came right up to where we had stopped. Who needs high-fibre diets when you can have 'olifant' scares for breakfast? Just as well M was driving or we'd still be there, a crumpled heap of metal and bone.

A few warthogs later we arrived at our next camp, Shingwedzi. Warthogs are not ugly, they are just wonderful characters.

Warthogs have some pretty sensible habits like kneeling to graze in comfort and entering their burrows backwards so that they can attack intruders with their tusks. Settled in at our new camp. M checked the spotters' board for the day as there are rewards for spotting unusual species or endangereds such as wild dogs. Talk about mad dogs and Englishmen out in the midday sun trying to win a free can of beer! M also did an immediate repair job on the ballcock in the loo. Can't take him anywhere without him having to get his hands in.

Set off for our twilight drive, hoping that the elephants had done a twilight flit, although I did notice that the car windows each had 'armour-plated glass' etched on them. Difficult to decide whether that was reassuring or not. Returned in time for our first safari night ride. Really fascinating but a fiendish wind, quite out of season, meant that we sat in the open-air truck with jumpers, anoraks and blankets. This was supposed to be South Africa's bushveld in the middle of summer. The ranger was very knowledgeable as well as diplomatic. With five searchlights, each equal to 750,000 candlepower, we saw and heard about life in the

African bush.

At the start we were told about our black knobbies, one per row: 'Push your knobbie when you want me to stop,' we were instructed.

M was a little peeved as he was in the same row as a nightjar enthusiast, who kept pushing the knobby whenever he saw a bird. In fact M was quite sure knobby pushing was the only excitement the nightjar fellow ever had, apart from the nightjars. Anyway, our ranger told us facts such as the leadwood tree being resistant to everything from termites to elephants. They can be 'upstanding' for over eight hundred years. His elephant story was about the time he had to back away from an oncoming elephant with a load of tourists not yelling 'Help, what do we do now?' but 'Hang on, we want a good photo.'

At the halfway 'convenience' stop, gun at the ready, our ranger told us about the time he stepped out for a pee in the dark without doing a 360° torch check. Recent rain had encouraged grass growth so he successfully watered a lioness, who stood up, looked at him in disgust and walked off. Some rangers have all the luck. Four hours later we dropped into bed, too cold to wash and wondering if it was any warmer in the UK.

Monday 12th December

Today's offerings included warthog mummy and tiny wartlets and a very pregnant hyena basking on the road. M feels sorry for hyena males as they have a very matriarchal society and the poor fellas are just skivvies and sex slaves. These were followed by six massive water buffalo, treetop munching giraffes (giraffe bulls feed at full stretch while cows bend down and any tough twigs and thorns are spat out). 'What, no elephants?' you ask, Well... half an hour before arrival at base camp, I was uttering my thanks to whom it may concern for my one-day elephant adrenalin reprieve, when we saw one on the road a good kilometre away. It was strolling along so I felt more confident about its existence, although M kept trying to scare me by saying it might have a co-stroller somewhere. Distance made my heart grow stronger.

'Well, if there is, it can't be that near.'

Nearly my famous last words as ten metres in front of us appeared the mate. It started towards us and M refuses to admit whether he knew that it was there all the time or not. Still, we are now quite adept at elephant getaways before we become elephant takeaways.

Midday arrival at Olifants Camp, like a paradise on earth, perched on a rocky outcrop with 270° vistas for miles over the Kruger. In rondavel 111 at the very edge we could see sunrises and sunsets beyond compare, watch miniature giraffes and zebras grazing below and listen to the sociable gruntings of hippos in the river below. We savoured every second of our two days spent there, a link with eternity. After this experience the time went into a haze and I gave up on dates in the diary and in fact I came home two weeks later with Olifants still touching my heart.

Our subsequent viewing included a family of hyenas with nine pups all living in a drain culvert. Pregnant mum lay in the sun-drenched road and refused to move so we carefully went round her. Later that day it was reported she had given birth. Another event was the ball of dung rolling across the road but of course it was a dung beetle doing its bit for the ecosystem with Mrs Dung Beetle hanging on for grim death. Talking of death it appears we just missed about a hundred vultures ravaging a dead giraffe. However, the same day we earned the gold tack award. The sightings maps in the camps have various coloured tacks for the different animals. The leopard has the gold tack for rarity. We were just beginning to think that nothing much was happening when a leopard ran in front of us into the scrub. Mind you, a few metres in and you would never have known he was there.

On the road to Crocodile Bridge we encountered a very large male rhino; twice the size of those you see in zoos. Placidly chomping at the side of the road, he couldn't give an eye blink about us. You could hear the crunching as he munched his way. The official classification of grazers and browsers definitely needs extending: rhinos are hoovers and elephants are bulldozers. Another entertainment is to watch baboons and monkeys at play. Adolescents taunt and cuff each other, while dads and grandads look on disdainfully or lie down in the road right in our way. Not that we minded as we could watch them for hours. They are so happy and uninhibited. Mothers and girls de-nit each other, while the juniors leap at each other, roll, somersault and cartwheel at great speed. We moved from the hyperactive monkey world to the slow, ponderous glide of the giant land snail, the length of a ballpoint pen, as he crossed the road, transporting his large, shiny, shell house on his back.

Writing this at the breakfast table while M goes for his second Gold Tack Award, because this morning we saw a magnificent leopard in full recline along the branch of a tree two metres up. They are beautiful; the markings, the proportions, the face, the eyes, when seen in the wider surroundings, are something special. Then he became a she, as she slowly stretched and moved into the undergrowth, where suddenly we spotted her two cubs larking about, tails flashing. M was thrilled to bits and I must say that a large part of the pleasure for me has been his youthful enthusiasm over his 'spots' large and small.

Then came the dreadful cultural and environmental shock as we left the park through the Numbi Gate. Well named, it strikes you numb as the sheltered paradise of the last few days is whipped away and you are surrounded by touts trying to push grotesque animal carvings through the window, open to avoid heat suffocation. Rotund elephants and elongated giraffes were thrust at us with cries of 2 rand (40p to you). There were also birds with skinny legs, which M concluded were failed giraffes. They all weighed a ton so we made flapping signs to indicate that we had to fly home and we would be overweight. The last shower of urchins spotted the half-packet of lemon creams (wonderful with real lemon juice in them). 'Sweeties, sweeties,' came the yell, so to make our escape I handed them over. Bit silly really, because as M pointed out later, we could have purchased a whole elephant for 2 rand and the biscuits had cost us 5 rand. Still, it did mean the boys could have their cake and eat it, or rather their biscuits and sell the elephants later.

Spent the night at the Nelspruit Formule I Hotel. Chatted to Bernie the manager. He used to live in Middlesbrough but fifteen years ago his wife left him so he came to South Africa on holiday. Settled in with Wendy, Afrikaans crumpet. His daughter visited England in the summer and was horrified at the fates of her old school pals – junkies, probationees, unemployeds and one-parent mums. We have not yet met one ex-UK who would go back to UK. Writing this in Pietermaritzburg, PMB for short, but I am now being interrupted by M in bath, about to come out and worried about the possible future exposure to cold air. Wimpus Maximus wishes me to turn off the air-conditioning. We are in the Hotel Capital Towers, not Fawlty Towers, with a room the size of a barn and an outsize revolving television. Rolled about until well after 11.00 p.m. watching a hilarious film *A Zulu on My Stoep*, about the antics of a black and white boy and how they meet up again in later life. After much hunting we managed to buy a copy, if you ever have a spare evening with nothing much to do.

On the day of the drive we travelled from Nelspruit to PMB in six hours – 600 kilometres which shows how good and empty the roads are. The next day was the day of the coincidence. We started by touting the Express Foto shops for the best deal on our seven films. We just wanted to see which animals we needed to concentrate on during our last two days at the Kruger. Having to take them at dawn and dusk, some of them were a fraction pale so we bought a posh album to put them in. At least they were cheaper than at home. Flying the length of Africa with a very large bag of children's clothes, we found that the Farm Community was closed for Christmas and for clothes. So now what were we to do with them? Then in the park we met a mixed race group of Salvation Army. Apartheid never seemed to reach them, thank goodness. Anyway they were delighted to have the clothes and as we talked it turned out that some of them knew our Dolly and Fred, whom we had met five years ago in the foothills of the Himalayas at Kalimpong. Some coincidence! That evening we went to a charity concert. Lovely choirs and large organ; ended with Jerusalem, very memorable.

The next day's five-hour drive was also very memorable. This was from PMB to Fanies Island by the Indian Ocean, pronounced Farnees by the way, in case anyone out there thought it might be an isle of ill repute or nudists. The drive was awful because the large lorries cut you up and the car did not have a great deal of oomph. Discussion as to why women drivers are not so decisive. In other words, why do women chicken out of overtaking, when men could have done it standing on their heads? Poor M was some-what frustrated by my turn at the wheel but we got there without standing on our heads. Just because I don't drive like his mother, a bat out of hell on a broomstick. Now we come to the day of the snorkel and I am writing this in the great Bay of Sodwana. Is it so named because every sod in

South Africa wana come here, because it sure seems so. Feel a bit out of sorts, as did when we came out of the Kruger this time last week. Can't decide whether it's the anti-malarials or having too much time to think or seeing what white humans do over here. Their money is very visible here on this beach – boats, four-wheel drives, gear, picnic equipment, canopies, chairs, games, and so on; not forgetting the African servant, who spends his or her time sorting out various family crises, such as the collapsing shade, the injured child or the over-blazing barbecue. In between they clean the car or fix madam's hair. Will anything ever really change? Even as a tourist it can make you feel ashamed of being white, something I never felt in India or Egypt. Perhaps it is because they do not seem to have the same *joie de vivre* but a sadness which slips down the generations.

Maybe we could all learn from the social system of the wild dogs. They live in packs whose close-knit structure is one of the peaks of mammalian social organisation. Their home range can be up to 4000 sq km and they can have up to fifty members. They are led by an alpha pair who usually account for all the breeding. Below them there is no definite hierarchy and submissiveness, not aggression, is the deciding factor in wild dog interaction. When a kill has been made the juveniles rather than the adults feed first. Some also guard while others feed. Frail, sick or weaning dogs beg for food by whining, nudging or licking. Food is then regurgitated, and so strong is the urge to share food, a single chunk of meat may pass from one dog to another through as many as four or five stomachs. Perhaps birth control and sharing are two features humans could adopt from this species. Very sadly they are now becoming very endangered.

After our 100 km drive down the dustiest track ever seen by us, the snorkelling honour was satisfied. He had to watch out for the high-speed boats shooting in to land as far up the beach as possible. The only shocking part was his close encounter with an electric ray. Sorry folks, but you have to have a bit of corn now and again. We did find a cure for corns – streaking across the baking sand in bare feet on the beach beside the Indian Ocean; not that you are aware of it until two weeks later and your soles start to peel.

At Fanies Island, Brian the warden was determined that his very first lot of Brits were going to have the works. This was in the form of dawn walk down a well-used hippo trail, not often used by humans, except Brian of course. He made a video of us for posterity, although most of it was my posterior as I was usually last, being nosy as usual. Strict instructions to go up the nearest tree if we found ourselves between a hippo and his watering or wallowing hole; not that the trees were that big anyway. Observed very large and very fresh hippo footprints in the sand and mud. On the return boat trip we observed jellyfish, thousands of them, shaped like light bulbs, socket and all. Our expert zoologists examined them and discussed the fact that they seem to have no brain – the jellyfish that is, because all they seem to do is to swim around in circles. Apparently they are asexual and reproduce by budding clones. Sounds more like *Star Trek* again.

The camp at Fanies was great fun with its resident monkey clan, warthog family and overnighting hippos. The monkeys stole a loaf of bread from one of the huts and shared it out. Then warthog junior tried to devour the poly-bag from the afore-eaten loaf, whereupon M did his Attenborough 'Save the Warthog' bit. We were not sure who was going to see who off first but the big bold M won without a speck of help from the other male campers, who just looked on. However, M still hasn't plucked up the culinary courage to sample the monkey gland sauce with carpet bag steak. Later that evening M had his second warthog encounter, when grandad warthog with his eighteen inch curved tusks gave him quite a bit of hassle when loading the car. We then had a beautiful drive through innumerable types of scenery (no wonder they call it The World) on to the old gold town of Barberton. Not deceased as a gold town as it produces about twenty per cent of SA's gold. Enrolled at the oldest hotel, the Phoenix. Tatty imperial style, but spacious and full of wacky old furniture. The info centre lady was a bit concerned when she heard that two very respectable English visitors were staying there. We did not disillusion her about the very respectable concept. Barberton nestles beneath the Makonjwa Mountains, in what used to be called the Valley of Death, because it was rampant with mozzies and tsetses. The men were pretty rampant as well and Cockney Lizz in particular became very well off as a result of auctioning her favours to the highest bidder at the end of the evening. Diggers paid in kind, gold dust, as well as the other, of course.

Christmas was spent at Sabie in the Drakensberg with a newly found – by chance – soulmate. We knew she was just for us when we spotted the Bach flower remedy books and other holistic literature. She reckoned we were heaven-sent to her as one rainy day M was able to fix her electrics, door handles, drawer handles as well as leading Maurene and her friends in a meditation, while yours truly minded the four waif and stray dogs in another room. Maurene is a real soft touch for forlorn animals. I think people leave them behind on purpose. So it came to pass that five days with Maurene came and went in a physical cloud and a mental haze in and around Sabie; a town almost lost in its own time and with no sense of urgency. Explored numerous waterfalls with names such as Lone Creek, Horseshoe and Bridal Veil. One double one is known as the Mac Mac Falls, not after the famous fellow traveller, M.A. Clark, but after all the Irish and Scottish Macs who used to live in the area.

The haze was there on Christmas Day when we went to the 1,000-foot escarpment viewpoint. From this place called God's Window you should see the view over the sheer drop which plunges the high veld into the low veld. Engulfed by thick cloud we decided that God was entitled to a holiday on Christmas Day. It was an unusual experience as we stood with other nutters from all walks of life, making remarks such as 'God has pulled the curtains', 'God has got a hangover', 'God'll be back in a fortnight'. Christians, Hindus, Muslims, Jains and Baha'is came together in camaraderie over God having the last laugh. We all pray to our different gods without realising that we are probably praying to the same one.

Michael and his Madams go to Prague!

Thursday, 1st June, 1995

Michael awoke at 4 a.m, excitement arising in his loins. After his customary Sugar Puff breakfast to arouse his latent energies, M was ready to gather up his three madams to set off on the grand journey to the fine metropolis of Prague. His choice of feminine entourage had been carefully made. There was Madam P with her convent upbringing; Madam B, artistic and impenetrable; and Madam J, adventurous and vocally vibrant. They were the real feminine elite of Punnetts Town in East Sussex. M was a traveller of world-wide experience but with his three madams this promised to be an adventure beyond limits. Star Trek would pale into insignificance. M was about to go beyond the bounds of any superman.

At 4.25 a.m. the Mills and Boon expectations of our hero were totally dashed as the madams arrived, tottering up the drive, full of early-morning sleep and average age fifty-seven plus. At that point the ever-courteous, gentlemanly M decided to regard the whole undertaking as a social service, rather than a sexual exploit. So he tucked all the baggage into the car – cases and madams – and set off into the red dawn just breaking over Tunbridge Wells. At least the madams are fairly docile, he thought; but by the time he reached the Royal Wells his opinion had changed.

A few miles along Newick Lane (supposedly the longest lane in England) the madams woke up. Even B usually a slow riser, was able to appreciate the red glow of the dawn after J had explained to her what it was. Meanwhile P carried out her 'I may be retired but I'm still a bossy teacher at heart' role by plying M with drinks and encouraging remarks.

Gradually M warmed to the whole situation as it occurred to him that he could be the recipient of various favours during the next five days even if they were gourmet rather than erotic in flavour. On the flight Madam P was tickled pink to have the handsome, brown-eyed, tanned and bearded M all to herself. Madams B and J, having had a non-convent, common education, wanted to sit in the back so that they could have a quick puff. Arrival at Prague and M completed the marathon task of dragging the madams to *Pension* Ganymede. This involved half-hour bus ride, three stops on metro and nine stops on tram. All went well until it was realised that the stop you start at is number one so they went one stop too far on the tram. M wondered if the whole trip was one stop too far as madams and baggage had to be negotiated up and down various sets of steps, ramps and underpasses to retrace one stop. That was before trying to cross the motorway!

At the *pension* life became rather complicated, as Madam Basso being the Punnetts Town community charge guarantor for M, otherwise known as Mr Clark, was to share a room with him. Mrs Clark, the right-hand neighbour, was to go in one single and Mrs Hallett, the left-hand neighbour, was to go in another single. Very respectable *pension* proprietor, not sure why Mr and Mrs Clark not together, handed the former the keys and if they had understood Czech it would probably have been 'Oh, get on with it and sort yourselves out.'

The three madams soon assigned themselves to keeping

M as happy as possible. B set a smart walking pace so that he did not have to hang around street corners. J made sure he had his little extras such as a second pat of butter at breakfast. P wrote the official travel log and kept his underpants clean. That Thursday afternoon they made their first foray into Prague and were soon totally lost in the Jewish quarter. Not much remains of the old ghetto but its history is preserved in the synagogues around the cemetery. Thousands of bodies were laid in tiers up to twelve and you can see innumerable gravestones all crammed in next to each other like rows of crumpled, decaying teeth. All this in a very small, tree-covered plot with rasping rooks overhead made it an eerie place to visit.

From then on M and his Madams drifted in and out of squares, streets and buildings as the mood seized them. There was so much to see it was difficult to adhere to any plan. The Madams adhered to M and everyone was happy. They saw all the beautifully built and decorated old buildings as well as the highly colourful art nouveau and the unusual cubist architecture. At 4 p.m. they strayed into the Old Town Square and watched the famous clock in action. Death, a skeleton, pulls the rope to start the drama. In his left hand he raises and inverts an hourglass. Two windows open and a parade of Apostles goes round. Vanity, greed and lust all do their bit and at the end the Cock crows and the actual hour chimes take place. The astronomical clock was completed by a master clockmaker, Hanus. His view of the universe was the earth at the centre and the clock imitating the orbits of the sun and moon around the earth as well as the sun and moon going through the twelve signs of the zodiac. A masterpiece of artistic mechanics; and to prevent Hanus recreating it elsewhere, they blinded him.

Friday 2nd June

M was awakened by the sound of J's posterior cheeks sliding into the bath in the room above. P was already writing up the log and went down to awaken B. Breakfast was civilised and included a discussion on future plans for the trip. Somehow there was a slight digression regarding the size of men's extra bits until the arrival of two leather-jacketed, gun-equipped policemen. M had a sudden call to the gentlemen's convenience. As all the Madams were interested in Impressionism, M led them to the Sternberg collection at the castle. Bit of a failure as many of the paintings needed a good clean and the name captions were too small for their failing eyesight. A few times there were loud reprimands from stony-eyed attendants: 'You be a metre away.'

'So why don't they put up some string to hold us back?' asked B.

By mid-afternoon they had wandered miles up and down cobbled passageways, having a wonderful time with so much to see. They moved on from grubby art to even grubbier religion around St Vitus's Cathedral. The interior with its fine architecture, stained-glass windows with amazingly vibrant colours and the Crown jewels was genuinely uplifting. The exterior reminded one of the less pure aspects of religion. Good King Wenceslas was mur-dered on his way to church on the order of his brother, Boloslav. Outside is the bronze ring to which he clung while being butchered. Another time the Prots tried to get rid of some notable RC's by throwing them out of the royal palace window. It was a fifty-foot drop but divine interven-tion allowed them to have their lives saved by landing on a dung lump – and that is not a load of rubbish!

B was totally enchanted by everything, 'I think I'll ask for political asylum,' she stated. She even fell hopelessly in love with the tannoy voice on the buses. In fact, the way she behaved on the final number 16 bus of the day, the others decided she would probably end up in an asylum. She was convinced that the driver was the tannoy and strolled up the bus to look at him. His looks and the vocal tone did not seem to match, so down to earth she came as the realised it was all pre-recorded. Nevertheless, one glass of red wine and she was any tannoy's woman, giggling away every time it spoke. All this was to the unamusement of a young Czech lass, who was trying to read Adrian Mole in Czech. Poor Michael, wondering why he had let himself in for all this, consoled himself by looking at the heaving bosoms on the soap ad hoardings and then guided his gaggle of gigglers home to bed – their own beds, it may be added.

Saturday 3rd June

At breakfast M realised that there were compensations as he watched the madams prepare titbits for his lunch. They were always ready to buy his ice creams and nuts without any ulterior motive. So generally refreshed, with his Dorling-Kindersley Eyewitness Guide to Prague under his arm and his madams in tow, M ventured forth once again for the first bus of the day. Fortunately in the cold light of the morning, sober as a Czech art gallery attendant, B was no longer in love with the tannoy. M smiled with relief, as he was wondering how he could cope with two besotted madams.

For J had fallen in love as well, with a young Russian artist in the Old Town Square, outside St Nicholas's Church of all places. The group had to form a protective shield around the innocent young man, while J fumbled in her lower underwear to pay him (for a painting, of course). M was beginning to worry about the wrath of the respective husbands on the return of their errant wives to Punnetts

Town. As it was, the miscreant women had already been plotting how to smuggle home a handsome, cloaked palace guard. M did point out they would have looked even better if they had removed the coat hangers from the capes. 'Poofed-up American footballers,' was his verdict.

The next church of call was St George's Basilica. This was the burial place of St Ludmilla, Bohemia's first female Christian martyr. As she prayed she was strangled by her daughter-in-law, Drahomira. Shows you should never trust anyone with a name like that. A visit to supermarket was next on the agenda. Somehow B became detached from the party and M was a long time gone searching for her. B returned and so did M, weak and with a silly look on his face. The madams soon saw why, a braless pair of perfect breasts in a thin skin-tight, pale blue T-shirt. It was M's turn to be guided home in a coma by his ever-willing madams. In view of M's weakened condition, this log will now be written up in the first person.

Later in the evening we set off to see Prague by night. It was like a gigantic Disney world including a firework display over the castle. A candlelit dinner with flambéed this and that also incorporated a group of musicians. J came over all unnecessary as they played her request until M pointed out his gaping flies – the fiddler's!

Sunday, 4th June

It was supposed to be Prague's marathon day but for us it was the Tram Marathon Day as most of the routes were redirected all over the place. Still, during one fifteen minute wait we had a quick but memorable organ recital in a large local church. The very walls seemed to vibrate and it really sent shivers down your spine. Eventually we reached the Loreto Church above the Castle, just to meet Czech custodianship at its worst.

J bought the tickets, very attractive picture glossies but she was in immediate trouble from custodian one for not showing the paper till receipts After strolling quietly through the peaceful cloisters, war broke out in the church of the Nativity. Frau Hitler two was holding forth in a very loud voice. J turned round and said 'Sh' to warn us, whereupon Frau Custody asked if we were German.

'Certainly not,' I replied. '*Wir sind Englisch.*'

Then she descended upon Michael to tell him about the fully clothed skeletons with death masks made of wax. Mission completed, she rounded on us lesser women and told us that she only wanted to speak to Michael, 'And for this I ask nothing of him.'

Not much, we thought, if we had not been there to protect him. Her parting shot was,

'If you no like Czechs, then you no come here.' M's reply has had to be censored although it had something to do with sex and frustration. The church itself just contained thousands of very cheeky and very dusty cherubs. So boldly we moved on to the Loreto Treasury.

Although this is worth millions, custodian three was a lot more serene, because it was all behind bulletproof, alarm-rigged glass. Nosy tourists could press their faces on the glass to admire the gems in their thousands on various church artefacts. The gold-plated diamond-encrusted monstrance shaped like the sun with its rays was simple and dramatic. Amazing what you can do with a large lump of gold and over two thousand large diamonds.

A last wander over the Charles Bridge took us home to Ganymede. We decided to eat with the locals. One local took me outside to admire the sunset with M calling 'You'd better bring her back.' How gallant of him. We both had a last night walk round Prague, while the other two madams soaked up the local culture in the form of wine and laughter.

Monday, 5th June

The last day. As I write this M is plane-spotting with his binoculars. The airport is small enough to have little planes as well as large ones and it's great excitement as he reads out the names and countries of origin. I suppose it makes a change from tits in the tram and keeping the madams under control. We were lucky to reach the airport at all, having descended from the bus at the wrong stop. Ourselves and some Germans were a little confused when we discovered the original airport all closed and not a soul around. An old lady informed us it was only used for the police. Our original Czech driver must have thought 'silly English' when we insisted on getting off and crossing the road to catch the bus to go back one stop to what we thought was the right airport. Poor M, all this plus Madams plus luggage. Overcrowding over Europe meant a two-hour delay and as planes scuttled around and past us it was like the M25 a few thousand feet up. So we made it safely home to Punnetts Town, five days and many memories later on.

'Where next?' asked the Madams, as they bade farewell.

M was not to be seen.

Zoomin' Zimbabwe

Tuesday, 3rd December, 1996

The time is 10 p.m. and it's off to Harare on Air Zimbabwe, UM 629 via the Bumi Hills. Not that we 'ummed and hawed much over this trip. *Sunday Mail* £480, seven nights B&B. Three-Star Victoria Falls Hotel with Jules Verne.

Monday 9 a.m. all booked. Really upset when we were told: 'Unfortunately you will have to stay at the five-star Elephant Hills Hotel'.

Ten hour flight was no problem except the immigration homework. Great ponderings over 'Have you, or any of your dependents, been convicted of any crime in any country?' Should we admit to the delinquency court summons from Mexico for not fulfilling our time share contract? Decided senile dementia would be a good idea.

Slow queue at Harare immigration and somehow we were last. Not a good thing as the officer decided to unload his problems on us. Apparently he had a dodgy heart from working so hard and I didn't have the nerve to say it was probably from talking so much. Harare Airport was pretty basic and we had to walk across the tarmac for our Zambia Express plane to Victoria Falls. Some confusion as the tannoy said 'Victoria Falls' and was it then 'on to Kariba' or 'not to Kariba'? Turned out to be the latter but bad luck if you wanted Kariba and thought it had said the first option.

Not helped by having to count along several planes and tough if you got it wrong as nobody checked boarding cards.

'Is this the smallest international airport in the world?' we asked as we landed at Victoria Falls. Luggage in a pick-up had to be caught very quickly as they offloaded it over a counter. Did have time to see six inch bugs on the walls. Reckoned they would need air traffic control to take off! Elephant Hills was superb. After a quick rest we did our first safari trek, 3 km round the grounds. We could not believe that every dawn and dusk we would be able to animal spot in our own grounds. Monkeys, mongooses, impala with their young, generations of warthogs and even young crocodiles wander around totally unhindered! Golfers have to give them all precedence and many a green suffers from the skirmishing of monkeys and the grubbing of warthogs. When the crocs are large enough to start consuming golf balls they are banished to the Croc Rescue Centre. At least there are no elephants. They were expelled for messing up the grounds with an excess of poo and broken trees. For a bit of extra excitement, the odd lion has has been known to scrabble under the fence, when meat on the outside is a little scarce. Five-star guests have plenty of flesh!

The sumptuous buffet meals contribute to that flesh. Waiters, with names like Reward, Lucky and Fortune, leap to your every whim. It made up for missing out on a little luck, fortune or reward as you might call it. Four days before, Jules Verne phoned down the list to find twelve to stay an extra week for free, as the return plane was over-booked. Somehow we missed the call but then we might have run out of things to do! Then we had another miss. The day after our arrival we made our first and probably last visit to the actual falls. Why? We went on the first day of the price rise from Z\$20 to Z\$200 – £1.20 to £12 –

simply by adding a nought to the old price. Nobody knew it was happening or we would have rushed down the day before.

Nevertheless, the falls were worth our journey. They were majestic, white and thundering, just as we expected. It reminded you that you were in the middle of Africa, despite the skinny-dippers splashing merrily but perilously in the pools at the top. M had a wonderful time with his binoculars. He has just read that Zimbabwe is aiming for high-cost, low-impact tourism, so that may account for the Fall price increase. After all, the rainy season has just started so you will see more water for your money. For us it was in half-flood but the rainbows were amazing. It is all caused by the geological fact that the Zambezi widens to 1600 metres or more and then plunges down a chasm around 100 metres deep. In the rainy season this means 545 million litres per minute with cloud of spray rising 500 metres into the sky. Hence the name Mosi-a-tunya, which means the smoke that thunders. For a full mile one set of falls gives way to another forming the largest curtain of water in the world. Eventually you reach the railway bridge joining Zimbabwe to Zambia. Instead of allowing the bridge to cross the Zambezi at a more convenient point, Rhodes decreed that train passengers on the bridge should not just see the spectacle but feel the spray. Despite the problems of building over the gorge the steel structure was completed in 1905. Rhodes died in 1902 so he was never able to 'steam' across himself.

One must of course mention Livingstone, who reached the Zambezi in 1851 and saw the Falls four years later. Going down into the gorge is not for the faint-hearted. Steep steps are provided now, but it is known as Chain Walk, as that was all you had in the early days to assist you down and up the very steep, wet and muddy, slippery slope. It was from the grassy ledge above that Livingstone first saw the falls. From that point he lowered a line to which he attached some bullets and a square of calico to measure the height of the falls. At 90 metres the weight lodged on a projecting rock, still some distance from the bottom and would go no further. In 1878 Serpa Pinto checked with a sextant, allowing himself to be held over the edge on a rope made from the shirts of his bearers. Names such as Danger Point and Knife Edge Promontory reflect the risk he took.

However, the hammerkop bird takes no risks with its nest, so we were told on our bike safari, or should I say 'sufferi'? More of that later and back to the Hammerkop. This insignificant brown wader takes six months to build its nest in a tree. Anything that floats past is used so the external appearance is large and scruffy. Internally there is a dome for the incubation chamber. This is connected to the surface on the underside by a passage, through which scraps of fish, droppings, and so on are ejected. The position of the entrance is almost fool-proof against predators.

With reference to predators, the Tonga tribe had the right idea. Children's huts were built on stilts and at night the ladder was removed. Would seem to be a good way to save on babysitters. Amazing Grace, our lovely, gentle rep, told us how predators often come in two-legged kits. The rest of her family were all coming to stay for Christmas (because she and her husband both had jobs), so she was busy buying cheap articles and ornaments to put around her house. Apparently they are real shockers. They say how nice something is in the house and then help themselves to it as a Christmas present. Grace is no fool and hides all her decent stuff at a neighbour's. Apparently if her husband were to die his siblings will move in and strip the place as their right. The only compensation Grace would have is to be offered another husband! They will also clean out any bank account but again Grace has it sussed. She has moved with the times with a 'hole in the wall' bank account card for quick cash extraction. If you are not on the ball, Grace told us, wives and children are left totally bereft. Grace had four children, two aged twenty-two and twenty, then two aged six and four. Being nosy I asked, 'Why the large gap?'

'I got the first two when I didn't have much sense,' was Grace's reply. I could have talked to her for hours.

Was it because M felt that he was a born-again, modern-day Livingstone that he decided that a bicycle 'sufferi' was a must? Why did we suffer? The saddles were a bare necessity metal frame and even the hotel handtowel draped thereupon did very little to cushion you during the four-hour sweltering, nerve-racking trek down narrow, boulder-infested tracks. M had bike number 13 so that was an omen from the start. Five minutes into our four hours his chain fell off. Nathan, our guide, soon had it restored. We could see that he had done it a few times in the past. He was equally proficient with M's puncture halfway round. Repair gear and spare tyres abounded in his side panniers.

'What happens,' I asked, 'if we have a really dire emergency?'

This question was prompted when seeing elephant footprints up to M's knee in depth and his girth in circumference.

Silly question.

'No problem, I radio and helicopter she arrive.'

Does anything worry a Zimbabwean? The very pregnant Anne-Marie told us that she would have a one-hour flight to the hospital. She had been given a special letter to jump the passenger queue. Looking at her I would have thought the letter was superfluous. Our last evening was one to remember – a sunset trip down the Zambezi with hippos grunting all around. Read afterwards that the so-called hippo yawn is in fact a keep-off signal. We did wonder how many fearless canoeists become hippo takeaways. While on food, vegetarians should miss the next two lines. The last-

258

night Boma Barbecue gave us the chance to sample cuts of impala, warthog and ostrich but unfortunately the croc was off.

We found an interesting recipe for elephant stew which involved a medium elephant, 20 bags of salt, 650 bushels potatoes, 12 bushels carrots. Allow six weeks to cut elephant into chunks, four to chop veggies, simmer for another week. Serves approximately three thousand!

We were somewhat relieved that we were not staying on the Zambia side of the falls as we would have been exposed to even more dangers. Zambia is not so tourist-minded as Zimbabwe. Fleas, lice and bedbugs are a common distraction. Locals recommend petrol or DDT for the lice: a total wipe-out and probably instant baldness. Incidentally M is no longer worried about the latter having seen a sticker on the back of a cranky Victoria Falls car saying, 'God only made a few perfect heads, the rest he covered with hair.' Bedbugs hide during the day. They look like lice but move like greased lightning once you become aware of their presence and switch on the light to see what is happening. Telltale blood marks on walls confirm their proximity. Local advice? Find another hotel.

Another hazard is crossing the border from Zim to Zam. Zim money has to be left with the border guard on the Zim side. The Zams are somewhat stamp-happy, four on your passport every time you go through, so you could run out of pages. Goodness knows what happens if you run late as the border closes at 18.00. We did wonder about crossing the border to Botswana but were well warned about the lack of timetables. Could we really trust bus companies with names such as the Shu-Shine Bus Co. and the Wankie Express? Malawi was also out as it would involve going on roads where lorry convoys race to overtake each other and there are lots of crashes, as well as craters marking spots where land mines planted by Mozambique guerrillas have exploded.

So we settled for seeing traditional life in the Victoria Falls locality. We wandered around a village and I chatted to the ladies weaving the larger baskets. Each of the larger baskets takes two weeks to make so you could make five and a half in elephant stew time! M spoke to the witch doctor but he was more of a fortune teller and not very forthcoming. Later on we saw some of the traditional spirit dancing which was very atmospheric until they performed an English love song with lots of 'apologetics' for 'unrequited loves'.

M was very taken with the Venda Grain Bin and thought the patterns would be good for our own wheelie bins to make our local life more shapely. Bins and baskets were also used to store dried moths, dried locusts, caterpillars and other delicacies. He also liked the idea of a Dare, an area set aside for old men to discuss affairs in complete privacy. Women could only come in with food and drink. So wait for it, Punnetts Town!

We ended up waiting for it. A cyclone in Mauritius meant that our Air Zimbabwe plane had to go on a passenger backlog mission. It did at least give us an extra, posh buffet lunch and an extra swim but with a ten-hour delay we still had five hours hanging around in Harare Airport. As it was we had to collect an umbrella from the brolley trolley to cross the runway, which looked more like the Zambezi. Lightning struck all around but we made it.

Letter from Sorrento

October 1996

Here we are in the Bay of Sorrento looking over Capri, the haunt of previous generations. Looking at old pictures, we wonder if they would recognise the area any more. Although the land mass is still splitting and sinking a centimetre a year (quite rapid in geological terms, M tells me), the actual bay still looks the same geographically. However, it is hard to see all the way round, as the pollution constantly masks the distant sweep of the coast and Vesuvius itself is very rarely visible as a clear outline. The vast industrial spread of Naples, the innumerable cars and scooters together with the ever-growing number of tourist coaches are taking their toll. It's so bad that when coaches re-enter Sorrento, they have to radio in from 5 km away to be told the best route to avoid the traffic. On our last day it took us an hour to go through Pompeii. Mind you, none of this is helped by the Italians having a total disregard for any one-way system. M has really enjoyed watching the havoc at the crossroads outside the hotel. Even pedestrians get fed up and climb over paralysed vehicles to carry on their way in the narrowest streets.

Yet the Italians are still the same – outwardly carefree, friendly and kind – with a couple of exceptions; Mussolini's grandmother and Mussolini's mother. The former ran the paper shop at the train station where you buy the bus tickets. Are you still with me? Anyway, heaven help you if you did not have the correct change. She just refused to serve you. 'Giva de Coinsa' was her stock phrase. If you were too slow she'd put the tickets away and you had to start again at the end of the queue. Mother Mussolini ran the toilet queue at Pompeii. 'You will stay in your place or be shot', then 'You will pay 300 lire or not be released'.

The Amalfi Drive is truly dramatic. Two thousand bends in thirty miles on a narrow bend have to be negotiated. Fortunately for the vertigoed M you hardly notice the perilous drops as your eyes are drawn to the emerald coastline with the mountains plunging into the sea. Positano still has some charm nestled in the mountains but it is expanding rapidly so it is losing its quaint image. On the drive it is one way for coaches so you return through the mountains and see the more rural aspect of Italy. It was more as I remember from twenty years ago.

Strolling round Capri was colourful with showers of bougainvillaea, hibiscus and morning glory trailing over pastel-shaded villas like rainbows. We were glad it was October. It must be difficult to see the colour of anything through the gaudy hordes of visitors in the summer. The Isle of Ischia was quieter but even there day visitors are ferried back and forth in jet boats and steamers to be scooped up by buses 'circumnavigating' the island. Our trip to Pompeii was a mixed blessing as our guide thought he was an immobile two-legged history book. Over one hundred coaches at the site meant there was a great deal of queuing. M reckoned the souls of Pompeii now feel well and truly downtrodden. Ercolano, however, had very few visitors and we were able to feel the atmosphere of life two thousand years ago before it was buried in 60 feet of lava mud. Goodness knows how they have managed to dig away the solidified mud to reveal pillars, stairs, deep-coloured mosaics and murals, marble baths, pots and even charred wooden beams. It must have been some blast. Unlike the Pompeians, the Ercolanos had time to flee.

The grand climb up Vesuvius was spectacular and it was a little disarming to see the swirling pockets of steam escaping from cracks in the solid lava. M's climb down was slightly hampered by his lumps of knobbly lava choking his shorts' pockets.

Really for me the trip was a bit of a pilgrimage as my father was killed in the Salerno Campaign. It is hard to say how I felt when I first saw his name on the sixth panel of the beautiful marble memorial at Cassino. With the peace of the war graves around you and the monastery of Monte Cassino gleaming on the mountains behind, it was almost unreal. As I left it seemed very strange to be leaving the name of your origins in that lovely but distant place. It was part of an organised coach trip but there were only two of us with any real reason for going, myself and an ex-soldier who was there at the time of the fighting. In a way I felt sadder for him as you could see the memories being stirred within him as he read the names of his mates on the shining white headstones. Forty-two thousand were killed in the whole campaign and the four thousand with no named graves have their names on the memorial. 'Their name liveth for ever more.'

There was a lighter side as our veteran recounted how the first wave of soldiers gathered up coins from deserted homes and set themselves up as money changers; L500 for £1, an inflated rate for those days! M was financially impressed. They also brought up supplies on mules but their iron shoes on the cobbles drew enemy fire, so gradually the poor old mules met with an accident over the mountain edge. Apparently his wife had arranged the visit as a golden wedding surprise and it was not until the day before that she told him they were going.

For us the big, bold adventure was on the last day – the

day of the hired car. Being Sunday we thought it would mean less traffic: joke. The morning was quiet but the later return into Sorrento was a nightmare. M's reactions to Italian maniac driving were amazing.

'How did you manage to stay so cool?' I asked.

'I've been studying them all week,' came the even cooler reply.

First stop on the day of the hired car was the Salerno Cemetery. I knew one of the graves would be Father's but of course one of the unmarked ones. It will be a question of what you believe when you read the following but it is good enough for me. M used his crystal pendulum to dowse for the possible grave; first the direction, then the block and then the row. We reached the row together and then fifteen graves along I spotted one unnamed plot with shrubs behind and mauve flowers in front. M's pendulum had already started to settle there and I felt that it was the right one – between two Scots Guards. It was as if my life had come round in a full circle as I reflected on what might have been, and it was reassuring to have M there.

The next meaningful experience was the Greek settlement at Paestum. We had a giggle when we spotted a little bus and a large bus next to each other from Campo Basso. 'Your Italian answer to Butlin's?' queried M. The Greek temples at Paestum are the most complete in the world so we felt we had a good taste of ancient Rome and Greece as well as volcanism and Italian traffic. Going home M complained about the weight of his hand luggage but if he wanted to bring home half a volcano, that's his own fault.

Arrivederci,

Pat and M